The Web of Victory

Earl Schenck Miers

THE WEB
OF
VICTORY

✳

GRANT AT VICKSBURG

Louisiana State University Press

Baton Rouge and London

Library of Congress Cataloging in Publication Data

Miers, Earl Schenck, 1910-1972.
  The web of victory.

  Reprint. Originally published: New York : Knopf, 1955.
  Bibliography: p.
  Includes index.
  1. Vicksburg (Miss.)—Siege, 1863. 2. Grant,
Ulysses S. (Ulysses Simpson), 1822-1885. I. Title.
E475.27.M64   1984   973.7'344   84-9717
ISBN 0-8071-1199-6 (pbk.)

For

STARLING

with affection

INTRODUCTION

Six weeks and a few days before General
Ulysses S. Grant left Memphis to assume personal command
of the campaign against Vicksburg, President Lincoln sent
his annual message to Congress. Only a short time before,
in a letter to General Carl Schurz, an old political friend,
Lincoln stated: "We lost the late elections, and the administration is failing, because the war is unsuccessful."
Now, heart full of doubt and hope, Lincoln approached the
conclusion of a long, thoughtful summary of the complex
difficulties 1862 had produced. The living spirit of the man
could no longer be stilled. For a moment the lawyer who
once had ridden the circuit set aside syllogistic reasoning;
the successful political candidate of two years ago who had
been forced also to become commander-in-chief over vast
armies fighting on far-flung battlefields no longer sought
either to explain or to apologize for past bungling. With an
eloquence that somehow always emerged in crisis, Lincoln
said:

"We cannot escape history. We of this Congress and this
administration, will be remembered in spite of ourselves.
No personal significance, or insignificance, can spare one or
another of us. The fiery trial through which we pass, will
light us down, in honor or dishonor, to the latest generation.
We *say* we are for the Union. The world will not forget that
we say this. We know how to save the Union. The world
knows we do know how to save it. We—even *we here*—hold
the power, and bear the responsibility. In *giving* freedom to
the *slave*, we *assure* freedom to the *free*—honorable alike in
what we give, and what we preserve. We shall nobly save,

or meanly lose, the last, best hope of earth. Other means may succeed; this could not fail. The way is plain, peaceful, generous, just—a way which, if followed, the world will forever applaud, and God must forever bless."

On the seventeenth of January 1863, the day that Grant arrived at Young's Point above Vicksburg, the editors of *Harper's Weekly* tried to answer a question that long had confounded Lincoln: "They say at Washington that we have some thirty-eight to forty Major-Generals, and nearly three hundred Brigadiers; and now the question is, have we one man who can fairly be called a first-class General in the proper meaning of the term?" The editors of *Harper's* frankly didn't know. The West, they conceded, had been "prolific of Generals of fair merit," with the understandable exception of Pope, who "struck his name off the list of competitors for fame by the disastrous campaign ending at Centreville." Of Grant the editors were cautious; they admitted that he had provided evidence "of enterprise, determination, and personal gallantry"; but the country was seeking something more—a man of success.

In another week the editors of *Harper's Weekly* extolled the battalions that moved by land and water along the Mississippi: "No monarch of Europe ever gathered together so many men, so many vessels of war, so many guns for any single purpose. In comparison with the force commanded by McClernand, Grant, Banks, Porter, and Farragut, the allied expedition to the Crimea was an insignificant affair. . . . The British army under Wellington, which carried on the Peninsular War, was less than any of the flying columns of our army of the Mississippi. . . . Should the war be finally settled by a pitched battle in the heart of Mississippi, as Jeff Davis predicts, the forces engaged will probably be twice as numerous as those that fought at Waterloo, and our army ought to exceed that of the Rebels by a large percentage."

Public interest at the moment centered not on Vicksburg but on Barnum's Museum in New York, where "the rage" had become especially "wild among the ladies" to behold Miss Lavinia Warren. The now venerable and wealthy Charles S. Stratton, who as Tom Thumb claimed that "he had kissed millions of fair faces," had found the twenty-nine pounds and thirty-two inches of Lavinia irresistible. On February 10 Tom would quit his "*quasi* retirement" in Connecticut to marry Lavinia at Grace Church. Reporters did not wonder at his choice. Lavinia, "a little lady of very fair proportions, decidedly of the plump style of beauty, with a well rounded arm and full bust," possessed "all the appearance of *aimable embonpoint*."

At Vicksburg Grant was deprived of the pleasure of dwelling upon Lavinia's exceedingly "animated and agreeable" complexion, her "very dark eyes," her "dimpled cheeks and chin." Before Grant was the report of what had happened when the *Queen of the West* attempted to run past Confederate batteries on the bluffs above Vicksburg landing. Against a rising river, troops under Sherman dug and swore, seeking to build a canal beyond reach of those batteries through which Porter's gunboats and ironclads could pass.

Few men ever possess the opportunity or encounter the risks that now confronted Grant. He, too, no longer could escape history. He, too, must "nobly save, or meanly lose."

Grant stood at the awakening of greatness. For long, bitter weeks he would struggle and grope. Then, like a flame before a moth, he would lure, dazzle, and sear his adversary. In twenty days his brilliance in command would emerge. He would become, in mortal judgment, immortal, if only for this achievement.

The Web of Victory is the story of how Grant reached those twenty days and what they portended. Part One sketches the influences that produced Grant at Vicksburg—

the influences he controlled, those he did not. Part Two tells how the flame smoldered, then burst into the scorching scenes at Port Gibson, Raymond, Jackson, Champion's Hill, Black River Bridge, Vicksburg. Part Three carries the reader through the forty-seven days of siege until the city capitulates.

The sources of this book are given by chapter in the appended material following the bibliography. Generally, spellings and punctuation have been modernized. No principal historic figure has been allowed to speak in direct quotation unless a source for his statements exists.

EARL SCHENCK MIERS

Stelton, New Jersey
June 1954

ACKNOWLEDGMENTS

F ROM the inception of this project, two of its warmest friends have been David C. Mearns, of the Library of Congress, and Harry E. Pratt, Illinois State Librarian, who first suggested many of the manuscript sources that were used. Percy Powell, of the Library of Congress, Margaret Flint, of the Illinois State Historical Library, Donald F. Cameron, librarian of Rutgers University, and Mark Kiley, librarian of the New York University Club, all rendered that type of assistance which has endeared them to a generation of working historians.

A special note of gratitude is due Paul M. Angle, director of the Chicago Historical Society, who offered numerous intelligent suggestions for the revision of the manuscript. For constant encouragement and assistance in securing material the author is indebted to Benjamin P. Thomas, Roy P. Basler, George Scheer, Roy E. Meredith, and Roger W. Shugg.

For my wife, who has typed the many revisions of this book with sweet tolerance for her husband's continued stupidity, I have the deepest sympathy. Finally, for unfailing faith in the outcome of the toil, I should be remiss if I did not acknowledge once again my affectionate appreciation to C. H. Wilhelm.

E. S. M.

Contents

CONTENTS

Illustrations

Maps

PART ONE

✳✳✳✳✳✳✳✳✳✳✳✳✳✳✳✳✳✳✳✳✳✳✳✳✳✳✳✳✳✳✳✳✳✳✳✳✳

Too Many Generals

1. PORTRAIT OF A GENERAL

H ELL, he's no general!"

At Young's Point, seven miles above Vicksburg, on a bleak January day in 1863, any of the Union soldiers gathered around the river landing could have made the remark. The man descending the gangplank scarcely looked worth two lines in the next letter home: a bare five feet eight inches of flesh hung on a slim frame that stooped slightly under even that strain. Weight about a hundred and thirty-five pounds. A mouth, one observer said, "of the letterbox shape," at least what could be seen of it behind a chestnut-brown beard. A wart on his cheek, just like old Abe Lincoln. And a face that somehow had a twist to it, with the left eye set a little lower than the right, and the high, rather square brow creased with wrinkles.

"There," Jake Wilkin of the 130th Illinois exclaimed, "is General Grant!"

A comrade shook his head—not derisive, simply unbelieving. "I guess not—that fellow don't look like he has the ability to command a regiment, much less an army."

Jake Wilkin said that they were mistaken about Grant; he had known the General in Illinois and Grant was all right. But many remained unimpressed. They watched Grant shuffle down the gangplank, slouch hat bent over a newspaper. The half of a cigar in Grant's mouth was all that seemed to fit with the pictures they had seen of him, and even the cigar needed a light. It was true, a friend admitted, that, judging by the sketches in *Harper's* or *Frank Leslie's Illustrated Weekly*, Grant might have been mistaken for a "burly beef-contractor"; and this trickery of the artist's pen

3

doubtless increased for many their disappointment on first meeting this near-runt of a man. But the more observant soon saw how really fine Grant's eyes were—eyes darkening from blue to gray and filled with warmth, good humor, even a twinkle. And when Grant spoke, his voice possessed a distinctive clarity and resonance. "It had a singular power of penetration," said Horace Porter, who later served on Grant's staff, "and sentences spoken by him in an ordinary tone could be heard at a distance that was surprising."

Mark Twain once said that he understood Wagner's music was better than it sounded; and Grant was a better general than he appeared. When Grant became interested in a subject, when he spoke with the gestures that characterized him in such moments—either raising and lowering his right hand or stroking his beard—the force of the man emerged: the quick grasp of his mind, the swift flow of his thought, the promptness of his decision. Horace Porter drew another picture of Grant. Writing out an order to his army, the General might decide suddenly that he required a paper on a near-by table. Grant would "glide rapidly across the room without straightening himself, and return to his seat with his body still bent over at about the same angle at which he had been sitting when he left his chair." No movement, no sound shattered the man's concentration. But it took time to know Grant. At first only his awkwardness appeared, his unmilitary gait, his inability to keep step even to the thumping of an army band.

In January of 1863 the best anyone could say for Grant was that he remained a general on trial. Lincoln had lived through a bad six months, culminating in the loss of the elections. When Hannibal Hamlin hailed the Emancipation Proclamation as "the great act of the age" and cried "God bless you for this," Lincoln replied cynically: "The North responds to the Proclamation sufficiently in breath; but breath alone kills no Rebels." From Carl Schurz came a sharp post-mortem on the elections: "*The result . . . was a*

most serious and severe reproof administered to the administration."
Bridling, Lincoln retorted: "You think that I could do
better; therefore you blame me already. I think I could not
do better; therefore I blame you for blaming me. I understand you *now* to be willing to accept the help of men, who
are not Republicans, provided they have 'heart in it.'
Agreed. I want no others. But who is to judge of hearts, or of
'heart in it'?"

The greatest cause of the President's irritation was his
generals. They all had the "slows." To Schurz, Lincoln
wrote bluntly: "I need success more than I need sympathy."
And determined to find that success, Lincoln had reshuffled
his high command. So prudent McClellan, who was "urged
by many Republicans and opposed by none," was gone and
Burnside commanded the Army of the Potomac. Buell had
been fired as commander of the Army of the Ohio and
Rosecrans now had a splendid opportunity to demonstrate
his theory that "sandy fellows" were quicker and sharper
than brunettes. In Louisiana, Nathaniel P. Banks had replaced Ben Butler, who, one of his critics thought, might as
well go home as Butler's bellicosity always would be most
effective with the factory girls in Lowell, Massachusetts.

Nobody really seemed to know about Grant, either Lincoln or the country. Part of Grant's misfortune was the way,
wherever he moved, ridicule followed him; and close on the
heels of ridicule, like a dog enjoying the scent of the fellow,
came rumor. General Ulysses S. Grant—a nation's enigma.
At Young's Point which should a soldier remember: the
Grant who had captured the heart of the North after Donelson or the Grant held responsible by many for the dismal,
bloody failure of thirteen thousand Union troops slaughtered
at Shiloh? Set a piece of red meat before Grant, the gossips
insisted, and the General's stomach turned squeamish. After
Shiloh, they asked, was that any special wonder?

Often the rumors grew uglier, more vicious. Grant was a
souse, an incompetent. Every day, some critics claimed, the

5

pressure mounted on Lincoln to rid the West of this drunken no-account before he brought on complete disaster. Soldiers heard that when Mrs. Grant was in camp the General never touched a bottle, but a soldier could easily grin at a story like this and ask what man didn't mind his p's and q's more circumspectly around the missus? With Grant, the whisperers said, one drink set him off. He became a fool then, and only God could guess when—or where—he would stop. Others contended that the main work John Rawlins performed on Grant's staff was to prowl the camps, day and night, seeing that the General kept away from the devilish stuff.

It was an easy step from denouncing such indiscretions to the argument that Grant, as commander of the Army of the Tennessee, represented a fluke. On a train traveling from Chicago to Cairo, Illinois, a reporter for the *Chicago Times* heard an officer speak derisively of Grant. Suppose Grant did command a department, what could you say for him? "He never did amount to anything, and never will," the officer exclaimed. "He has been kicked out of the United States Army once, and will be again. He is nothing but a drunken, wooden-headed tanner that will not trouble the country very long."

On trains, in the army, wherever one heard discussed the war that the North once had believed it could win in ninety days and now realized it could lose, sooner or later the question was raised: What was the basis of Grant's reputation, anyhow?

2.

Grant's early service in the war came under a group of commanding generals who, in the end, all tried Lincoln's patience to the point of breaking. First John C. Frémont ruled over the newly organized Department of Missouri to which Grant was assigned, and the style of Frémont's headquarters at St. Louis impressed William Tecumseh Sherman as "a more showy court than any king." Billy Sherman was quick-nerved and loose-tongued in those days. One visit to Frémont agitated his easily ruffled temper. Sherman looked at the hangers-on who had followed the Pathfinder from California and said sarcastically: "Where the vultures are, there is a carcass close by." Sherman was unacquainted then with the commander Frémont had placed at Ironton, the terminus of the St. Louis and Iron Mountain Railroad.

At Ironton, Grant toiled earnestly at the task of curbing the highly secessionist spirit of Missouri. With no staff, with eight cannon but no artillerymen to fire them, yet with a locomotive that the imaginative Frémont had supplied for running errands, Grant saw the humor in the situation. In his first report to St. Louis he said the men and officers under him were trained so ineffectively that he feared any "resistence would be in the inverse ratio of the number to resist with." He would improve these conditions "in two days more." Where artillery, cavalry, and the quarter-master's department functioned at all they were "yet quite deficient." Many of the horses, he found, were "barefoot."

A steadiness of will to make a place for himself, a good humor and even temper that quickly won friends, a thoughtful, administrative efficiency marked Grant's command at Ironton. He had need to marshal all his wits, for a Georgian brigadier general of considerable reputation threatened Ironton from the south with a not unsizable force.

There was a ludicrous quality in the circumstances that pitted William J. Hardee against Grant. *Hardee's Tactics,* a translation of a French military work, was the drill manual for both armies. Earlier Grant had secured a copy of Har-dee's book, studied one lesson, and set himself to the commendable task of mastering another lesson each day until he had gone through the volume. He lined up his regiment, then encamped "among scattering houses with enclosed

7

gardens," and found that if he attempted to follow the lesson he had studied he "would have to clear away some of the houses and garden fences to make room." Grant's interest in *Hardee's Tactics* ended there; moreover, what Hardee had translated "was nothing more than common sense and the progress of the age" applied to the system Scott had used in the Mexican War. So at Ironton Grant could regard the reputation surrounding Hardee with cynicism; but his conscience troubled him at what reaction might result if his officers ever discovered that he had "never studied the tactics" that he used.

Meanwhile in southwestern Missouri a nasty little action was fought at Wilson's Creek and General Nathaniel Lyon was saved from sharp reprimand for an ill-planned assault by falling in the midst of a scorching battle. Frémont grew jittery. Grant still prepared to meet Hardee; he rented wagons, arrested a clergyman who doubled at spying, and thought wistfully of how nice it would be if he had somebody who could shoot his eight cannon. Then, as battle seemed imminent, Grant was replaced in command by General Benjamin M. Prentiss.

Grant went to Jefferson City, once more coming under the direct command of a general Lincoln would view wryly —John Pope, an opinionated, pugnacious, politically conniving fellow whose place in history seems to stem, perhaps unfairly, from the fact that another general said bluntly he preferred Pope no more than "a pinch of owl dung." Grant was not the general; he tried to get along with everyone. During the Mexican War, Grant had fought under both Winfield Scott and Zachary Taylor, and whereas he had admired Scott's splendor in "all the uniform prescribed or allowed by law," he had been more naturally drawn to Taylor, who dressed for comfort. Scott had relied on the opinions of staff officers in reaching a decision; Taylor had judged for himself and had done "the best he could with the means given him." Both at Ironton and Jefferson City,

Grant copied much of the spirit and style of Taylor, of whom he remembered: "No soldier could face either danger or responsibility more calmly than he. These are qualities more rarely found than genius or physical courage."

The post at Jefferson City largely duplicated the difficulties and discouragements of Ironton. To use Lincoln's phrase, Grant was learning that the job of command could be "like trying to shovel fleas across a barnyard." Again he faced the problem of reorganizing an inefficient command; again he had artillery without artillerymen (but no locomotive for running errands); again, when he had organized an expedition to chase the Confederates under that redoubtable Tennessean Ben McCulloch out of Springfield, Missouri, another general arrived to take over Grant's command.

Apparently nobody wanted to let Grant fight, or so Jesse Grant believed when he observed how his son was being shunted around the state of Missouri. Grant replied soothingly to the old man's outburst of temper. He was not being discriminated against, Grant wrote. Actually, he had been "laboriously employed." Jesse still felt huffy over the waste of his boy's military talents, but Grant moved cheerfully to his next post at Cairo, Illinois. If Jesse really possessed an eye for military strategy, he must have recognized the importance of this river town where the southernmost tip of Illinois thrust like a wedge between Kentucky on the east and Missouri on the west.

Grant felt content to return to the free soil of his adopted state. His thoughts were drawn to his home in Galena, and Galena also reminded him of John A. Rawlins.

When the firing on Fort Sumter had roused Galena as it had stirred every town with an ounce of gumption for the Union, Rawlins had spoken at a mass meeting at the courthouse. Everyone in the town had respected this grave young man who had done better than most had expected. His old man had drunk a lot, the scuttlebutters said, winking; hadn't really tended his farm at all, but young John had;

and the boy had gained a decent sort of education in district schools and a near-by seminary. Later Rawlins hung out his lawyer's shingle; he was as good a Democrat as anyone could find in the whole of Jo Daviess County.

With the gift of the natural orator, Rawlins appealed to his townsmen that evening to submerge political differences in the face of the common peril: "It is simply country or no country. I have favored every honorable compromise; but the day for compromise is passed. Only one course is left for us." Logic, vigor, idealism flowed through the utterances Rawlins made. Grant felt deeply moved. He had decided then that he would never forget the speech, or the man who delivered it. Now at Cairo he wrote to the Galena Democrat. Would Rawlins like to serve on his staff? The jokesters had begun to say that "Grant's special and general orders could be picked up in the streets of Cairo oftener than they could be found in his office." Obviously he needed someone. Rawlins replied that Mrs. Rawlins had died, that he must set off for her family home in New York state, but that if Grant would wait he would be glad to accept the offer. Grant decided to wait.

Meanwhile Grant's attention focused on the movements of Leonidas Polk, the Episcopal Bishop turned Confederate general who liked to baptize fellow officers on the battlefield. At times the Bishop acted as though he took his orders from heaven rather than from Richmond. When the delicate balance of Kentucky's border-state sentiments made any invasion of its territory hazardous, Polk ignored Jefferson Davis, talked with God, and "seated himself" behind cannon and entrenched lines opposite Columbus, Kentucky. Such were the Bishop's persuasive powers that by telegraph he converted Davis to the belief that his actions were justified by "the necessity."

Polk also convinced an alert Grant of what "the necessity" must be, and in a manner that would have warmed the heart of Taylor, Grant showed his independence of decision. Paducah, the military gateway to the Cumberland and Tennessee rivers, must be occupied; so while Governor Morton moaned into any ear that would listen, "If we lose Kentucky now, God help us," Grant moved. Under the nose of an over-trusting Polk, Grant occupied Paducah and so shattered the Bishop's faith that he let Richmond berate the heathen North for breaking the neutrality of Kentucky. Grant had acted without specific orders, but with sound military sense: once the Union held Paducah, a desperate battle was the smallest price the Confederates must expect to pay to gain a defensive line along the Ohio River. Whereas headquarters in St. Louis eventually sanctioned the movement, Grant's initiative also drew sharp rebuke. It seemed incredible that Frémont could add anything more to his mismanagement and bad judgment, but once the Pathfinder began to explore the regions of his emotional instability as a commander, almost limitless areas appeared to open before him.

3.

At last Lincoln's patience broke, and the Presidential ax fell upon the neck which Frémont's arrogance had stretched to such astonishing lengths. For a time the command of the department in which Grant served would pass to Major General David Hunter, but soon another shift would see Major General Henry W. Halleck taking over at St. Louis. Now Grant encountered someone with whom he would have to live—with varying degrees of nervous strain—for almost the remainder of the war.

With justification Halleck could be called an ambitious schemer, a malicious gossip, a dangerous juggler of the truth, and a man who often mistook his hulking shadow for the image of his innate ability, but no fair-minded critic could call Halleck a fool. His nickname was "Old Brains," and a high, sloping forehead was his most prominent feature. At the age of thirty-one he had written *The Elements of Military Art and Science*—a good text, in use for twenty years—and had translated from the French Baron Jomini's *The Political and Military Life of Napoleon*. When finally Winfield Scott recognized that he was too old for the supreme command, Scott had tried to delay the appointment of a successor until Halleck could return from his station on the Pacific coast. But Lincoln wouldn't wait, and picked McClellan.

In November 1861 the forces in the West had been divided into two departments—the Army of the Mississippi under "Old Brains" and the Army of the Ohio under Don Carlos Buell. Of Buell much could be said, but nothing more telling than the fact that discipline and delay were his distinguishing characteristics; McClellan had seen him as one of the great generals of the war, and as no one could really start McClellan moving, it was perhaps unimportant that Buell also stalled easily. But it wasn't unimportant to Lincoln. Always partial toward the Unionist loyalists in mountainous Tennessee, the President wanted Buell to march the Army of the Ohio from Louisville to Knoxville and threaten Virginia in the rear.

Lincoln's strategy was reasonable, but Buell was full of objections. Two hundred miles of country roads separated Louisville from Knoxville—a fine trek to expect of him with winter breathing down his neck! And how long, the querulous Buell would like to know, would "friendly neutrals" remain amenable if they were subjected on one hand to Northern impressment of supplies and on the other to raids by the Southern cavalry? A Rebel army under Albert Sidney Johnston frowned menacingly at Buell from its base at Bowling Green, Kentucky; Confederate forts blocked the Mississippi below Cairo, rendering Federal gunboats ineffective; and Confederate control reached up the Tennessee to Fort Henry and up the Cumberland to Fort Donelson. Buell wanted to defeat Johnston (ultimately, at any rate) and he did grasp at once the importance of the Tennessee and the Cumberland as lines of supply. So Buell proposed that he should march for Nashville and Halleck should be sent up the Cumberland. Knoxville could wait.

Understandably, Grant failed to figure in any of these discussions that began to upset Lincoln, McClellan, and Buell. Sitting almost Buddha-like in headquarters at St. Louis, Halleck preferred to ignore the whole issue. "Old Brains" wanted command of both Buell's army and his own, although how he intended to use either remained at that moment among the carefully guarded secrets of war. At Cairo, Grant strained impatiently. He had asked permission to attack Columbus, but weeks passed, St. Louis ignored the request, and Polk dug earthworks and mounted 142 heavy guns. In the ear of a sympathetic Rawlins, intent on learning a new job, Grant's remarks doubtless grew nettlesome. Rawlins tidied the office and waited hopefully.

Then, unexpectedly, Grant got into a fight, though through no intentions at headquarters. Frémont advanced against the Confederates under Price in Missouri, and Grant was asked to make demonstrations along both banks of the Mississippi to keep Polk from sending reinforcements against Frémont. Opposite Polk's frowning guns at Columbus stood three wooden shanties bearing the euphonious name of Belmont. Here with three thousand raw recruits Grant struck a Confederate force of about equal size under General Gideon J. Pillow. After four hours of sharp fighting Pillow abandoned the camp in disorder. Under the guns of Columbus, Belmont was untenable, but against orders the victorious Yankees pillaged the camp and shouted and cheered officers who must make patriotic speeches. Grant set the camp on fire to stop this nonsense. Across the river Polk's guns belched a withering fire, and Pillow, joined by three fresh regiments, placed himself between camp and river to cut off the retreat to the Yankee gunboats.

Panic seized Grant's raw troops. Pleas to surrender were

shouted. But Grant stood firm. "We must cut our way out as we cut our way in," he said. Grant's coolness under fire prevented the seeming rout; Pillow's attack on the Federals in flank came as they reached the shore. It was too late.

Grant numbered his casualties at 498 and those of the Confederates at 966. Despite his inability to quote from *Hardee's Tactics*, Grant returned in a jubilant spirit to Cairo. Polk had been too well occupied to divert troops into Missouri. But Rawlins understood that his commander also had suffered an item of deep personal grief—Belmont had cost Grant his horse and bay pony, his saddle and equipment, personal property valued at two hundred and fifty dollars. For Grant, that was a staggering sum.

In December 1861 McClellan fell ill, and Buell and Halleck were more or less left to their own devices. "Old Brains" declared that sixty thousand men would be required for any move up the Cumberland and the Tennessee; as he could spare no more than ten thousand troops for the venture, he obviously intended to do nothing. Then an event occurred that made Halleck feel as though a hair had been wrenched from his head by which to suspend the sword of Damocles. Halfheartedly, Buell dispatched a division under General George H. Thomas toward Knoxville, and that stouthearted Virginian, about midway to his objective on the nineteenth of January, won a small, unexpected, but thoroughly satisfactory battle at Mill Springs. This success, redounding to the credit of Buell's army, unhinged the doors of Halleck's inertia. All at once he saw that he might scrape up as many as fifteen thousand troops to send up the rivers under Grant.

Why Halleck picked Grant is largely a guess, and yet Grant's relative obscurity at that moment would not have been unattractive. If there was one thing "Old Brains" didn't want to discover, it was a hero. Grant looked safe. The relationship between Halleck and Grant was, as a matter of fact, somewhat chilly. Grant had found occasion to run up to St. Louis and meet Halleck personally, and had been received "with so little cordiality" that he had returned to Cairo "very much crestfallen." Perhaps Grant sensed why Halleck had chosen him for the expedition up the rivers. Perhaps not. Grant certainly wanted the opportunity; he had ambition, too.

Grant moved on the first of Feburary supported by a force of Federal gunboats. Fort Henry on the Tennessee defied basic principles of military engineering: set on low ground, it was a miserable work to defend, and before Grant arrived the place already had been abandoned in favor of Donelson. The few Confederate gunners who remained at Henry were expected merely to delay the Yankees. Grant accepted their surrender on the sixth, and plunged on toward Donelson on the Cumberland River.

The War in the West approached another climacteric. Easterners must have found difficulty understanding the sweep of the fighting beyond the Alleghenies. The theater of operations dominated by Lee and the Army of Northern Virginia would involve only parts of Maryland, Pennsylvania, and the Old Dominion State; between Bull Run, where this fighting began, and Appomattox, where it ended, the distance was little more than a hundred miles. But when one drew a finger along the 95th meridian, and thus approximated an irregular line between Louisiana and Minnesota, one covered the three thousand miles which the Western war affected.

Logic governed the pattern of that fighting. Operations that had carried Grant to Paducah and Belmont had been part of the strategy to guarantee the neutrality of Kentucky and Missouri and seal off the Ohio from Confederate armies. Now, at Henry and Donelson under Grant, the Union moved to an offensive action, seeking the control of hundreds of miles of navigable rivers that would permit Yankee gunboats to sail deep into Alabama.

Grant, hastening on to Donelson, found the weather turning cold. Numerous inexperienced troops, having enjoyed a succession of warm days, discarded or forgot their blankets. Then snow swept the camps; the temperature fell to twenty degrees below freezing; and the Union boys groaned with frostbite. Some of the attacking soldiers froze to death. Disease in many forms prostrated others. Roads, first flooded, then iced with ruts, made any passage of troops hazardous and painful; the fleet must travel a long distance to reach Donelson, again promising slow movement of supplies.

Cigar atilt, chin jutting, Grant reached the plateau near the great bend of the Cumberland where the hillside water batteries and bastioned earthworks of Donelson commanded a fortress of one hundred acres. To the north of Donelson the waters of Hickman Creek had overflowed, constituting an impassable barrier. To the south flowed Indian Creek, and here, too, stretched the narrow road to Nashville by way of Dover and Charlotte. To the west high ridges marked the network of brooks emptying into Hickman and Indian creeks. Rifle pits and abatis fortified these ridges; nine Confederate batteries covered any land approach to Donelson.

But Grant had his chance and he acted with audacity. To capture Donelson meant also the fall of Nashville, for once Federal gunboats could sweep past Donelson, they could easily destroy the single suspension bridge that gave the Rebels their only avenue of retreat across the Cumberland. Grant's lines of investment were slim, his soldiers were hungry, the weather was foul, but his flair had grown almost telepathic. At Paducah, Kentucky, William Tecumseh Sherman felt it. Sending men, food, messages to Grant, he didn't conceal his admiration for the commander in the field. By then Sherman had been ousted from one command and had wanted to quit the army. But now he thought he would like to fight once more—under Grant. Sherman puffed on his cigarillo, threw it away, lighted another—it was hard for him to wait. And yet his faith grew. The War in the West had begun to move.

Not all of Grant's luck proved bad. His first good fortune was the fact that the commanding Confederate general, Gideon J. Pillow, fulfilled Grant's hunch that if Pillow were scratched on the hand, he "might irritate the sore until . . . convinced . . . he had been wounded by the enemy." Pillow didn't linger to observe how the attack fared, but turned over the command to Simon Bolivar Buckner and slipped across the Cumberland with Confederate Secretary of War Floyd and five thousand troops for an escort. Once the Rebels broke free, cutting a road open toward Nashville; then a confusion in orders recalled the graycoats into the fort, and Grant promptly blocked the road. But greater luck for Grant was the fact that the bad lessons of the Mexican War had not yet been unlearned. In another year generals in both armies would feel less contemptuous of fighting behind entrenchments; at Donelson, as one of Grant's lieutenants shrewdly remarked, the Rebel commander "threw away his army by fighting outside his works." Sad and wiser, Buckner came forward to accept Grant's laconic "No terms but immediate and unconditional surrender."

Now Halleck had exactly what he didn't want. When the North learned that twelve thousand prisoners had been taken at Donelson—that at last it could claim a major victory—Grant became the nation's darling. The March first issue of *Harper's Weekly* would depict the stirring scene as Donelson fell with a dreary Confederate atop the earthwork waving a white flag. The following week the cover would be devoted to a full-page portrait of Grant—"The Hero of Fort Donelson." The editors of *Harper's*, alert to what the public wanted, kept the story alive in succeeding issues. The interior of the fort was delineated in detail so that the formidable size of the bastion could be appreciated. "The capture of Fort Donelson," extolled the jubilant editors, losing their heads entirely, "is probably the culminating point in the struggle between the United States Government and the malcontents."

Each new expression of adulation for Grant seared more deeply the burning pride of Halleck and McClellan. The telegraph wires thrummed between Washington and St. Louis as one disjointed nose vied with the other. Without permission, Halleck blustered, Grant had run off toward Nashville; moreover, Grant's army was demoralized; moreover, complained Halleck, "I can get no returns, no reports, no information of any kind from him. Satisfied with his victory, he sits down and enjoys it without any regard to the future." Previously Halleck even had hinted that "Grant had resumed his former bad habits," although the source of this intelligence was obscure; if he had asked Rawlins, the authority on the subject, he would have learned nothing. Sputtering over the wires from Washington came tart advice from McClellan: "Do not hesitate to arrest Grant at once if the good of the service requires it. . . ." Halleck demurred: "It is hard to censure a successful general immediately after a victory." Experts give varying opinions on the causes for Grant's difficulties after Donelson. Some will hold that the worst that can be charged against Grant is the indifference and carelessness he exhibited in letter-writing; others see in the aftermath to Donelson the independence of action that had brought reprimand from Frémont after Paducah, and they say that on the same impulse Grant pursued the Confederates toward Nashville and momentarily lost touch with Halleck.

In any case, McClellan, nourishing the tantalizing vision of a sodden Grant, and Halleck, flipping the pages of *Harper's Weekly* as though they had been woven of nettles, were not conjuring up any excuses. At last Halleck acted, and, Grant wrote bitterly, "in less than three weeks [after the victory at Donelson] I was virtually in arrest and without a command." Lincoln, grateful to discover a general without the "slows," affixed his signature to Grant's promotion to major general. Then Buell was moved to Nashville, Halleck placed in command of both Western departments, and the surface tension lessened.

4.

But Halleck almost came out completely on top after Shiloh.

The warm, balmy spring of 1862 brought the scent of peach blossoms to Shiloh Meetinghouse at Pittsburg Landing on the Tennessee. Along the yellow bluffs of the river Grant had encamped forty-five thousand men and leisurely awaited another thirty-seven thousand under Buell from Nashville. At Corinth, only twenty miles away, Albert Sidney Johnston commanded forty thousand Rebels. Johnston had fought Mormons at sixteen degrees below zero in the Rocky Mountains; Zach Taylor had called him "the best soldier he ever commanded." Johnston had no intention of allowing Buell to join Grant before the issue was drawn.

Afterward at least one reporter wondered if the initial in Grant's name stood for "Surprise," for the General clearly possessed no notion of the impending peril. His patrols seemed scattered, almost carelessly alerted. He ignored instructions to dig entrenchments, holding to the still prevalent West Point theory, as Charles Francis Adams said, "that fieldworks made the men cowardly." Shy and silent, Grant roamed the camps, quick to smile with sympathy at wan soldiers who tried to shrug off diarrhea by calling it "the Tennessee quickstep."

Grant had found a new friend those spring days in Sherman. Rumor-mongers had once proclaimed Sherman mentally unbalanced, but the aftermath of Donelson had given Grant a bellyful of nasty gossip and he judged the man as he found him—an alert, hard-cussing, two-fisted son of the Midwest with a sound head for military strategy. They made an odd pair side by side—Grant squat, composed, confident, and Sherman lanky, nervous, his red head full of fears and suspicions. "We are in great danger," Sherman said privately at Shiloh. But he wouldn't carry this worry to Grant. If the commander expected no attack, then neither did he. Reporters heard him arguing that the Confederates were not such fools as to leave their base and attack the Yankees in theirs.

"The distant rear of an army engaged in battle," Grant said later, "is not the best place from which to judge correctly what is going on in front." On Sunday morning, the sixth of April, Grant breakfasted comfortably at the beautiful Cherry House, where he had set up headquarters nine miles from his front lines. From far off came the distinct sound of firing. Grant dug spurs into his horse, but by the time he reached Shiloh disaster had struck. The Confederates, seizing the initiative, had found the entire Union army exposed to attack. In blood and agony and sometimes utter confusion, brigade battled brigade, mob pitched into mob. Irresistibly that first day Johnston's Rebels drove Grant's Yankees toward the river. Four horses were shot from beneath Sherman; the 40th Illinois, the 13th Missouri ran out of ammunition; and Dan McCook of Sherman's staff swore his heart out at the thousands of soldiers cringing under the yellow bluffs, who, "not satisfied with their own infamy, were discouraging our troops newly arrived." Johnston was killed and the Confederate command passed to Beauregard, the hero of Sumter. Toward nightfall Buell's troops began to arrive and the seeming rout for Grant was averted; with morning the remainder of Buell's army reached the field and drove out the enemy. Beauregard's retreat was orderly, and Grant failed to pursue. Again a mistake was marked down by critics against his military career.

When the fighting at Shiloh ended, a Yankee wrote home: "We made the field of battle ring with hymns of praise to God!" No explanation anyone might offer could lessen the nation's shock at the more than twenty-three thousand casualties the two armies had suffered. On the eleventh a grim-lipped Halleck arrived to take command in person; he advanced so cautiously on Corinth that the town was completely evacuated when he reached there. But "Old Brains" made certain that Grant didn't escape the lash of his anger; again he accused Grant of drunkenness, this time of being too drunk to mount a horse during the battle. The charge was serious, but once more unsupported; for a private convicted of intoxication on duty the sentence might range from hanging to imprisonment and hard labor, and his only hope was that Lincoln would intervene and mitigate the sentence.

The spring days along the Tennessee remained warm and balmy; for Grant they were filled with growing bitterness. Around Shiloh Meetinghouse the scent of peach blossoms had been replaced by another odor. Civilian surgeons and Sanitary Commission agents, arriving at Pittsburg Landing in a constant stream, beheld the dead on the field, the groaning wounded in their meager shelters. Huddled around campfires, soldiers related grisly stories—the terror of Shiloh remained a haunting specter. Visitors to Shiloh, Sherman testified, "caught up the camp stories, which on their return home they retailed through their local papers, usually elevating their own neighbors into heroes, but decrying all others." The lieutenant governor of Ohio lashed out at Grant in an abusive verbal attack.

Sherman returned from Corinth one day to hear that Grant had asked for a thirty-day leave and was going away. Straightway Sherman rode to Grant's headquarters—a group of four or five tents behind a sapling railing. Rawlins stood outside and greeted the other with a sober nod. Office and camp chests were piled up outside the tents—everything had been made ready for the General to leave next morning. Inside, Sherman found Grant "seated on a campstool, with papers on a rude camp-table; he seemed to be employed in assorting letters, and tying them up with red tape into convenient bundles."

The account of the subsequent remarks between Grant and himself that Sherman gave in his memoirs was greatly prettified. The scene depicts none of Sherman's excitability under emotional stress, quotes none of the damns and God-damns that punctuated his conversation in such moments, never once lets him pound the table. Sherman knew that his own grasp of "war, military history, strategy, and grand tactics" surpassed Grant's; but Grant had something more that the Union army desperately needed. So Sherman pictured himself as quietly asking what he probably thundered: Was it true Grant intended to quit?

"Sherman," Grant said, "you know that I am in the way here. I have stood it as long as I can, and can endure it no longer."

On another day—under other circumstances—the remark would be made that Grant was the "creator" of the Western army and that Billy Sherman was its "idol." At that moment neither deserved this accolade. Sherman stormed. Grant couldn't quit. Suppose he ran away— "events would go along, and he would be left out." But if he hung on, weathered Halleck's sharp tongue and the fools who were wise by hindsight, "some happy accident might restore him to favor and his true place." What if the reporter for the *New York World* had renamed him Ulysses Surprise Grant? And what did they call *him*? Crazy Sherman!

Grant wavered. The wounds in his sensitive nature had been cut deep. Those wounds continued to itch and burn. Grant wouldn't commit himself one way or the other. Time must decide, he said. But Grant promised to think the matter over and not to leave without seeing Sherman once more or at least communicating with him.

Sherman, ordered to Chewalla soon thereafter, just didn't know. Grant might stay. He might not. Then a short note revealed that Grant had reconsidered. He would stay. Exuberantly Sherman replied: ". . . you could not be quiet at home for a week when armies were moving. . . ."

Grant must have smiled.

5.

In the East McClellan's campaign on the Peninsula collapsed. With a disheartening sputter, the cries of "On to Richmond" faded. In Virginia, Robert E. Lee began to think seriously of invading the North.

Lincoln stirred restlessly. He was through with McClellan. Still, he wanted some military man close to the White House on whom he could rely. Whatever singular success the Union forces had enjoyed had been in the West. Lincoln couldn't make up his mind whether or not Halleck was really the man he wanted for general-in-chief; Halleck, quite satisfied with commanding in the West, afraid of Washington and its politicians, didn't want to go. Halleck's reluctance, his insistence that he actually had little to offer the Eastern theater of operations, brought out a perverse stubbornness in Lincoln. At first he had decided he must see "Old Brains" before committing himself; now he wouldn't wait. Halleck was appointed general-in-chief.

And so "the happy accident" that Sherman had foreseen developed, and Grant took over the command of the Federal forces at Corinth. Subsequently Grant's base would be moved to Memphis, whence he could look down the Mississippi—toward Vicksburg and the final campaign that could win the war in the West.

The town that the Methodist minister Vick had founded on a hairpin bend of the Mississippi stood on cliffs that rose abruptly for two hundred feet or more above the water. Years before, visiting Vicksburg, Daniel Webster had called it the "terraced city of the hills"; but Jefferson Davis saw it more realistically as "the Gibraltar of America." Below

Memphis, Vicksburg was the first high ground on the Mississippi, and its strategic importance was enormous. A railroad, running east from the city, connected with other roads leading to every significant point in the South; across the river another railroad ran west to Shreveport, Louisiana. With Vicksburg the Confederacy was geographically united; without Vicksburg the Mississippi became a knife cutting the empire of the South into disintegrating sections. Understandably formidable batteries frowned down on the river from the heights of Vicksburg, and forts stood at every critical point by which a Union army might approach this bastion.

Whether Grant could take Vicksburg—whether the Northern army possessed a general capable of taking it— was at least problematical in January 1863. Grant, arriving at Young's Point that bleak day, did not mitigate the risks. The campaign for Vicksburg to that moment was not going well—in fact, it progressed dismally. The general who came down the gangplank, head bent over a newspaper, faced an unhappy duty. Frayed nerves and smoldering tempers surrounded him. He understood why. Sherman actually was at the seat of the trouble—Sherman, who virtually had stolen another general's army, certainly over that general's wish and in all likelihood over the expressed wishes of the President and the Secretary of War.

Grant would like to soothe ruffled feelings if he could, but difficulties obviously stood in the way of that happy prospect when one of the participants in the quarrel was an angry admiral who distrusted all West Pointers, and another was a political general who not only disliked West Point graduates, but was also a sulky honeymooner.

2. THE DISGRUNTLED BRIDEGROOM

ALONG the lower Mississippi, January can become a dreary month, with cold, misty mornings and dank, gray days. General John A. McClernand stood at the entrance to his headquarters and gazed with dull eyes at the cheerless countryside. The general's nerves and temper, always somewhat delicately balanced, now teetered dangerously under a succession of emotional stresses. The bride he had married at the age of fifty-one had gone home, and her final embrace had not disguised for either the humiliating knowledge that the triumphant honeymoon they had planned had ended badly. From deep sockets McClernand's dark, introspective eyes scowled sullenly. Conspiracy and betrayal were indelicate words, but the mind of the prairie politician had been taught to recognize how unpleasant reality could become. The present situation was rotten, really sickening.

The crisis over which McClernand brooded had brought Grant to Young's Point. To Grant's practical mind there was only one way to deal with a wound that had been festering for months: scrape it clean and give it the chance to heal. Perhaps someone could explain why there was any need for a showdown over who should run the war on the Mississippi—McClernand or himself—but privately Grant must have suspected that he was embroiled in the sort of mess that always developed when military decisions grew out of political love-making. Lincoln and his Secretary of War had fumbled the matter right from the start—whether through carelessness or callousness no one could say.

In the spring of 1861, shortly after Lincoln issued his second call for troops, Grant and McClernand met. The place was Springfield, Illinois, the state capital. The invigorating sunniness of the day could not dissipate the edginess of those gathered at near-by Camp Yates, where ten regiments of militia, organized to serve the state for ninety days, must be mustered into the Union army for a period of three years. Rag-tag recruits, often drilling with broomsticks until muskets arrived, and probably growing sated with the saloons and whores that began to clutter the streets of Springfield, balked at this extended commitment of service in larger numbers than anyone cared to admit. Grant felt the general uneasiness. He had come to Springfield to accept command of the 21st Illinois. Grant liked his boys, and found them "of as good social position as any in their section of the State"; but in almost the next breath he confessed: "I found it very hard fcr a few days to bring all the men into anything like subordination."

Governor Richard Yates, John A. McClernand, Grant, each wanted to hurry along the muster with as few hitches as possible. To use Grant's words, Illinois continued to encounter difficulty in bringing all parts of the state "into anything like subordination" on the issues of the war. The sixteen counties of southern Illinois—"Egypt"—had been settled originally by several families from the deep South, and the political temper of the region was such that even the noses of dogs twitched at the mention of Abe Lincoln and the youthful Republican party. Secessionist talk in southern Illinois charged the atmosphere with the brittleness of any of the border slave states, and moving Federal troops through these counties involved the same risks that existed in Kentucky or Missouri. Almost every bridge must be guarded.

But there remained Democrats in Illinois who felt as touchy as Republicans over this split in loyalty. John A. McClernand, member of Congress, had been an outstanding advocate of unity; it was thoroughly appropriate for him to be in Springfield that day to address the troops and speed up the muster in a climate of political harmony. With McClernand appeared a fellow Congressman named John A. Logan, who owed his power and influence to the renegade Democratic majority in southern Illinois.

26

2: THE DISGRUNTLED BRIDEGROOM

Grant knew no more about this pair than what he had read in the papers. That he stood between two men, one of whom would become a lifelong friend and the other one of his bitterest enemies, events of the next few months would disclose. At that moment Grant felt no hesitancy in having McClernand talk to the boys in the 21st Illinois, but the more he thought about Logan, the less his mind seemed at rest. Grant had lived in Missouri and knew the virulence of the secessionist crowd; the reputation of the southern Illinois population was to him bitter fact rather than political myth. But Logan's smile attracted Grant. The fellow possessed charm. Down in Egypt it was reported that Logan knew enough people by their first names to form his own Congressional district. Logan—"the Gallant Egyptian"— could out-swear most of the young blades and, if the need arose, out-drink them. But Logan's following set as his first virtue the fact that he was scrupulously fair-minded. At the age of ten he had acquired his initial local renown for a proclamation tacked to a tree:

> I give notice to all squirrels to keep out of this corn-field. If they don't keep out they will be shot.
>
> John A. Logan

McClernand addressed the troops. Then "the Gallant Egyptian" mounted the platform. Years afterward Grant still would declare that Logan's appeal that spring afternoon seldom had been equaled "for force and eloquence." Logan "breathed loyalty and devotion to the Union"; the boys in the 21st Illinois "almost to a man" enlisted for three years. In Grant's experience the Democrats were proving the real orators of the war—first Rawlins in Galena, now Logan in Springfield.

But Grant should have scrutinized McClernand more closely. The deep lines around McClernand's mouth suggested his pride and ambition; austerity and vanity dominated his bearing, and when he walked his stride became energetic and aggressive. The Scotch-Irish in McClernand made him both stubbornly dogmatic and delicately sensitive; he believed, and with justification, that he had inherited the diadem of Illinois Democracy once worn so brilliantly by Stephen A. Douglas. It was in this role that Lincoln also viewed McClernand, seeing him as an old political rival from his home state and home town who now had turned friend. From former days in Springfield, the President remembered McClernand at a rally in Edwards' Grove, predicting that Douglas was a sure winner in 1860; he remembered that McClernand had appeared for the claimant in Springfield's first fugitive-slave case, and, as head of the Democratic Club, had stood eager and ready at all times to swap verbal blows with the Young Men's Republican Club organized by "Billy Herndon, Lincoln's Man Friday." But the fighting edge of McClernand's temper had been demonstrated by more than the power of his lungs. When the editor of the *Springfield Journal* offended McClernand with certain published criticisms and refused to apologize, McClernand caned the journalist in public.

Both politics and sentiment led Lincoln to want Illinois stanchly aligned with the Union. For any man to succeed as President there must exist in his personality, in the political sense, a touch of the Casanova. He must woo willingly and well when the opportunity arises—not promiscuously, as in the case of Buchanan, but with the restraint of good sound sense so that he only winks at wantons with their hearts in the right place. Somewhat in this spirit, Lincoln had no need to hesitate when McClernand wanted a place in the army to award him the rank of brigadier general. With a trace of self-consciousness, the President confessed to a White House caller from Illinois: "There is General McClernand . . . whom they say I use better than a radical [Republican]." In the photographic files of the hustling Mathew Brady reposed a negative of Lincoln standing between a McClernand looking ridiculously un-Napoleonic with hand thrust inside his coat and an Allen Pinkerton looking ludicrously like the traditional sleuth in a checkered shirt and bowler hat. The picture, taken at McClellan's headquarters, represented a period when Lincoln, still green both at command and the Presidency, had not begun to separate his military sheep and goats.

2.

Grant, the West Pointer, could view McClernand much more dispassionately. Political generals invariably became military liabilities—or so Grant had learned if he paid any attention to his lessons at the Academy. No one could have expected Grant to feel impressed by McClernand's one previous lick as a soldier in the Black Hawk War. Lincoln had engaged in the same squabble and cheerfully admitted that he had not seen any "live, fighting Indians," although he had encountered "a good many bloody struggles with mosquitoes." Likely, in Grant's opinion, McClernand's experiences had been no more telling; and yet when Grant slipped into Paducah under the prayerful procrastination of Polk, his report to Frémont included acknowledgment of the efficient assistance McClernand had rendered in equipping the expedition. McClernand likewise had fought well at Belmont. After that engagement, however, Lincoln should have been forewarned that McClernand saw foggily through the eyes of his own self-interest. Congressman Washburne, who had visited his home-state boys at Belmont, dropped by at the White House to shed a few of the fleas McClernand had lodged in his ear. Lincoln took time to write McClernand "not an official but a social letter." His Springfield friend must not feel neglected if supplies were lacking, or if he did not know his precise destination; "our good people have rushed to the rescue of the Government, faster than the government can find arms to put into their hands."

At Donelson, Grant began to sour on McClernand. A very sick man, sitting in shawls and stocking cap on the porch of his summer home at Mount McGregor, Grant after long years still railed bitterly at the memory of how at Donelson McClernand had attacked an enemy's battery "without orders or authority." Grant's recollections ran on harshly: "Of course the assault was a failure, and of course the loss on our side was great for the number of men engaged"; for the first time, "hospitals were overcrowded." Later, when the Rebels almost cut their way out of Donelson on the road to Nashville, it would be McClernand's division that "scattered . . . in full retreat" through lack of ammunition rather than lack of gallantry when "there was an abundance of ammunition near by lying on the ground." Tartly Grant commented: "At that stage of the war . . . not all our commanders . . . had been educated up to the point of seeing that our men were constantly supplied with ammunition during an engagement."

Grant's distrust of McClernand grew after Donelson, for that was Grant's way. His faith was hard to shake when he liked a man, even though this trait would write the word "Grantism" into history as a derogatory term, but he also could dislike thoroughly and grudgingly. At Shiloh many Union regiments ran out of ammunition, but Grant's *Memoirs* would ignore this fact; indeed, his remarks concerning McClernand during those bloody two days would be restricted to how McClernand had reinforced Sherman and had "profited much by having so able a commander supporting him." Actually, McClernand fought well at Shiloh; Sherman's own report cited how he "promptly and energetically responded" and "struggled most determindedly."

After Shiloh, McClernand arrived in Washington one bright September day excited by a plan that he wished to put before the President. Let him go into Illinois and raise his own army, McClernand urged, so that he might charge down the Mississippi and capture Vicksburg! What the general wished to do fitted into Lincoln's own deliberated notions of how the war must be fought.

3.

"The war can never be brought to a close until that key is in our pocket!"

The speaker, pointing to Vicksburg on a map of the South, was Lincoln. The year was 1861. The idea, in part, was borrowed. His audience was McClellan.

David D. Porter, a young naval officer, had stimulated the President's excitement. New Orleans, Porter claimed, easily could be taken—and now, Lincoln instructed McClellan, plans must be formulated for a combined land and naval attack so that New Orleans could be used as a base of operation against the whole of the Mississippi controlled by the Confederacy. The general-in-chief always liked to work on plans, especially when they in no way involved him in the field, and by spring McClellan was ready to order General Ben Butler, commander of the Department of the Gulf, to co-operate with the navy in an expedition intended to snatch everything from New Orleans to Vicksburg. Lincoln assented, excited and enthusiastic.

Porter accompanied the expedition as commander of the mortar flotilla. Sylvanus Cadwallader, who represented the *Chicago Times* at Vicksburg, characterized him pointedly: "Porter was vain, arrogant, and egotistical to an extent that can neither be described nor evaluated, and you know his calibre completely. He possessed many polite accomplishments but very few qualities of a great naval commander." However, Porter could tell a story with verve and color. New Orleans capitulated with little more than a token resistance from its batteries, and as Flag-officer David G. Farragut led the Western Gulf Squadron past the Chalmette batteries Porter saw ships, cotton, steamers, and coal ablaze. The shore and docks were crowded with a shouting, defiant horde. "There was no insulting epithet these maniacs did not heap upon the heads of those on board the ships," Porter said. "It was as if bedlam had broken loose and all its inmates were assembled on the levee at New Orleans."

Farragut landed his forces—amid a city in an uproar "such as was perhaps never before seen in this country," Porter declared. And the "polite accomplishments" attributed to Porter drew a vivid picture: "All the vagabonds of the town, thieves, ragpickers, abandoned women, the inhabitants of the slums, all were abroad, their faces distorted by passion, the riffraff hobnobbing with the well-to-do, and all animated by a common hatred of the detested Yankee." Men smashed in the rice tierces, Porter said; women—not necessarily abandoned—scraped up all they could gather; what was left went into the river with a shout: "The damned Yankees shan't have it!"

In a few days a reasonable degree of order, sanity, and subservience had been restored to the "Queen City of the South." Meanwhile Ben Butler appeared to grow fond of the varied divertisements of New Orleans; as Farragut pointed out that the job of taking Vicksburg remained, Butler manifested increasing reluctance to budge. Furthermore, the ten thousand troops Butler had brought to aid Farragut on his river sally he now decided must remain with him in New Orleans. "This failure to act promptly," Porter said, "cost the Government many lives and millions of money."

Farragut pushed on to Vicksburg, lacking the mortar support he felt he needed and aided on land by an eventual concession of three thousand troops under General Thomas Williams, who, Porter grumbled, as "they attempted nothing" were "perfectly useless." Farragut's ships passed Vicksburg "with very little loss," but "the soldiers in the hill forts refused to stay shelled out." Moreover:

2: THE DISGRUNTLED BRIDEGROOM

. . . The fortifications of Vicksburg were scattered over the hills in groups, the guns fifty yards apart, and concealed from view. The heavy shells would whistle over the ships, throwing up the water in spouts and occasionally crashing through the vessels' timbers, to let the invaders know how well Vicksburg was fortified. . . .

The whole power of the Confederacy had been set to work to save this Gibraltar of the Mississippi, the railroads poured in troops and guns without stint, enabling it to bid defiance to Farragut's ships and the mortar flotilla. . . .

Our combined fleet lay there and gazed in wonder at the new forts that were constantly springing up on the hill tops . . . while water batteries seemed to grow on every salient point. It was evident enough that Vicksburg could only be taken after a long siege by the combined operations of a large military and naval force. . . .

When Secretary of the Navy Welles carried into a Cabinet meeting Porter's report on how Butler had forsaken the operation against Vicksburg, Lincoln doubtless began to lose faith in the generalship of this politically powerful Massachusetts Democrat. Other idiosyncrasies—some military, some not—soon became manifest. Butler was not an attractive man; he squinted; one wag called him a crosseyed cuttlefish; he antagonized or insulted virtually everyone, from European consuls to the average housewife; and for years after his stay in New Orleans night vases with the general's visage painted within were a popular curio of the war (prostitutes, it was said, adored them). The Department of the Gulf needed someone better than Butler. With expanded forces, an army from New Orleans could push up the river to meet another army coming down the Mississippi. Thus might the key of Vicksburg be pocketed! Later an expedition could push out from Louisiana along the Red

River into Texas. The scheme entranced Lincoln. Perhaps the President felt that if he replaced one Massachusetts political general in the field with another he would strike a nice balance. So Butler was succeeded by a general known to the voters of the Bay State as Nathaniel P. Banks. Very quickly the army renamed him Nothing Positive Banks.

McClernand, filled with his plans for investing Vicksburg from the north, seemed to Lincoln to offer the reasonable teamwork required for Banks. Stanton came over from the War Department, listened, and assented, perhaps somewhat vaguely, for in drawing up the order that implemented McClernand's proposal Stanton achieved a masterpiece of ambiguity. Both Lincoln and Stanton played the whole affair very close to their vests; Halleck, trying to establish himself in Washington at the unwanted job of general-in-chief, did not receive for weeks the slightest hint of the plan that the President and the Secretary of War had worked out with Lincoln's fellow townsman. Meanwhile McClernand hustled back to Springfield in quest both of an army and a wife. He had every reason to believe he operated directly under the White House and the War Department.

The order eventually released in respect to McClernand poses so many basic contradictions that it is possible neither Lincoln nor Stanton knew how to explain them to Halleck. McClernand would be authorized by this order "to proceed to the States of Indiana, Illinois, and Iowa, and to organize the troops remaining in those states and to be raised by volunteering or draft." Then, "with all despatch," he was to forward these troops to "Memphis, Cairo, or such other points as may hereafter be designated by the General-in-Chief." But Memphis remained the only logical point, and, technically, any forces sent to Memphis belonged under the command of Grant's Department of Tennessee. Stanton tried to meet this conflict: "When a sufficient force, not required by the operations of General Grant's command shall be raised, an expedition may be organized under General

McClernand's command against Vicksburg and to clear the Mississippi River and open navigation to New Orleans." Stanton really compounded absurdity—where else, except for Vicksburg, should Grant aim? A copy of these orders marked "confidential" went to McClernand on the twentieth of October. Lincoln's accompanying note, however, permitted McClernand to show the order "to Governors, and even others, when, in his discretion, he believes so doing to be indispensable to the progress of the expedition." Lincoln expressed his "deep interest" in McClernand's activities and desired the expedition "pushed forward with all possible despatch, *consistently with the other parts of the military service.*"

Would McClernand realize that the last of these aces the President slipped him was actually a joker?

A beautiful October yielded to the clear crispness of November. In Springfield the bridegroom-to-be rustled up recruits for his army and thought pleasantly of the future. A brilliant army record, a term perhaps in the Senate, and then—who could say? Dreams of the Presidency were not new in Springfield. Lincoln had lived with them; so too had Stephen A. Douglas.

4.

In the field during these months of negotiation among McClernand, Lincoln, and Stanton, an unsuspecting Grant faced bitter fighting. That fall of 1862 found the Confederacy playing for high stakes. Popular sentiment, already wavering in the Lincoln administration as the elections approached, might crumble entirely if the military thinking in Richmond prevailed. Lee's Army of Northern Virginia, having defeated Pope soundly, invaded Maryland. Along the Ohio the Confederate Bragg kept step with Buell on his way to Louisville. Grant, worried over the reinforcements he had been called upon to send Buell, could see the tight spot in which he had been placed: "If I too should be driven back, the Ohio River would become the line dividing the belligerents west of the Alleghenies." And the trap that the Confederacy tried to spring on Lincoln Grant saw with equal clearness: "To say at the end of the second year of the war the line dividing the contestants at the East was pushed north of Maryland, a state that had not yet seceded, and at the West beyond Kentucky, another state which had been always loyal, would have been discouraging indeed."

Grant took stock of his situation. His entire force "of all arms" was less than fifty thousand. Two divisions were spread along a line touching Corinth, Rienzi, Jacinto, and Danville; another division and two brigades, with cavalry and artillery, were at Corinth. These forces constituted Grant's left wing, commanded by Rosecrans. General E. O. C. Ord, astride two railroads—the Mobile and Ohio from Bethel to Humboldt and the Mississippi Central from Jackson to the crossing of the Hatchie River at Bolivar—held the center. Sherman was at Memphis, with two of his brigades thrown out as far as Brownsville to cover the crossing of the Hatchie River by the Memphis and Ohio Railroad. Grant might well draw a deep breath; what actually confronted him, he recognized afterward, was "two and a half months of continued defense over a large district of the country . . . where nearly every citizen was an enemy ready to give information of our every move."

The Battle of Iuka—or perhaps Grant should have called it the "Battle of the Wrong Wind"—followed. The Confederate general, Sterling Price, had earned no affection from loyalist Missourians; hard-bitten, bitter veterans of the Missouri regiments claimed that wherever Price went within their borders mothers, sisters, wives, and sweethearts were raped. Some twenty miles east of Corinth on the Memphis and Charleston Railroad, Price struck at Iuka on the thirteenth of September. Colonel R. C. Murphy of the 8th Wisconsin guarded the place with a handful of men.

Murphy fled. Grant guessed Price's real objective—to shuttle troops into Tennessee to help Bragg. Reinforcements, brought up to Corinth from Bolivar and Jackson, gave Ord a command of nearly eight thousand men; Rosecrans, commanding the district of Corinth, had nine thousand "movable" troops. About four days' march to the south lurked the Confederate general Earl Van Dorn. Grant saw instantly that he must get at Price before Van Dorn joined him. So Ord was told to move by rail to Burnsville, some seven miles west of Iuka, and either to wheel around and intercept Van Dorn if he should dash suddenly at Corinth; or, as Grant hoped, to join with Rosecrans bringing his troops by the roads through Jacinto and Fulton.

Price was tough, but so was Edward Otho Cresap Ord. He had fought Seminole Indians in Florida, Mexicans at Monterey, Rogue River Indians in Oregon, and Spokane Indians in the Washington Territory; he had also fought Confederates at Dranesville, Bull Run, and Ball's Bluff before coming West with the reputation that if "there was a fight to be scared up, Ord would find it." So, completely in character, Ord fought a nasty skirmish at Burnsville, and Grant learned that part of "Old Rosy's" forces had moved so slowly he could not possibly reach Iuka before two the following afternoon.

The roads were bad, a march of over twenty miles separated Rosecrans from Iuka, and his troops would not be much good for fighting when they reached there, anyhow. Ord was notified of Old Rosy's delay, and was ordered "to be in readiness to attack the moment he heard the sounds of guns to the south or south-west." Then the wind proceeded to blow the wrong way. On the nineteenth neither Ord in the field nor Grant, waiting at Burnsville, heard anything. Rosecrans's column came down to Barnett's Corners, where the road from Jacinto to Iuka forks to the east, and found the enemy waiting. Alone, betrayed by the wind, Rosecrans fought a short engagement in which "his loss was considerable for the number engaged." A courier finally reached Grant with this intelligence; the hour was late, no road connected Burnsville with the position Rosecrans occupied, and Ord could not attack until early next morning. Price, however, pulled out of Iuka during the night along the Fulton Road that Rosecrans neglected to guard. Grant admitted disappointment over the results at Iuka, but still he retained his high opinion of General Rosecrans.

William Starke Rosecrans, with his large red nose, so that "Old Rosy" described him precisely, had been at West Point with Sherman. He had always liked leisure, a good time; a favorite story was how he and Sherman had risked expulsion by running down to Benny Haven's tavern, a mile away on the Hudson, to eat oysters at night. Signs on tents reading "Dog-hole No. 1 . . . Sons of Bitches Within" made Old Rosy, now a general, howl gleefully. He could swear eloquently and generously—although never, his conscience as a converted Roman Catholic made him point out (and Rosecrans professed a deep, almost perpetual interest in spiritual matters), did he blaspheme God. He could also drink like a fish, preferring a good dash of whisky with his water.

None of these traits disturbed Grant. He just wished Old Rosy had been more careful about letting Price get out of Iuka. But now Van Dorn seemed to disclose his intention. Debonair Earl—the following May a civilian would assassinate Van Dorn and charge the general with amorous indiscretions—wanted to strike the Mississippi above Memphis. Union forces at Helena, Arkansas, could have balked Van Dorn, but Grant exercised no command over them. Then Van Dorn revealed "a deeper design"—joined by other Confederate troops, he aimed for Corinth. On the fourth of October, Van Dorn made, Grant said, "a dashing attack," in the hope of capturing Rosecrans before reinforcements could come up. Van Dorn thus could occupy Corinth and use the Federals' own defenses to hold "at bay" all Union troops as they arrived. Old Rosy cussed and fought; Van Dorn's boys charged gallantly and penetrated Yankee lines for a time, but, in the end, were "driven back with great slaughter." Rosecrans failed to follow up orders to pursue Van Dorn the moment he was repelled. Grant chafed and repeated the order. Still Rosecrans lingered. Ord, joining Hurlburt's reinforcements, caught the head of Van Dorn's retreating column at the Hatchie River and drove them back "in a panic." Confederates, pushed off the bridge in their frantic retreat, drowned. Even with a late start, Grant said, "if Rosecrans had followed the route taken by the enemy, he would have come upon Van Dorn in a swamp with a stream in front and Ord holding the only bridge." So where Iuka could be called the "Battle of the Wrong Wind," Corinth became, at its close, the "Battle of the Reluctant Rosy."

Now official Washington intervened. On the twenty-fourth Rosecrans was relieved and soon Grant "was delighted" to learn of Rosy's promotion to a separate command to succeed Buell. On the twenty-fifth—just five days after Lincoln had sent McClernand his "confidential orders"—Grant was placed in command of the Department of Tennessee. Within twenty-four hours Grant was suggesting to Halleck "a forward movement against Vicksburg."

3. "TIRED OF FURNISHING BRAINS"

GRANT remained eager to seize the initiative. On the second of November he launched *his* campaign against the "Gibraltar of the Mississippi." But an old axiom of war imposed a nettlesome obstacle. "Large bodies of troops," Grant had been taught, "must operate from a base of supplies which they always covered and guarded in all forward movements."

At that moment Grant's army straddled three railroads. The Mobile and Ohio was held from a point approximately twenty-five miles south of Corinth to Columbus, Kentucky; the Mississippi Central, joining the Mobile and Ohio out of Bolivar, also rested under Grant's control along that distance; and the Memphis and Charleston from Corinth east to Bear Creek likewise was in Yankee hands. In late October the enemy under Pemberton had been reported headquartered at Holly Springs, "much reinforced by conscripts and troops from Alabama and Texas"; from the Federal base at Jackson, Tennessee, Grant advised Halleck that he intended to draw three divisions from Corinth and two from Bolivar, and start a general movement for Grand Junction. "If found practicable," Grant wired the general-in-chief, "I will go to Holly Springs, and maybe to Grenada, completing railroad and telegraph as I go."

Grant felt fretful, however. He talked of a forward movement when his entire command of thirty thousand appeared capable only of holding his present lines and might be hard pressed to do that if kept on the defensive. But Grant saw an alternative to avoid that danger—a bold move straight against the enemy's "unsubdued, and not yet captured, territory." The Confederates had fortified their positions along the Tallahatchie River and occupied both Holly Springs and Grand Junction on the Mississippi Central. Grant went back to his maps. The strategy taking shape in the General's mind his troops soon would be calling the "Tallahatchie Expedition"; its objective was to approach Vicksburg from the north and east by land.

Grant's boldness paid. Within six days he reached Grand Junction and La Grange, with a sizable force thrown along the railroad for seven or eight miles to the south. Grant's army, well rested through September and October, was full of fight and swagger. Morale ran high.

No one was more impressed by this fact than Sylvanus
Cadwallader, reporting on Grant's activities for the copper-
head, "jingo" *Chicago Times*. There was a marked difference
now between the opinion Cadwallader held of Grant and
the one he had formed traveling by train to catch the river
steamer at Cairo. Soldiers and officers had crowded the cars.
They had expressed their minds freely: "Grant was used up
at Belmont—he was drunk all day—his troops were driven
from the field. . . . Prentiss of Illinois had been sacrificed
at Shiloh—McClernand was the coming man, perhaps—
Lew Wallace [he would one day write *Ben-Hur*] had few
equals, perhaps no superiors—Rosecrans was the most
brilliant officer in the West—Sherman was crazy. . . . But
Grant—" Even then Cadwallader had appreciated the
jockeying inevitable among soldiers over "the long list of
Western generals coming into prominence"; most of
Grant's detractors, he had noticed, had fought under
Rosecrans or were from Crawfordsville, Indiana, where
Lew Wallace had raised the 11th regiment of Indiana
Volunteer Infantry.

In the field Grant was liked, even loved. Troops caught
up the relaxed, jocular spirit that made Grant on a march
more inclined to talk about "Illinois horses, hogs, cattle, and
farming, than of the business actually in hand." Individual
regiments were proud, competitive, pugnacious. One day a
chaplain bragged to Colonel Gabe Bouck of the 18th
Wisconsin of how religion was spreading among the boys of
the 7th Iowa. He had, the chaplain boasted, "just concluded a series of precious refreshings" in the camp of the
Iowans; seven members of the regiment had been baptized.
A "glowering storm" spread over "Gabe's green and bilious
countenance"; turning on his camp stool, he roared:
"Adjutant! Adjutant!" When "that meek functionary"
appeared, Gabe, "with a satanic grin," yelled: "Detail
fifteen men to be baptized tomorrow morning at ten o'clock.
I'll be eternally God-damned if the 7th Iowa or any other

regiment shall ever get ahead of the 18th Wisconsin!"

Grant enjoyed camp pranks. The 124th Illinois, newly recruited, arrived "in all the pride and circumstances of war." They couldn't be formed in a straight line in an hour, Cadwallader said, but had new tents, new arms, a full band, trunks full of clothing, and most of the comforts of home. Veterans pounced on them. A detachment of the 124th, successful in a day's foraging for "chickens, turkeys, ducks, geese, pigs, sheep, butter, eggs, vegetables, and such other delicacies," were tried on their return before a mock court-martial, the food was confiscated, and the raw youngsters were hoodwinked into paying fines "for a breach of military discipline." A couple of nights later the vets went out and stole the tents over the heads of half the regiment. Hearing these stories, Grant burst into "uproarious laughter."

On the march down from Bolivar to La Grange, the same crowd slipped out of hand. Stragglers from McPherson's corps, ranging over the country for miles, frequently grew "lawless and destructive." Houses were plundered, plantations burned. The Wisconsin boys behaved as badly as any; an "immense concourse of camp followers" trailed behind them. Later, at Oxford, the cavalry found a cache of liquor and "behaved scandalously." Negroes were robbed of their watches and paid off "in green express labels stolen from the depot." Cadwallader wrote a stinging story for the *Chicago Times* about such abuses, then worried that he might be sent out of the Department for the sharpness of his criticisms. But Grant admitted the censure was deserved. A reporter, he said, was at liberty to report anything that had happened; but "predictions" of pending operations were forbidden.

2.

Many problems plagued Grant at Grand Junction. Delay had been inevitable with the necessity of repairing the railroad from Bolivar and the collection of forage. The unforeseen hindrance was the thousands of Negroes—"of all ages and both sexes," Grant said—who streamed into Grand Junction and slowed down his advance to a virtual standstill. Rawlins sensed quickly Grant's annoyance and concern. How could this horde of countrabands be kept from starvation? Army regulations permitted Grant to employ the able-bodied as teamsters, cooks and pioneers, and to feed them out of army stores, but only a handful would be saved this way.

Rawlins listened and Grant talked; then Grant listened and Rawlins talked. The Galena ex-lawyer had a bold, resolute mind. He had learned well the nature of both his job and his commander since Cairo. Those close to Grant eventually discovered that the longer he was separated from his wife, the more nagging grew his thirst. His heavy drinking on the Pacific coast after the Mexican War that had forced him to resign from the army wasn't any mystery to those who knew about the strand of Julia's hair in the locket he wore around his throat. Anyone living as intimately with Grant as Rawlins could guess what was happening; confidentially, in a letter home, Sherman admitted that Grant was drinking again. Rawlins played the faithful watchdog, confessing in time that he was the only one when Julia was not with Grant who could "stay . . . & prevent the evil consequences." Rawlins lived in torment with the problem, and no one could understand his position, he wrote, "unless the blighting shadow of intemperance had hung like a pall over one's pathway all his life and shaded the consummation of his fondest hopes and made him from its continuous presence fear to ask himself the question, 'and to die a drunkard'?"

Now Rawlins took a firm hand with Grant. Whenever the General failed to express himself clearly in writing, the lips of Rawlins tightened, for he knew that Grant had been "where the wine bottle had just been emptied." It was in the nature of Rawlins to speak out whenever it pleased him; he insisted on verifying every dispatch Grant sent, and rewriting dispatches if necessary so that they conformed to the facts as understood at headquarters. Grant's easygoing, mild disposition was not disturbed by Rawlins's aggressive temper, his inflexible will. They worked well in harness— the one exploding, the other nodding good-naturedly, and neither yielding on an essential conviction.

For the problem of the Negroes they managed a solution. Around Grand Junction on the deserted plantations cotton and corn had ripened. They would employ men, women, and children above the age of ten to save those crops. A fixed wage was set for the Negroes, the quartermaster paid twelve and a half cents for a pound of cotton picked and ginned, then shipped the cotton north to be sold by the government at a profit. The freedman, Grant boasted, became "self-sustaining"; the money "was not paid to them directly, but was expended judiciously for their benefit." Later the Negroes chopped wood for the river steamers. What the Negroes thus earned, Grant said, proved "not only sufficient to feed and clothe all, old and young, male and female, but to build them comfortable cabins, hospitals for the sick, and to supply them with many comforts they had never known before."

Another irritation appeared that Grant could not solve so easily. With increasing persistency newspapers carried the rumor that McClernand was to have a command independent of Grant and was to conduct his own campaign against Vicksburg by an operation down the river. "Two commanders on the same field are always one too many," Grant said bluntly. What did Halleck know of this? "You have command of all men sent to your department and have permission to fight the army as you please," Halleck wired back. The general-in-chief's huffiness was easy to imagine. Lincoln had dragged him to Washington and then had planned this strategy behind his back.

Halleck's reply reached Grant on the twelfth of November; he needed no other spur. Next day his cavalry was in Holly Springs, forcing the Confederates to fall south of the Tallahatchie. His success seemed remarkably easy; he should have wondered why.

Instead, Grant thought of Sherman. Three days later he was off to meet Billy at Columbus, Kentucky. There were no opinions Grant couldn't express now to Billy, and few that Sherman ever kept to himself at any time. The conference at Columbus, Grant said, dealt with "general plans." Doubtless there was also reference to a remark attributed to McClernand that he was "tired of furnishing brains for the Army of the Tennessee."

3.

To a Rebel across the picket line, one day during the Vicksburg campaign, a Union officer spoke freely:

"You don't know me, perhaps. My name is Sherman. My enemies in the North sometimes call me 'Crazy Sherman'; but, in my sane moments, I have said this war may last seventeen years yet; and I know of no place where I should so soon spend seven of them as right here, before Vicksburg."

S. H. M. Byers, who told the story, concluded: "The Rebel said 'Good day,' and returned to the forts, where it was soon whispered around that, with such a man besieging them, the city was doomed."

Sherman was the man who came back. In those months when Grant was taking Paducah, then revealing his fighting qualities at Belmont, Sherman had seemed on his way out of the army in disgrace. One day his young son Willy raced into the house, eager to tell his mother: "Papa's crazy!" A headline in the *Cincinnati Commercial* stated bluntly: GENERAL WILLIAM T. SHERMAN INSANE. The text that followed mixed half-truth with personal enmity:

The painful intelligence reaches us, in such form that we are not at liberty to disclose it, that Gen. William T. Sherman, late commander of the Department of the Cumberland, is insane. It appears that he was at the time while commanding in Kentucky, stark mad. We learn that he at one time telegraphed to the War Department three times in one day for permission to evacuate Kentucky and retreat into Indiana. He also, on several occasions, frightened leading Union men of Louisville almost out of their wits by the most astounding representation of the overwhelming force of Buckner and the assertion that Louisville could not be defended. The retreat from Cumberland Gap was one of his mad freaks. When relieved of the command in Kentucky he was sent to Missouri and placed at the head of a brigade at Sedalia, when the shocking fact that he was a madman was developed by orders that his subordinates knew to be preposterous and refused to obey. He has of course been relieved altogether from command. The harsh criticisms that have been lavished on this gentleman, provoked by his strange conduct, will now give way to feelings of deepest sympathy for him in his great calamity. It seems providential that the country has not to mourn the loss of an army through the loss of mind of a general into whose hands was committed the vast responsibility of the command of Kentucky.

Sherman had tried to tell Lincoln he dreaded the responsibility of a command and under no condition wanted one. But circumstances forced the President to send him to Kentucky. Sherman had performed badly. He had mothered his troops until they began calling him "Old Sugarcoated"; but toward the press he had exhibited only truculence and secrecy. It had become a common rumor that the antagonized reporters were out to cook Sherman's goose; and the anxieties that tormented him had given them ample opportunity. Consumed by ridiculous hallucinations that the enemy was about to overwhelm him when the Confederates were nowhere within reach, Sherman *had* retreated when he should have advanced. He *had* demanded extravagant reinforcement; his gloomy, nervous statements *had* reduced many citizens of Louisville to jittery exhaustion.

Sherman's political connections and Halleck's military ambitions in the West had combined to give Billy a second chance. Sherman's brother John in the United States Senate, his stepfather Tom Ewing, whom his party would have been glad to push as a favorite-son candidate for the Presidency, both wrote Halleck. Would "Old Brains" give Sherman something to do around headquarters? Halleck grew suddenly interested in Billy; to Senator John Sherman he wrote: "I have the fullest confidence in him." A generosity in Halleck's nature, a deep understanding of Sherman's problem that Halleck expressed in kindness and patience and encouragement, a mind both cautious and calculating that served as a crutch under Billy's crippled ego, produced an affection that even Halleck began to feel deeply. But there was something more: even though a youthful Halleck had written a good text on military science, Sherman disclosed a grasp of such matters that "Old Brains" recognized, respected, and appropriated. But Halleck deserved something in return; alone, at first, he managed Sherman's rehabilitation. There would be genuine sentiment in the note Halleck wrote Sherman when finally "Old Brains" left for Washington to become general-in-chief. In confidence, Halleck confessed:

> The change does not please me, but I must obey orders. Good-by and may God bless you. I am more than satisfied with everything you have done. You have always had my respect, and recently you have won my highest admiration. I deeply regret to part with you.

47

Part One: TOO MANY GENERALS

To Halleck, a grateful Sherman wrote:

> You should not be removed. I fear the consequences.
> . . . Instead of that calm, sure, steady progress which
> has dismayed the enemy, I now fear alarms, hesitations,
> and doubt. You cannot be replaced here and it is too
> great a risk to trust a new man from the East.

The verb "fear" used twice in one short paragraph disclosed that Sherman's temperament might still be described as "nervous-sanguine." But the salvation of Billy, started by Halleck, Grant completed. Sherman felt drawn irresistibly to "the tenacity of a Scotch terrier" in Grant; of one of Grant's orders he exclaimed with pride: "If Wellington could have heard it he would have jumped out of his boots." And Sherman admired Grant as a person—especially the "amiable weakness" of his love for his children, "not only pardonable, but attracting the love of all who did not suffer the consequences." Sherman had a large family; at one period he had succeeded in keeping his wife almost constantly pregnant.

During the siege of Henry and Donelson, when Sherman first experienced the magnetism of Grant, "Every boat that came up with supplies and reinforcements," Grant recalled, "brought a note of encouragement from Sherman, asking me to call upon him for any assistance . . . and saying . . . I might send for him and he would waive rank." At Shiloh Sherman seemed to find himself more fully; he was shot twice, once in the hand and once in the shoulder, and a third ball passed through his hat; but Sherman neither lost his head nor his heart. Reporter Albert Richardson eulogized Sherman at Shiloh as a warrior with "face besmeared with blood and powder"; and Grant said: "A casualty to Sherman that would have taken him from the field that day would have been a sad one for the troops engaged."

So, as friends of mutual respect, of hard times and good

48

times together, Grant and Sherman met at Columbus, Kentucky. Grant, looking across the table, saw first the flaming red beard, the glitteringly intense hazel-colored eyes, the ceaseless impatience with which Sherman puffed on a cigar "as if it were a duty to be finished in the shortest imaginable time." Sherman's jumpy nature led him to pace the floor when he talked; a question, an answer, he would be as likely to throw at the window or door as at Grant. This habit once had virtually convinced Secretary of War Cameron, Stanton's predecessor, that Sherman was unbalanced; but Grant knew better. He could reach Billy's mind and steady it.

Between them some decision must be made as how best to handle McClernand. Could Sherman march two divisions down the Mississippi and join Grant? Billy said he could. Within two weeks Sherman was ten miles north of Oxford with three divisions.

Meanwhile in Washington the general-in-chief brooded over Lincoln's private war along the Mississippi. Halleck's fingers remained well stuck in that pie. To help Grant, he ordered troops out of Helena, Arkansas, to cut the road in the rear of the Confederates—a shrewd maneuver, but, unhappily for Grant, the damage could be quickly repaired.

December came on. Grant reached Oxford, patched up the railroad from the Tallahatchie northward on piles the enemy left standing. What he needed most now, Grant decided, was a competent commander watching affairs in Memphis. Sherman got that job. Grant's orders to Billy left no doubt that he intended to have the jump on McClernand. In part, Grant directed:

. . . On your arrival at Memphis you will assume command of all troops there, and that portion of General [Samuel R.] Curtis's troops at present east of the Mississippi River, and organize them into brigades and divisions in your own army. As soon as possible move

49

with them down the river to the vicinity of Vicksburg, and with the co-operation of the gunboat fleet under command of Flag-officer Porter proceed to the reduction of that place in such manner as circumstances, and your own judgment, may dictate.

Prudently Grant communicated what he had decided to Halleck; and with equal prudence he left for the general-in-chief to read between the lines his true motive—"I doubted McClernand's fitness; and I had good reason to believe that in forestalling him I was by no means giving offense to those whose authority to command was above both him and me."

Had Grant lacked "good reason" for his action, Halleck could have supplied it. He had washed his hands of McClernand. Let Lincoln and Stanton fuss over that problem. It would be a good idea, Halleck told Grant, to collect twenty-five thousand troops at Memphis for the Vicksburg expedition. Whether Grant or Sherman went down the river to command, Halleck reaffirmed, was Grant's decision to make.

4. A BLEAK YULETIDE

IN SPRINGFIELD, McClernand began to grow restive. On the twelfth of December he had notified Washington that he was ready to take command of his army. A day passed, another, without an answer. McClernand's mouth grew thinner. December fifteenth, sixteenth, seventeenth—and yet no reply. McClernand could stand the suspense no longer. To both Lincoln and Stanton he dispatched the same urgent wire: "I believe I am to be superseded." Within a day new instructions sped from

THE MISSISSIPPI THEATER

Washington to Grant: he must divide his command into four army corps and place the one that was to operate down the Mississippi under McClernand.

Grant's annoyance became as obvious as his half-smoked cigar. He wanted to concede nothing to McClernand. Already he had worked out his plan with Sherman: "If the enemy should fall back I would follow him even to the gates of Vicksburg. I intended in such an event to hold the road to Grenada on the Yallabusha and cut loose from there, expecting to establish a new base of supplies on the Yazoo, or at Vicksburg itself, with Grenada to fall back upon in case of failure." Grant still couldn't think of an army subsisting on the country for supplies.

The order to give McClernand a corps to command reached Grant on the eighteenth of December, and, Grant contended, "The order was obeyed without any delay." This statement at best was a half-truth. Confirming orders went to Sherman and McClernand, but a Confederate cavalry raid succeeded in cutting telegraph wires and two days elapsed before the message reached McClernand—a delay, Grant insisted doggedly, created purely by circumstances beyond anyone's control.

That cavalry raid was proof, as Christmas approached, that the Confederates were determined the Yuletide season must not pass without one or two Rebel remembrances for Grant. The failure of reluctant Rosy after Corinth to follow Van Dorn into the swamp while Ord controlled the bridge over the Hatchie River now produced new regrets. On the twentieth of December, Earl Van Dorn rode hard and rode straight into Holly Springs, which served as Grant's secondary base of supplies. Again, as at Iuka, the Union garrison was under command of Colonel Murphy of the 8th Wisconsin. After Iuka Grant had been urged by Rosecrans to drop Murphy as untrustworthy, but, touched by the colonel's youthfulness, Grant had demurred. So Old Rosy did not bear all the responsibility for the disaster that now smote Holly Springs. Whether Murphy acted through "disloyalty" or "gross cowardice" became quite an academic matter beside the result: the Yankee garrison of fifteen hundred captured by Van Dorn, all munitions, food, and forage (worth a million in value) either destroyed or confiscated.

Van Dorn's boys had caught Grant's forces by surprise, and a staff officer set frantically to burning important Union dispatches while the streets of Holly Springs echoed with the hoofbeats of the yelling Confederate cavalry. Van Dorn pushed on eagerly—first to a point west of La Grange where he could cut the Memphis and Charleston Railroad, and then, by a detour to the right, to strike the Jackson and Mississippi Railroad a few miles above Grand Junction. If Grant wanted a lesson in how unwieldy his line of communication had become, debonair Earl appeared delighted to supply that tutelage.

And Grant did not need to look far to find another Rebel mentor intent on teaching the same lesson. Nathan Bedford Forrest, slave-trader by profession, high-tempered, capable of disemboweling an enemy with a penknife one day and arranging a religious revival the next, hater of whisky and smut, had few rivals as a cavalry leader. Sherman called him "that devil Forrest" and he was all of that to the Yankee cause. Cadwallader said that "he was the only Confederate cavalryman of whom Grant stood in much dread"; when a raid was threatened, Grant asked at once: "Who's commanding?" The Confederate generals Rodney or Wheeler he dismissed lightly, but Forrest made him "apprehensive because the latter was amenable to no known rules of procedure . . . and was constantly doing the unexpected, at all times and places." When Forrest set out to tear up a railroad it stayed torn up, sometimes for the duration of the war. Now, co-operating with Van Dorn, Forrest struck behind Grant's lines, helping to cut the railroad between Jackson, Tennessee, and Columbus, Kentucky—cutting it to stay cut. For over a week Grant was left without any means of communication north; for more than two weeks his army subsisted without regular issue of rations or forage.

Grant's judgments grew bad. At Holly Springs he issued an order that the *New York Times* described as "one of the deepest sensations of the war":

> The Jews, as a class violating every regulation of trade established by the Treasury Department and also department orders, are hereby expelled from the department within twenty-four hours from the receipt of this order.
>
> Post commanders will see that all of this class of people be furnished passes and required to leave, and anyone returning after such notification will be arrested and held in confinement until an opportunity occurs of sending them out as prisoners, unless furnished with permit from headquarters.
>
> No passes will be given these people to visit headquarters for the purpose of making personal application for trade permits.

If Grant wanted to upset a nest of hornets, he had his wish. Overnight, cotton dropped fifteen cents a pound in Memphis. News of the order, racing across telegraph wires, erupted into angry editorials, meetings of protest, and telegrams seeking intervention from the President. Grant tried to backtrack. His intention, he declared, had been merely to free the army from merchants, speculators, and peddlers who were trading with the soldiers at exorbitant profits. Grant and Rawlins were notorious in their hatred for cotton-buyers; both men, Cadwallader said, were "implacable enemies" of such merchants and "no persuasions, appliances, nor artifices could deceive or mollify them for an instant."

Cadwallader supplied an interesting motivation for

Grant's unprecedented action. During the time that Grant's headquarters were at Oxford, Cadwallader claimed,

> . . . he was surprised by a sudden visit from his father then living at Covington or Newport, Kentucky. The General was glad to see him; showed him every possible attention; and enjoyed his society for a day or two without unpleasant interruption. But several Cincinnati gentlemen of Hebrew persuasion soon appeared, and notably a Mr. Mack of the wealthy firm of Mack Brothers, and posed as the personal friends of "Uncle Jesse." These the General also treated handsomely for his father's sake until he learned the real object of their visit to be to obtain special permits and privileges to buy and ship cotton. It seems that playing upon "Uncle Jesse's" cupidity, these men had entered into a partnership with him for that purpose, they agreeing to furnish all the capital needed, and he to obtain the trade permits from his son, Gen. Grant. The impudence of these mercenaries was of course surprising, but the most astonishing feature of the whole transaction was that the father could have been so ignorant concerning his own son. The General's anger was bitter and malignant towards these men, and greatly intensified the mortification he felt at their having entrapped his old father into such an unworthy undertaking. The first train north bore them swiftly homeward, accompanied by "Uncle Jesse" with a stupendous flea in his ear. This was his last visit to the army. The order expelling all "Jews" from the department was issued immediately.

If the story Cadwallader recounted was correct, Jesse, returning home, acted strangely, for in a letter to Congressman Washburne he defended his son's order by insisting that it "was issued on express instructions from Washington." Jesse likely felt that the highly revivalistic spirit of the times supported him, for this was an age when, one Midwesterner told a friend, there warn't any fun—next to a woman—better than a good camp meetin'. Forrest wept both in battle and at religious revivals; Old Rosy kept his staff officers awake until four in the morning discussing the soul and in all likelihood the number of angels God could stand on the head of a pin; Brigadier General Ebenezar Dumont, in ordering the arrest of a sutler of Jewish extraction, burst out in anger at the poor startled fellow: "If it hadn't been for just such damned cusses as you, our Lord Jesus Christ would be alive and well until this day!"

Grant had been raised a Methodist, but not in the spirit of violent zeal that usually had distinguished Methodism in Ohio; Jesse hadn't cottoned to revivals: the "holy laugh" of the "penitents' pen" had chilled his blood. Horace Porter declared that Grant "rarely, if ever, spoke about his own religious convictions." A criticism Grant would one day try to answer came from a clergyman disturbed because so many climactic moments of the war in which Grant was involved occurred on Sunday—Shiloh, the surrender of Donelson, Chancellorsville, the capture of Petersburg, the surrender at Appomattox. Grant explained that he tried to begin his military operations on a Monday but delays invariably carried him into midweek, "and when the fighting actually begins it is the end of the week." This circumstance, the clergyman felt, remained "unfortunate."

Perhaps in part Grant's order could be explained by the fact that the age also was one in which caricature was rampant—in Black Sambo, Uncle Sam, the hook-nosed peddler. Caricature thought loosely; it employed "Jew" not so much as designating a race or a religion as specifying a type of merchant. Whatever the order's motivation, Cadwallader admitted that "its effect would have been to drive from Memphis many well established general merchandise and clothing firms." Lincoln intervened on the fourth of January, and through Halleck revoked the order, but not, as Cadwallader suggested, because Grant's star had not "at that time reached its zenith." A fortnight later Halleck explained to Grant: "The President has no objection to your expelling traitors and Jew peddlers, which I suppose was the object of your order; but, as it in terms proscribed an entire religious class, some of whom are fighting in our ranks, the President deemed it necessary to revoke it."

In the field Grant's judgments likewise betrayed him. Apparently his scouting reports, if they existed, were not reliable. In later years Grant would read in the "diary of a lady who accompanied General Pemberton in his retreat from the Tallahatchie" that the Confederate retreat was "almost a panic." Grant could only express surprise at this intelligence and add sadly: "Had I known the demoralized condition of the enemy, or the fact that central Mississippi abounded so in all army supplies, I would have been in pursuit of Pemberton while his [Forrest's] cavalry was destroying the roads in my rear."

But Grant remained a general trapped behind an axiom of war. When after Corinth he had ordered his troops back, with the reluctant Rosecrans at last accelerated and wanting to go on, Halleck had nudged Grant gently: "Why not reinforce Rosecrans and pursue the enemy into Mississippi, supporting your army on the country?" But the hint hadn't registered. Now Grant's first thought was not of grand strategy, but of his base of supplies. He sent his cavalry to drive away Van Dorn, while he concentrated on replenishing his supply base at Grand Junction.

Grant simply hadn't thought through the whole problem, and the failure would cost him dearly—in time, in men, in matériel. What would the interruption in his communications north mean to Sherman, poised at Memphis? Was a campaign into the interior of Mississippi really necessary?

2.

Grant's conflict was not alone within himself. He had not yet grown to understand fully the nature of the commander opposing him, whom he had met once before under rather unusual circumstances. Perhaps Grant recalled that incident of the Mexican War when the Americans had advanced upon the *garita* at San Cosme along the aqueduct road. The troops moved slowly, cautiously, an arch at a time. Grant, striking out to explore the terrain for himself, saw a church off to the south. The belfry commanded the ground back of San Cosme. Grant possessed the same flair that he admired in Zach Taylor: he could make a decision to fit the moment. An officer of the *voltigeurs* agreed to give him a mountain howitzer with a crew to work it. Ditcheş breast-deep in water were waded; the howitzer was disassembled and carried across a piece at a time. At the church the priest politely refused admission to Grant and his party. In fumbling Spanish the young Captain explained to the priest "that he might save property by opening the door, and he certainly would save himself from becoming a prisoner, for a time at least"; and besides, Grant "intended to go in whether he consented or not." The priest, Grant said humorously, "began to see his duty in the same light that I did." With the howitzer mounted on the belfry, Grant lobbed shots into the enemy lines and threw the Mexicans into confusion. But he never denied his luck: "Why they did not send out a small party and capture us, I do not know. We had no infantry or other defenses besides our one gun."

General William J. Worth, commanding the American troops at San Cosme, sent a courier to express his pleasure at Grant's alertness and effective action. The young lieutenant who bore these congratulations held out his hand and Grant shook it warmly. He liked the cut of John C. Pemberton that day; the same young lieutenant, now General John C. Pemberton, had in October 1862 assumed command of Confederate forces at Vicksburg.

"He is a soldier—a thorough soldier—and the character of the soldier has stamped itself upon his whole mind and bearing," declared the *Charleston Mercury* in praising John C. Pemberton. His technical proficiency in military science no one disputed; in his knowledge of artillery, he could outstrip many generals. But, the *Mercury* also must confess, Pemberton "was not a 'popular man.' His habitual reserve and occasional brusqueness of manner forbid." Actually, Pemberton came to Vicksburg a man of deep psychological conflicts; he had been a person who, all through his life, had got astride his conscience, as though it were a pure white charger, and had ridden it stiff-legged from one emotional emergency to the next. Always he must be more right than others around him—at West Point, in the army, at home.

Young John Pemberton grew up in Philadelphia, the second of thirteen children. Early playmates included George B. McClellan, whom Halleck had superseded as general-in-chief, and George G. Meade, who would command the Army of the Potomac against Lee at Gettysburg. But at West Point emerged a sort of compulsive quality in Pemberton that set him at odds with everything that might have been expected of him. He liked the Southerners best among his classmates at the Academy—Bob Chilton, who was later Lee's chief-of-staff; Jubal Early, Bill Walker, Braxton Bragg, Bill Mackall, all destined to become Confederate generals; Arnie Elzay, a prime defender of Richmond, and others. His later army service carried him not only into the War with Mexico, but also to twenty different military posts as widely separated as Florida and the Indian-infested wilderness of Minnesota. Confederate General Dick Taylor remembered him at his first station in South Carolina as one who "imbibed the tenets of the Calhoun school"; to Jubal Early, Pemberton had seemed "noted for his liberal and States-rights sentiments, and for his affiliations with the young men of the South."

Another event occurred while Pemberton was garrisoned at Fort Monroe that turned him further toward the South in sentiment. Martha (Patty) Thompson was one of the belles at Old Point Comfort; her family owned steamship lines operating out of Charleston and Norfolk to many European ports; and Pemberton, in the vernacular of the day, made "a good match." The War between the States faced both Pemberton and his wife with a choice of sides. One of Patty's sisters married Benjamin Pollard Loyall, who would serve as an ensign aboard the Confederate *Merrimac;* but Loyall's sisters in turn married Northerners—David G. Farragut and Alexander Pennock.

For Pemberton the division of family loyalty became deeper. Old Winfield Scott, clearly courting Pemberton, offered him a colonelcy; Pemberton's two younger brothers, Andrew and Clifford, joined the Philadelphia cavalry troop; but Patty would be writing North, as Pemberton buffeted the influence of Scott and family: "My darling husband, why are you not with us? Why do you stay? Jeff Davis has a post ready for you." Pemberton did not stay long thereafter. "I feel that if this grief and mortification *must* come upon me, that I must accept it, and submit to it— we have done all we can—John believes it would be the most honorable and right—'tis only for us he hesitates," his mother wrote her favorite daughter-in-law in trying to describe the "horrid state of suspense" which Pemberton soon resolved for her.

Pemberton's first duty was at Norfolk, where as a lieutenant colonel he organized Virginia's cavalry and artillery. In November 1861 he moved to Charleston, now a brigadier general under Lee; and when, the following March, Lee was transferred to Richmond, the command of the coast from South Carolina to Florida went to the Northern-bred states'-righter. Charleston and Pemberton rubbed from the start.

There was not in Pemberton's disposition any of the flexibility of the soldier under Sherman who sucked persimmons to pucker up his mouth to fit the size of the rations they issued him. Into headstrong, hot-tempered Charleston, where braggadocio was not uncommon in a hero like Beauregard, came Pemberton as rigid, as cold, as disturbingly foreign to native temperaments as an ice sliver down the back. He aroused suspicion when he stood on military protocol and refused to discuss openly his plans for defense. He created resentment—in fact, seemed to fly straight into the face of Southern sentimentality—when he proposed the dismantling of Sumter, no less now than a shrine to the independent power of South Carolina. He insulted, though through unintention, the wrong Charleston family in the proud, mighty, and not unvindictive Rhetts. Women pleading for their husbands for permits to take cotton through the lines—a little profitable extramural trafficking with the enemy did not overweight some consciences in Charleston—found Pemberton, when he refused to violate the law, "an unfeeling brute."

Governor Pickens refused no Rhetts, no Simons, no Gadsdens; they wanted Pemberton to go, and go he must, Pickens urged Davis. The President balked; he would be "satisfied to have [Pemberton] in any position requiring the presence of an able General"; but Pickens knew how to play states'-rights and Pickens prevailed.

Davis could take at least one sly poke at Pickens; he raised Pemberton to lieutenant general, along with Stonewall Jackson, James Longstreet, and William J. Hardee, so that he placed him with the cream of the Confederacy's military crop. Then Davis gave Pemberton the command in Mississippi, and, as one Vicksburg paper said, the government at Richmond at last demonstrated that it had not "failed to appreciate the vast importance of preserving this important region" and Mississippians were not "to be put off and imposed upon with one-horse Generals until the enemy had succeeded in placing us under his hoof." Certainly Pemberton's stature was not diminished, in either Richmond eyes or those in Mississippi, by the orders that sent Van Dorn into Holly Springs and set Forrest to tearing up the railroad from Jackson to Columbus. Set to the fixed objective of holding Vicksburg at any cost, Pemberton would never bend.

Inflexibility opposed to inflexibility produces stalemate. Grant could see this. Someone had to yield a fixed idea. Grant did. His reward would be greatness.

But events, at the moment, had moved beyond Grant by the time he scrapped the campaign into the interior and moved back to Holly Springs. As Grant traveled to Oxford via Grand Junction and La Grange his mind began to see the new shape of fighting. On all sides rumbled Grant's commissary wagons, scouring the vicinity for supplies to last two weeks and discovering that they might bring in enough for two months. Then, in time, he would see the fuller meaning of this fact—that an army with five days' rations might subsist on the country for twenty—and he would make of twenty such days a chapter in military history studied around the world. Meanwhile, however, he must contend with failure, among other difficulties.

3.

On the day after Christmas, McClernand, his wife, and bridal party reached Cairo, Illinois. The cheerless river town magnified the bridegroom's own depressed feelings. Grant's telegram, finally reaching Springfield, had said McClernand was to command the army corps against Vicksburg, but McClernand's mind grasped the none too subtle difference between operating under Grant's Department and commanding the independent army Lincoln and Stanton had promised him. McClernand stood by the boat railing and held his wife's hand.

An uncomfortable situation confronted Grant. McClernand arrived in Memphis. Where, asked McClernand pointedly, was his army? Grant faced the ticklish problem of explaining that there wasn't any army—at least not in Memphis. McClernand's troops had gone down the river with Sherman on the nineteenth of December—but only in strict accordance with instructions from Halleck, Grant insisted forcefully.

McClernand's bride—she was his own sister-in-law, said Sherman's wife, intending no compliment—waited patiently with her party. The bridegroom must have wondered which of his legs Grant was trying to pull. Grant said that he had wired on the eighteenth, and Sherman had left Memphis on the *nineteenth*. Indeed, if such an "occurrence of accidents" explained his predicament, McClernand thought, no better word than "strange" described that "occurrence."

On the thirtieth of December, still sustained by his adoring wife, McClernand started down the Mississippi to find his army. Of how greatly the ardor of the honeymoon may have been quickened or dampened by all these events, history has gained no record.

5. BILLY'S BEDEVILMENTS

On Christmas Day, Sherman reached Milliken's Bend, about ten miles above Vicksburg. Although he had stopped at Helena, Arkansas, long enough to pick up a division under General Frederick Steele, he had generally pushed right along, in the belief that this was a good way to make off with another general's army. "Time," said Flag-officer Porter indulgently, "was an important factor . . . that could not be lost by delaying . . . to collect siege tools, etc."

Sherman came down the river in high spirits. He not

only sent a map, but also a rousing letter to each of his division commanders—Steele, George W. Morgan, A. J. Smith, Morgan L. Smith. In part, Sherman exhorted:

. . . The river, above Vicksburg, has been gained by conquering the country to its rear, rendering its possession by our enemy useless and unsafe to him, and of great value to us. But the enemy still holds the river from Vicksburg to Baton Rouge, navigating it with his boats, and the possession of it enables him to connect his communications and routes of supply, east and west. To deprive him of this will be a severe blow, and, if done effectually, will be of great advantage to us, and probably the most decisive act of the war. To accomplish this important result we are to act our part—an important one of the great *whole.* General Banks, with a large force, has reinforced General Butler in Louisiana, and from that quarter an expedition, by water and land, is coming northward. General Grant, with the Thirteenth Army Corps, of which we compose the right wing, is moving southward. The naval squadron (Admiral Porter) is operating with his gunboat fleet by water, each in perfect harmony with the other.

Sherman did not trouble to explain to his subordinates why, in the haste of organizing this river expedition, he had neglected to bring pontoon bridges. Instead, admitting that Forrest's raiders had damaged seriously the railroad in the rear of Grant, which might "disconcert" Grant somewhat, Sherman went on predicting how everything would work:

. . . At the Yalabusha General Grant may encounter the army of General Pemberton, the same which refused him *battle* on the line of the Tallahatchie, which was strongly fortified; but, as he will not have the time to fortify it, he will hardly stand there; and, in that event, General Grant will immediately advance down the high ridge between the Big Black and Yazoo, and will expect to meet us on the Yazoo and receive from us the supplies which he needs, and which he knows we carry along. . . .

Billy said again: "We must do the work quickly and effectually." Surprise was that he wanted.

Porter's gunboats and ironclads had cleared the way for Sherman along the Yazoo. Porter felt expansive and accepted philosophically the loss of the *Cairo* to a torpedo. In October he had been made Flag-officer of the Mississippi Squadron under the direct supervision of the Secretary of the Navy, which meant, specifically, that he took no orders from Halleck or anyone else in the army! Porter claimed that before he left Washington for his new duties on the Mississippi, the President had informed him of the part McClernand was to play in the campaign against Vicksburg. The prospect evidently had depressed him, and he was as eager as Grant or Sherman to outrun the prairie politician to his objective.

Sherman disembarked his forces on an island across from Walnut Hills, which were part of the high bluff on which Vicksburg was situated. A single plantation afforded the only clearing on the island, and the trees dripped miserably from the heavy rains that in recent days had drenched the area. A broad, shallow bayou—"evidently an old channel of the Yazoo," Sherman said—separated the island from Vicksburg. On the right Old River Bayou stretched cheerlessly; on the left stood narrow Chickasaw Bayou, far too deep to be forded.

"A general has seldom had so difficult a task assigned him," Porter declared in appraising Sherman's situation. Around the "innumerable bayous" bridges or corduroy roads must be built. "It was killing work," Porter said. Again, the only approaches by land led "through dense swamps or over boggy open ground, where heavy guns were placed, so as to mow down an advancing army." Again, Porter listened to the wind "howl like a legion of devils, though which side it was howling for, I have no idea." Again, "even a small force could hold the place against a vastly superior one." Only at one point could Porter see any chance for Sherman to attack Vicksburg, and that existed simply because the Rebels "never supposed anyone would attempt to penetrate swamps where men had to wade up to their middle in mud and water."

But Sherman, set to an objective, could be as immovable as Pemberton. He had not yet learned to improvise, as he would do so well in later months in Georgia when, to Grant, he was like a ground-mole disappearing under a lawn: "You can here and there trace his track, but you are not quite certain where he will come out till you see his head." Sherman decided that he could use two roads across Chickasaw Bayou. Over the road near the head of the bayou General Morgan was to lead his division. Across the other road, about a mile lower down, the 6th Missouri Infantry would cross.

The force inside Vicksburg Sherman estimated at fifteen thousand under the command of Confederate Generals Stephen D. Lee and Martin Luther Smith. On the morning of December 29 he felt ready to strike. Porter's gunboats opened with a diversionary fire on Haines' Bluff. Sherman, seeking first to make a lodgment "on the foothills and bluffs abreast of our position," showed Morgan the place where he must cross the bayou.

"General," Sherman claimed Morgan replied, "in ten minutes after you give the signal, I'll be on those hills."

There was reason to respect Morgan's fighting qualities; Morgan had left college to fight in the regular Texan army, had been cited for gallantry by the Ohio legislature after the Mexican War, and as a division commander under Buell had routed the Confederates out of the Cumberland Gap.

66

But Morgan was also a contradiction: he would maintain the Union at any cost, and damned interference with the state institution in the South. Personalities, however, were not the paramount issue just then.

Sherman saw his first danger in too quick an assembling of enemy reinforcements on his front. The firm ground beneath the bluffs of Vicksburg was narrow. Not three hundred yards from the bayou poised an enemy battery. Rebel infantry waited on the spurs of the hills beyond. To succeed at all, he realized, he must disguise his real point of attack by opening the assault at the flanks. Sherman launched his drive. Along the whole Yankee line the heavy artillery opened fire. Viciously, the Rebel batteries replied.

DeCourcey's brigade of Morgan's division crossed first and dropped to the bank, pinned there by the Confederate infantry fire. Frank Blair, who had stumped Missouri for Lincoln and then resigned his seat in Congress to fight, brought his brigade over the bayou bridge. Sherman might see Blair as "erratic and unstable" as a politician, but now Sherman could view another side of Blair: "He was noble and intelligent as a soldier." Blair pushed beyond the bank to the foot of the hills. But he was unsupported. Evidently Morgan's watch had stopped. His "ten minutes" stretched out to hours as Blair staggered under the blasting crossfire from the Rebel infantry. Blair reeled back; his casualties approached five hundred. Thayer's brigade, which might have supported Blair, lost its direction and never did cross the bayou. Nor did Morgan in person. Meanwhile, the 6th Missouri, crossing on the lower road, encountered a steep bank. Directly overhead a battery blasted down on them. "The men," Sherman admitted, "actually scooped out with their hands caves in the bank, which sheltered them against the fire of the enemy, who, right over their heads, held their muskets outside the parapets vertically and fired down. . . . We could not recall the men till after dark, and then one at a time."

Sherman had failed badly. He thought of renewing the attack in the morning, but everything stood against that— his heavy losses, the element of surprise that had been dissipated, Porter's advice. Then he decided to find a place below Haines' Bluff whence to make a new attack. Under cover of darkness on the thirtieth a brigade of Steele's division crept up the Yazoo, disembarked about daylight, and dashed into the hills. But just when Steele's boys were supposed to move in concert with Porter and the guns back at Chickasaw Bayou, nature intervened. They were fogbound.

A more bedeviling end to the old year was difficult for Sherman to imagine: "The rain, too, began to fall, and the trees bore watermarks ten feet above our heads, so that I became convinced that the part of wisdom was to withdraw."

The new year started no better. Vicksburg became full of noises and rumbles. Trains pouring into the city, battalions of men clearly visible marching up toward Haines' Bluff, could only mean the arrival of reinforcements either from Bragg in Tennessee or from Pemberton at Grenada. Since leaving Memphis, Billy had received no word from Grant.

2.

In the midst of all Sherman's troubles, McClernand arrived at Vicksburg. Despite the meeting with Grant at Columbus, despite Porter's avowal that he had been told in Washington of the President's intention, Sherman could say with a straight face "it was rumored he had come down to supersede me." Sherman came down the Yazoo, all virtue if not all guile.

Most of the surprises were for Billy. Said McClernand: "Grant was not coming at all." Said McClernand: Grant's "depot at Holly Springs had been captured by Van Dorn. . . . [Grant] had drawn back from Coffeeville and Oxford to Holly Springs and La Grange. . . . Quimby's division was actually at Memphis for stores." Said McClernand, assuming command of the Army of the Mississippi: his forces would be divided into two corps, one to be commanded by Morgan, who may have rewound his watch by now, and the other by Sherman.

Billy knew what was in store for him; again the North would raise its old cry: "Repulse, failure, and bungling!" Tartly he said there was no bungling on his part: "I never worked harder or with more intensity of purpose in my life." And then he struck a more philosophical note: "Had we succeeded, we might have found ourselves in a worse trap, when General Pemberton was at full liberty to turn his whole force against us."

Sherman's touchiness brought trouble that eventually would reach Lincoln. So great had been his wish to leave Memphis in secrecy that he had forbidden "all citizens, traders, and women" to accompany the army. A group of correspondents smuggled their way on board the transports —Thomas W. Knox of the *New York Herald*, Richard Colburn of the *New York World*, Junius Henri Browne of the *Cincinnati Gazette*, A. H. Bodman of the *Chicago Tribune*, and Albert D. Richardson of the *New York Tribune*. These reporters witnessed Sherman's defeat at Chickasaw Bayou. Sherman, in Cadwallader's phrase, "got wind" of that fact and ordered their immediate arrest.

No act could have been more in character. From the time Sherman had been called crazy his hatred for the press had smoldered. Actually, Cadwallader had come into the Department of the Tennessee to obtain the release from the Alton penitentiary of the brother-in-law of the publisher of the *Chicago Times*. Sherman had arrested and confined him—true, at Grant's suggestion—for an outrageous story about Rebel ironclads at Pensacola. Cadwallader confessed that at this time "nearly all army correspondents were in bad odor at all army headquarters" and unfriendliness toward the scriveners was "especially prevalent among West

Pointers." In candor, Cadwallader listed the grievances that could be charged against them: they lacked politeness but not conceit, some "almost unblushingly took the contract of 'writing up' some Colonel to a Brigadier Generalship, for a specified consideration in dollars," others gave fulsome and undeserved praise to officers who would pay their "whisky bills and horse hire," and the "more despisable" purloined papers and orders and secretly hung around tents at night "hoping to hear conversation that could be used by their papers." In order to avoid such "odor," Cadwallader had determined, while with Grant, to procure his own outfit, ride his own horse, and pay his own expenses "liberally rather than parsimoniously."

Sherman's temper, always at a low boiling point, rose to spouts of angry steam at the reporters who had spied on his army at Chickasaw Bayou. But, said Cadwallader, "the correspondents must have had some 'friend in court,' " for they escaped to Porter's flagship and "were thus beyond the jurisdiction of Gen. Sherman." The stories they wrote were not very complimentary; the old story of Sherman's insanity was revived; and such had been the nature of the Chickasaw Bayou expedition that they "could without much apparent malice put him in a very unenviable light."

But Sherman would have his revenge.

3.

Except for these fulminations, however, the remarkable bounce in Sherman's personality came out now. The bad defeat was behind him. He would find a success elsewhere. Under his prodding, an adventure in Arkansas followed that was justified as sound military strategy without the bizarre embellishments of comedy and burlesque that also developed.

From a boy belonging to the crew of the steamboat *Blue Wing*, out of Memphis for the Yazoo with mail, coal, and ammunition, Sherman learned that a Rebel boat had darted out of the Arkansas River, captured the *Blue Wing,* and carried her up the river to Fort Hindman. This Confederate stronghold, called the "Post of Arkansas," sat some forty miles above the mouth of the river and was reported garrisoned by about five thousand troops. Sherman believed the fort would be "easy to capture from the rear." Twelve years afterward he could infuse not a little passion in telling of subsequent events:

. . . At that time I don't think General Mc-Clernand had any definite views or plans of action. If so, he did not impart them to me. He spoke in general terms of opening the navigation of the Mississippi, "cutting his way to the sea," etc., etc., but the *modus operandi* was not so clear. Knowing full well that we could not carry on operations against Vicksburg as long as the Rebels held the Post of Arkansas, whence to attack our boats coming and going without convoy, I visited him on his boat, the *Tigress,* took with me a boy who had been on the *Blue Wing* and had escaped, and asked leave to go up the Arkansas to clear out the Post. He made various objections, but consented to go with me to see Admiral Porter. . . . It must have been near midnight, and Admiral Porter was in *deshabille.* We were seated in his cabin, and I explained my views about Arkansas Post and asked his co-operation. He said that he was short of coal, and could not use wood in his ironclad boats. . . . Porter's manner to McClernand was so curt that I invited him out into a forward cabin where he had his charts, and asked him what he meant by it. He said that "he did not like him"; that in Washington, before coming West, he had been introduced to him by President Lincoln, and he had taken a strong prejudice against him. I begged him, for the sake of harmony, to waive that, which he promised to do.

Porter, having asserted the authority of the Navy, now capitulated completely. "Suppose I go along myself?" he asked Sherman. Billy felt pleased. But McClernand suddenly decided that he didn't want to be left out. He would go, too; in fact, there was no need to disembark his troops already on the steamboats—he would take his whole force. The adventure up the Arkansas that Sherman had plotted for a personal coup had, in a matter of minutes, attracted almost everything but the weather prophet who in Washington was driving Lincoln to distraction with suggestions on how to time military operations and the elements.

McClernand's army, convoyed by Porter's gunboats (including three ironclads, for which he could now spare the coal), reached the mouth of the White River on the eighth of January, proceeded next day through the "Cut-off" to the Arkansas, and pulled in just below Fort Hindman. Early the following morning Stuart's division moved up the river and soon fell into a sharp engagement with a Rebel force dug in behind earthworks extending from the river across to a swamp. Sherman took Steele's division through the swamp to the firm ground beyond and was marching up toward the rear of Hindman when McClernand overtook him. The Rebels, McClernand said, had abandoned their position in front of Stuart and fallen back into the fort. Sherman recrossed the swamp. A bright moonlight night made reconnoitering easy; the whole Rebel force *had* fallen back either into or around Hindman. Sherman

> crept up to a stump so close that I could hear the enemy hard at work, pulling down houses, cutting with their axes, and building entrenchments. I could almost hear their words, and I was thus listening when, about 4 a.m., the bugler in the Rebel camp sounded as pretty a reveille as I ever listened to.

Daylight revealed the full scale of Confederate activity during the night—a new line of parapet connecting Hindman on the riverbank with the swamp to its left or rear. McClernand now "had a man up a tree, to observe and report the movements." At ten o'clock McClernand wanted to know what Sherman was waiting for. Open up with the gunboats on the river, Sherman advised; the assault "must be simultaneous along the whole line."

Out on the river Porter viewed Fort Hindman with grudging respect. Its thirteen guns included two ten-inch Columbiads, one nine-inch Dahlgren. Four layers of heavy railroad iron covered the Columbiads; the Dahlgren was well sandbagged. The fort left only twenty feet of bank in its front; Porter, scanning the works, felt "they could defy a naval force three times as strong as that now about to be brought against them." But the Confederates had set their range buoys for gunnery practice at twelve hundred feet. "All these calculations," Porter reported, "we upset by the *DeKalb* leading, and the *Cincinnati* and the *Louisville* close behind her, running up and taking position close to the fort where the current was slack and the vessels could maintain their positions without any difficulty; while the other vessels could take such positions in the river as best suited [them] and throw in shrapnel from their small shell guns."

With "the clear ring of the navy guns" a savage land fight opened. Except for two small gullies, the ground in front of Sherman was "a dead level." A few standing trees and scattered logs on the ground gave him his only cover. But Sherman's boys went forward nicely, "once or twice falling to the ground for a sort of rest or pause." The fire they kept up from behind the trees and logs, Sherman declared, was "so hot . . . that the Rebel troops fired wild." He could see the flags of the gunboats over the parapet of Hindman. Rebel gunners scampered out of the embrasures and fled into the ditch behind them. White flags appeared suddenly all along the parapet, and Sherman, entering the Confederate line, didn't wonder at the capitulation: "There was a horse battery, and every horse lay dead in the traces."

The Confederates were bad-tempered. Colonel Garland declared the fort had surrendered; General Deshler, commanding a Rebel brigade, said *he* hadn't surrendered and refused to stack arms; General Churchill snorted that he hadn't given the order to give up but didn't see what he could do about it now. Churchill turned angrily on Garland, and Deshler sputtered at Churchill. Sherman, "wishing to soften the blow of defeat," inquired if there was a relation between the disgruntled general and the Deshler family in Columbus, Ohio, that he knew. The Confederate replied "in an offensive tone," and, Sherman said, "I think I gave him a piece of my mind that he did not relish."

Eventually, however, a verbal cease-fire was effected. But Sherman stepped from one astonishing situation to another:

> . . . I found General McClernand on the *Tigress*, in high spirits. He said repeatedly: "Glorious! glorious! my star is ever in the ascendant!" He spoke complimentarily of the troops, but was extremely jealous of the navy.[1] He said: "I'll make a splendid report"; "I had a man up a tree"; etc. I was very hungry and tired, and fear I did not appreciate the honors in reserve for us, and asked for something to eat and drink. . . .

Colonel Garland, who had surrendered the fort, spent the night with Sherman, for "there seemed to be a good deal of feeling among the Rebel officers against Garland." On straw, "saturated with the blood of dead or wounded men," both slept quietly through the night.

---

[1] As though to set the edge of McClernand's teeth aching, Porter contended: "It seems that the garrison of the fort belonged to the Confederate Navy and determined to surrender only to the U.S. Navy." Cf. David D. Porter: *The Naval History of the Civil War* (Hartford: 1886), p. 291.

6. DECISION AT YOUNG'S POINT

AT YOUNG'S POINT the feeling that the campaign against Vicksburg suffered most of all from too many generals deepened as Grant talked with Porter, Sherman, McClernand. The admiral he found petulant and vindictive, but Sherman knew why: "McClernand's report of the capture of Fort Hindman almost ignored the action of Porter's fleet altogether." Crossly, too, McClernand was claiming that Grant "disapproved" the movement up the Arkansas, and Sherman contended that Grant would approve when "he learned of our complete success." To Halleck in Washington, Grant soon considered it "my duty to state I found there was not sufficient confidence felt in General McClernand as a commander, either by the army or navy, to insure his success. Of course, all would cooperate to the best of their ability, but still with a distrust. This is a matter I made no inquiries about, but it was forced upon me. As it is my intention to command in person, unless otherwise directed, there is no special necessity of mentioning this matter." If Grant wished to please Halleck with a touch of artfulness, he should have succeeded; he left no one but Halleck to direct "otherwise," elevated Sherman and Porter to speak for entire branches of the service, then sought audiences with them so that the issue might be forced upon him!

But McClernand remained far from idle, and for obvious reasons ignored both Grant and Halleck in the bristling letter he dispatched to Lincoln:

> . . . I have determined, at whatever personal cost to myself, to address . . . you, upon a subject of the deepest interest. . . .
>
> I charge Maj. Genl. Henry W. Halleck with willful contempt of superior authority, and with utter in-

competency for the extraordinary and vital function with which he is charged as Genl-in-Chief. . . .

I charge him with incompetency on many grounds: 1st., For want of eminence in any profession, or calling, previous to his appointment as Maj. Genl. . . .

Without ever having fought a battle, he curtailed the success of our arms at Fort Henry. . . . Before Corinth, . . . he permitted the enemy to escape. . . . Since he assumed the functions of General-in-Chief, scarcely anything but disaster has marked the experiences of our arms. . . .

Without genius, justice, generosity, or policy, his continuance in command will not only involve new levies to fill up the wasting ranks . . . but must be attended by accumulating disaster. . . .

Grant had interests that reached beyond how to handle McClernand. When General Williams had substituted for Butler the summer before in lending land support to Farragut's ill-fated river sally against Vicksburg, Williams had set his troops cutting a canal some ten or twelve feet wide and about as deep straight across the peninsula from Young's Point to the river, a distance of about a mile. Williams expected that the river, when it rose, would carve its own channel through the ditch, allowing Yankee gunboats and transports to cross the peninsula opposite Vicksburg. Halleck was anxious that Grant should "direct your attention particularly" to this project, adding "the President attaches much importance to this." Grant thought he understood the source of Lincoln's interest, as the President had navigated the Mississippi "in his younger days" and knew "its tendency to change its channel, in places, from time to time." Lake Providence was no more than part of the old bed of the Mississippi. However, the report Grant sent Halleck on the canal General Williams had started was not encouraging: the ditch actually had left the river "in an eddy, and in a line perpendicular to the stream, and also to the crest of the hills opposite, with a battery directed against the outlet." The canal Grant now proposed would "debouch below the bluffs on the opposite side of the river, and give our gunboats a fair chance against any fortifications that may be placed to oppose them."

Grant studied his maps, rode over the ground where he could, talked and listened. It was true, he wrote Halleck, that "the intolerable rains"—in Arkansas, Sherman and McClernand had encountered a heavy snowstorm the week before—made impossible for the winter any effective operation from Milliken's Bend. But Grant's mind remained open. The facts, the gossip, the opinions he sifted. He told Halleck: "Once back of the entrenchments on the crest of the bluffs, the enemy would be compelled to come out and give fight, or submit to having his communications cut and be left to starve." He felt, too, that "both banks of the Mississippi should be under one commander, at least during present operations."

2.

Within a day Halleck replied: "The President has directed that so much of Arkansas as you may desire to control be temporarily attached to your Department. This will give you control of both banks of the river." And Halleck offered Grant some very sage advice: "You must not rely too confidently upon any direct co-operation of General Banks and the lower flotilla, as it is possible that they may not be able to pass or reduce Port Hudson." Banks would do everything in his power to "form a junction" with Grant at Vicksburg, Halleck said, and "at least" Banks would "occupy a portion of the enemy's forces and prevent them from reinforcing Vicksburg." Halleck still hoped for something better out of Banks, but he said so with tongue in cheek.

Lincoln, Stanton, Halleck had all chilled toward Banks.

77

Part One: TOO MANY GENERALS

What impulse had motivated the President to decide that "the Bobbin Boy" could command with effectiveness in Louisiana no one could say. Perhaps Lincoln had been impressed by Banks as an industrious young fellow who, trained to the trade of a machinist, had worked himself up to the point where prior to the war he had succeeded George B. McClellan as president of the Illinois Central Railroad. In politics Banks had been distinguished more for agility than performance in office; he had revived the Democratic party in Massachusetts through a coalition of waning Whigs and frustrated Free Soilers, had then thrown in with the American or "Know Nothing" party, and had finally emerged as a Republican. But, Lincoln would learn, gifts of grit and gabbiness do not necessarily produce a Marlborough before Blenheim. Banks had fought in the Shenandoah, and been taught a lesson in generalship by an ex-schoolmaster named Stonewall Jackson; and at Cedar Mountain had fought with Franz Sigel, where he had looked good because Sigel could never look better.

Such was the nature of "the Bobbin Boy," however, that he wasted little time in disillusioning Lincoln. Before leaving for the Gulf, Banks sent the War Department a requisition for supplies that would have taken months to fill. Stanton was easily stretched to the limit of patience; he sent the requisition to the President. Irritably, Lincoln wrote to Banks, wondering what, for example, Banks had in mind ordering these vast amounts of supplies when "where you are going, you have no use for them." Banks must now back up his fine statements about swift and effective action, Lincoln asserted, "or your expedition is a failure before you start." The President said: "You must be off before Congress meets." Banks thought he could wriggle out of this unhappy involvement by again becoming a "Know Nothing"— the whole mess, Banks declared, was the fault of "an officer who did not fully comprehend my instructions."

6: DECISION AT YOUNG'S POINT

Lincoln recognized his mistake in appointing Banks, decided to do something about it, and then apparently lost heart. In late January 1863 the President sent Stanton a draft of a letter to Banks which would have restored Ben Butler to command, and in which he hoped Banks would not believe the President "indifferent" to his feelings and honor. Lincoln told Stanton that the restoration of Butler to command of the Department of the Gulf must be "so managed as to not wrong, or wound the feelings of Gen. Banks." But the President's letter never went to Banks and Ben Butler was never returned to New Orleans.

But the President did write and send a letter that aided Grant more than he ever suspected. Before Lincoln was McClernand's bitter tirade against Halleck, who had "contumaciously refused to recognize me in the relations contemplated" by the President and the Secretary of War. Lincoln replied to McClernand: "I have too many *family* controversies (so to speak) already on my hands to voluntarily, or so long as I can avoid it, take up another. You are now doing well—well for the country, and well for yourself—much better than you could possibly be if engaged in open war with Gen. Halleck. Allow me to beg that for your sake, for my sake, & for the country's sake, you give your whole attention to the better work."

For Grant's purposes, the coercive influence of this letter could not have reached McClernand at a better psychological moment. Upon the field at Vicksburg there was going to be but one commanding general and his name was Ulysses S. Grant. General Order No. 13 reduced McClernand to command of the Thirteenth Army Corps as one unit within the Department of the Tennessee and charged him with "garrisoning the post of Helena, Ark., and any other point on the west bank of the river it may be necessary to hold south of that place." A sharp correspondence between McClernand and Grant preceded the transmission of this order to Washington. Were his forces to be reduced, howled McClernand; where did his authority begin and end? Grant mustered what patience he could: "Instead of weakening your force, it will strengthen it by about 7,000 men. . . . All forces and posts garrisoned by the Thirteenth Army Corps are under your command, subject, of course, to directions from these headquarters." In reply McClernand was grudging and grumbling: "I acquiesce in the order for the purpose of avoiding a conflict of authority in the presence of the enemy."

In the days of Grant's first command at Ironton it had been unthinkable for subordinates in the field to deal directly with the aloof and untouchable Frémont. Grant had addressed his first dispatches to Captain John C. Kelton, Frémont's assistant adjutant general. Kelton, now a colonel, was Halleck's assistant adjutant general in Washington, and it was to Kelton on February 1 that Grant addressed a copy of General Order No. 13, the two letters from McClernand, his one reply. Kelton had become the thread connecting Ironton with Vicksburg. "If General Sherman had been left in command here, such is my confidence in him that I would not have thought my presence necessary," Grant informed Kelton.

3.

Rawlins brought the reports to Grant for review. On January 29 the water in the old canal dug by Williams's troops was five feet deep, "and river rising." In the bayous around Vicksburg, at the old river bed that had become Lake Providence, Federal scouts probed for a route around the Confederate bastion on the bluffs. A ram made ready to run the Vicksburg blockade. The *New York Herald* reporter Thomas W. Knox returned, and Sherman arrested him and had him court-martialed, although Cadwallader suspected that "the court was selected with a view to Knox's final acquittal and a sort of left-handed vindication of Gen. Sherman." Billy was criticized for conduct "unworthy of his position"; Grant sent Knox out of the Department. But another sequel remained. Traveling straight to Washington, Knox secured the President's permission to return. Grant spoke privately to Knox. The reporter's return was ill-advised; Grant could judge the situation better than Lincoln; future trouble would certainly ensue "if he remained within Sherman's reach." Cadwallader said: "Knox took the hint—and the first steamer up the river."

Grant shrugged. Bigger issues remained. If he wanted to get at Pemberton, he must first fight a river. Soon soldiers said of Grant that he looked like Napoleon—a little bigger and "not so dumpy."

PART TWO

✶✶✶✶✶✶✶✶✶✶✶✶✶✶✶✶✶✶✶✶✶✶✶✶✶✶✶✶✶✶✶✶✶✶✶✶✶✶

The Moth and the Flame

7. FIGHTING THE RIVER

McCLERNAND had his fingers in many pies. In early January 1863, while the issue was drawn over whether Grant or McClernand would command the Vicksburg campaign, McClernand's chief aide, Major Walter B. Scates, arrived in Washington with two lengthy letters for the President. McClernand wrote that "a gentleman of the first respectability just arrived from the Rebel army" brought suggestions of "import from officers of high rank in the Rebel service, who were formerly my warm personal and political friends." Stepping from the role of warmaker to peacemaker, McClernand told the President: "These officials desire the restoration of peace and are represented to be willing to wheel their columns into the line of that policy. They admit that the South West and the North West are geographically and commercially identical."

On January 8 Lincoln responded bluntly. The President hoped that McClernand would understand "a coarse, but an expressive figure." He had issued the Emancipation Proclamation and could not retract it, thus: "Broken eggs can not be mended." To a general fighting in the heart of a country where in some seventy years since the invention of the cotton gin a plantation system had grown with slavery as its essential foundation, Lincoln stated in unequivocal language the position he took:

> After the commencement of hostilities I struggled nearly a year and a half to get along without touching the "institution"; and when finally I conditionally determined to touch it, I gave a hundred days fair notice of my purpose to all the states and people, within which

time they could have turned it wholly aside by simply again becoming good citizens of the United States. They chose to disregard it, and I made the peremptory proclamation on what appeared to me to be a military necessity. And being made, it must stand. As to the states not included in it, of course they can have their rights in the Union as of old. Even the people of the states included, if they choose, need not be hurt by it. Let them adopt systems of apprenticeships for the colored people, conforming substantially to the most approved plans of gradual emancipation; and they may be nearly as well off, in this respect, as if the present trouble had not occurred, and much better off than they can possibly be if the contest continues persistently.

As to any dread of my having a "purpose to enslave, or exterminate, the whites of the South," I can scarcely believe that such dread exists. It is too absurd. I believe you can be my personal witness that no man is less to be dreaded for undue severity in any case.

If the friends you mention really wish to have peace upon the old terms, they should act at once. Every day makes the case more difficult. . . .

As the winter wore on, as a long, hard war became the only course by which the bleeding parts of the Union could be restored, Lincoln reputedly confessed to another general: "I have been praying to Almighty God for Vicksburg." The President, this reputed letter said, had "wrestled with Him, and told Him how much we need the Mississippi, and how it ought to flow unvexed to the sea, and how that great valley ought to be forever free, and I reckon He understands the whole business from 'A to Izzard.' . . . We are going to win at Vicksburg. . . . I can't tell how soon. But I believe we will. For this will save the Mississippi and cut the Confederacy in twain; and be in line with God's law besides."

Grant faced the long winter months, taking the problems as they came. Public opinion solidified against him. The *Cincinnati Commercial* decided that either "negligence" or "imbecility" must account for the state of affairs developing at Vicksburg. Mary Livermore, the woman suffragist, rising to her first public fame through her work with the Sanitary Commission, visited Grant at Young's Point and gave "the lie to the universal calumnies then current." Miss Livermore insisted that the General possessed a "clear eye, clean skin, firm flesh, and steady nerves." But rumors persisted, public opinion grew more adverse, and the War Department in time would take the extraordinary step of sending an emissary to judge the man and the situation in person.

Meanwhile Grant kept plugging. Nobody not at Vicksburg could understand how the threat of smallpox could spread aboard Grant's headquarters boat. Characteristically, the Negro roustabout who brought the menace to the *Magnolia* saw nothing wrong in his actions. Why shouldn't he use the discarded coffin for a bed on the boat deck?

The situation was ready-made for another eruption of temper from Rawlins. Yet the Negro had acted innocently. Rawlins could tongue-lash the old fellow, if it helped; the real culprit remained the weather. After Sherman's hapless assault at Chickasaw Bayou, heavy rains swelled the river. A strip of land between the bank of the Mississippi and the levee afforded the only area for burying the dead, and the elements, in a wicked and capricious mood, continued to grumble and growl over that exception. Days without rain became few. The river rose steadily, sloshed over the strip, and turned the place into a mudhole. Cadwallader watched the teams "still contriving to drag through to the transports for supplies." The reporter had known happier experiences: the teams would strike the end of a box or coffin "and heave it clear out of the ground."

The Yankees, Cadwallader said, tried reburying the coffins "a little deeper." The Mississippi hissed and swirled,

87

crept over the strip in other places, and left teamsters and gravediggers struggling in a quagmire. Some talked of seeking dry ground elsewhere, but, asked the realists, who wanted to cart those coffins for miles to find any such spot? So the dead were reburied once more, this time on the side of the levee. The embankment, in Cadwallader's description, was "literally honeycombed with such excavations."

Word of this plight traveled northward. A father arrived with a metallic casket and ordered his son's body disinterred and transferred for better protection. The empty wooden coffin was left on the levee. The Negro roustabout spied it. For over a week he kept it secreted aboard the *Magnolia.* At night his slumber was undisturbed by the fact that the coffin's previous occupant had died of smallpox.

Rawlins had the boat fumigated from stem to stern. The staff waited. Time alone could tell if the contagion would spread, and, if so, how far.

2.

The smallpox scare aboard the *Magnolia* passed. Halleck continued to reflect Lincoln's interest in the canal. On the thirteenth of February he wired Grant: "Cannot dredge-boats be used with advantage on the canal? There are four lying idle at Louisville, belonging to Boston, Robinson & Co., canal contractors." Ten days before, Grant had encouraged Halleck: "Work on canal progressing as rapidly as possible." But Grant's heart had begun to go out of the endeavor. The river still rose; coffins still popped out of the mud. William S. Duff, Grant's chief of artillery, scouted Lake Providence, searching for an alternate route. More than dredge-boats were required to fight the variable moods of the Mississippi.

The necessity to revamp or to abandon fixed ideas was about the only constant factor that any longer confronted Grant. Sherman's assault across Chickasaw Bayou had demonstrated the folly of trying to attack Vicksburg on either flank, and even a child might guess that Pemberton had been strengthening these points of potential invasion. Halleck already had blasted any sensible hope of Banks ascending the Mississippi; to Cadwallader, Porter might be "by all odds the greatest humbug of the war," but now rather succinctly the admiral commented that Grant "had to depend upon his own resources." Meanwhile Grant's scouting reports would have been utterly worthless if they had not revealed the facility with which the Confederates were ferrying supplies into Vicksburg via the Red River. Large quantities of bacon and corn reached the city from this source, and, Pemberton admitted, the Rebels felt so secure in these operations that "the rapid rise of the river" was thought a greater danger than the threat of Yankee gunboats.

Grant viewed the situation realistically. As long as Banks, either through reluctance or inability, left Port Hudson under Confederate control, supplies would continue to flow along the Red River. Grant saw Porter; if Nothing Positive was going to be worthless to them, they would have to take the matter in hand. The best chance would be for Porter's fleet to accept the risk of running the batteries at Vicksburg, get below the city, blockade the river, and thus hasten the evacuation of Port Hudson.

The night of February 3 was picked for the test run. The ram *Queen of the West*, Colonel Charles R. Ellet commanding, was assigned the "perilous duty." Porter spoke extravagantly of Ellet—appropriately his middle name was Rivers—as a "gallant young fellow, full of dash and enterprise"; the ram, the admiral said, was "a very frail one." Once more Porter wrote his orders with one hand holding the pen and the other clutching the pulse of history. Go downstream under low speed, the admiral instructed; keep close to the righthand shore, allowing sufficient steerageway; put in no fresh coal after starting, as "the smoke might betray you"; permit no lights to show from the stern passing the town, "enabling them to rake you"; at the wharf lay the Rebel steamer *City of Vicksburg,* which Ellet should disable by striking twenty feet forward of her wheel. Porter intended to forget nothing, including his grievance at the sinking of the *Harriet Lane* at New Orleans in 1862. Porter coached Ellet: "Think of the fate of that vessel while performing your duty, and shout 'Harriet Lane!' into the ears of the Rebels." Nor need the moment end there: "If you can fire turpentine balls from your bow field pieces into the light upper works, it will make a fine finish to the sinking part."

Ellet started at four thirty in the morning, relying on the darkness to shield his passage of the Vicksburg batteries. But Porter's orders had omitted to say how to readjust a wheel that wouldn't operate properly. An hour was lost in repairs. Streaks of sun lighted the progress of the *Queen of the West* when at last she rounded the hairpin bend of the Mississippi and approached the city. Rebel guns opened fire, but, Ellet reported, "we were only struck three times before reaching the steamer."

A man conscientious to duty, Ellet would have snarled "Harriet Lane!" into the ears of the Rebels if circumstances had permitted. The *City of Vicksburg,* however, lay in such position that if Ellet had run obliquely into the steamer, the bow of the *Queen of the West* would have "glanced." So Ellet was forced to come partially around to strike, and "at the very moment of collision the current, very strong and rapid at this point, caught the stern of my boat, and, acting on her bow as a pivot, swung her around so rapidly that nearly all her momentum was lost." Even so, Ellet remembered "the incendiary projectiles" recommended by Porter. A Rebel shell from a sixty-four-pounder crashed onto the *Queen of the West.* Ellet still fired his turpentine balls. The steamer burst into flames.

To borrow Ellet's own concise words, "The enemy, of

course, were not idle." Confederate shells ripped through the cotton bales barricading the starboard wheel of the *Queen of the West,* and now Ellet had a taste of fire-fighting:

. . . The flames spread rapidly, and the dense smoke, rolling into the engine room, suffocated the engineers. I saw that if I attempted to run into the *City of Vicksburg* again, my boat would certainly be burned. I ordered her to be headed downstream, and turned every man to extinguishing the flames. After much exertion, we finally put out the fire by cutting the burning bales loose. . . . We were struck twelve times, but, though the cabin was knocked to pieces, no material injury to the boat or to any of those on her was inflicted. About two regiments of Rebel sharp-shooters in rifle pits kept up a continuous fire, but did no damage. The *Queen* was struck twice in the hull, but above the water line. One of our guns [was] dismounted and ruined.

Ellet reached Natchez at about midnight and barely missed capturing a Rebel colonel in Vidalia, a town across the river. Next day, sailing up the Red River, the hunting proved livelier and more rewarding. A side-wheel steamer, the *A. W. Baker,* tried to escape by running ashore; "numerous Rebel officers sprang into the water," but Ellet bagged five captains, two lieutenants, and a number of civilians, "among them 7 or 8 ladies." The steamer *Moro* yielded "110,000 pounds of pork, nearly 500 hogs, and a large quantity of salt, destined for the Rebel army at Port Hudson." A short distance beyond, Ellet destroyed "25,000 pounds of meal, awaiting transportation to Port Hudson." Stopping at a plantation to discharge the ladies captured aboard the *A. W. Baker,* Ellet spied the *Berwick Bay,* seized the steamer, and found her "laden with supplies for the Rebel forces at Port Hudson, consisting of 200 barrels of molasses, 10 hogsheads of sugar, and 30,000 pounds of flour. She had also on board 40 bales of cotton." It was a good day's work and Grant wired Halleck with enthusiasm: "One of the rams ran the blockade this morning. This is of vast importance, cutting off the enemy's communication with the west bank of the river."

3.

To Major General John A. Dix at Fort Monroe, Virginia, Lincoln dispatched the first of many plaintive appeals he would write in succeeding weeks: "Do Richmond papers have *anything* about Vicksburg?" Yet visitors to the *Magnolia* found Grant easily approachable, a fact that impressed Frederick Law Olmsted. The sentry—or "apology for one" —who guarded the gangway stopped no one. Olmsted, perhaps, failed to see himself as a distinguished guest, but, as secretary of the Sanitary Commission, he had led a vigorous fight to reorganize the Army Medical Corps and to save Union forces from "death from the frying-pan." To Olmsted, Grant was more "liable to interruption than a merchant or lawyer"; Olmsted heard one caller say: "I hain't got no business with you, General, but I just wanted to have a little talk with you, because folks will ask me if I did." But despite Grant's gentleness, modesty, and "exceedingly kind disposition," Olmsted recognized "a man of strong will . . . and of capacity underlying these feminine traits."

Grant's own quarters were in the ladies' cabin; here he worked on a table near the stove. Before him in early February was the report Duff had sent Rawlins from Lake Providence. A connection between the lake and river, Duff felt, was "entirely practicable." Grant could only hope for the best. A network of bayous linked Lake Providence with Red River. But the water in the lake was eight feet lower than the surface of the Mississippi. A channel must be cut through the levee, equalizing the two water levels; then, it was thought, the larger boats could pass from Baxter Bayou into Bayou Macon and thence into the Red River.

Grant reserved judgment. There were other schemes for outwitting Pemberton behind the natural obstacles of water, swamp, and forest that protected him. Another route Grant considered was through the Yazoo Pass into the Coldwater, Tallahatchie, and Yazoo rivers. "This route, if practicable," he informed Washington, "would enable us to get high ground above Haines' Bluff, and would turn all the enemy's river batteries." A third possibility was by way of Willow and Roundaway bayous; thus Grant could leave the Mississippi at Milliken's Bend and come in at New Carthage.

Any enthusiasm Grant once had held for the canal started by General Williams dwindled steadily. Soldiers toiled daily, trying to widen and deepen the old ditch. A half-mile or more above the old entrance a new start was made to take the canal into the river at an acute angle with the current; but sometimes Cadwallader wondered if Grant hadn't decided "the army would be in better condition by reason of such temporary work . . . than by lying idle in camp." On the ninth of February neither Halleck nor Lincoln would receive encouragement from Grant's brief report on the canal. Work was "much retarded"; the continuous rise of the river "has kept the army busy to keep out of water." Sherman detailed five hundred men a day from each of his two division, and was glad that they weren't all drowned. The narrow levee and the few steamboats abreast of the camps gave the only refuge. Mrs. Grove's house, where Sherman had established headquarters, was surrounded by water. A plank walk, built on posts from the levee, provided gingerly support for his nervous legs.

But the morale of the army remained unshaken. One reason had impressed Olmsted: Grant, he had found, was "one of the most engaging men I ever saw. . . . Those about him become deeply attached to him." Then, too, it was the nature of the Midwesterner to turn a cheerful face to adversity. Even Anthony Trollope, visiting Missouri and Illinois, conceded that "no race of men requires less outward assistance than these pioneers of civilization. Food, newspapers, and brandy-smashes suffice for life; and while these last, whatever may occur, the man is still there in his manhood. . . . Dirt, dishonesty, and morning drinks are his vices."

8. THE HARES AND THE TORTOISE

CHARLES RIVERS ELLET doubtless took pride in the wisp of mustache that an old photograph retains with difficulty. Ellet was only nineteen—young for growing a mustache, younger still for holding the rank of third commander of the ram fleet—but he accumulated navy tradition more quickly than the soft black down would thicken on his cheeks and upper lip. Ellet's father had died of a wound at Memphis, and the son had gone in a rowboat to accept the surrender of the city.

Perhaps Porter sensed how swiftly life was running out for the young officer; eight months after Ellet stirred Northern hearts by running the Vicksburg batteries and disrupting Rebel shipping in the *Queen of the West*, the boy would be dead. That Porter placed a youth in his teens in command of a craft virtually qualifying as a gunboat led to sharp criticism. Still, confronted by Ellet's intense eyes, his firm mouth, his round, fighting chin, it was easy to overlook his youthfulness; and toward armchair critics generally, Grant had summed up the only livable attitude: "I always admired the South, as bad as I thought their cause, for the boldness with which they silenced all opposition and all croaking, by press or by individuals, within their control."

With Ellet aboard the *Queen* had sailed A. H. Bodman, whom readers of the *Chicago Tribune* knew as "Bod." In the dispatch the reporter was writing of Ellet's exploits ran a note of admiration and of exhilaration. The *Queen* now had anchored in the Red River at the mouth of the Black, a point eighty-five miles from Gordon's Landing, where, it was believed, the Confederates had constructed heavy fortifications. Bod, however, wrote cheerily of air "as balmy as June in our Northern climate," of trees "decking themselves in green," of men "walking about the hurricane deck in their shirt sleeves." This was the way to live in mid-February! "We could not help," Bod said, "commiserating poor Northerners, shivering before coal fires—'on ice.' "

Yet disquieting rumors persisted. In addition to the fortifications at Gordon's Landing, scouts insisted that heavy Rebel guns also supported Harrisonburg, near the head of Black River. Here was a situation where Ellet's youthfulness could reveal its thin edge—in indecision, saying first they'd make for Gordon's Landing, then thinking the target had better be Harrisonburg, then settling once more on Gordon's Landing. For a time Ellet's mind swished like a cow's tail, then fixed at last on Gordon's Landing as the striking-point for the *Queen*. Bod told readers of the *Tribune*: "We moved as rapidly as the tortuous nature of the stream and the ignorance of our pilots would admit, in the hope that we should reach the position and commence the attack before nightfall." Among Ellet's "incentives for speed" was the report that the steamer *Louisville* recently had passed up the Red River with a thirty-two-pound rifled gun intended for the gunboat *William H. Webb*, then lying at Alexandria.

Once more luck played into young Ellet's hands. At ten o'clock the steamer *Era No. 5* hove into sight, half turned in an attempt to escape, and felt a shot across her bow that passed through the cookroom, demolished a stove, and wounded a Negro cook. Officers and passengers swarmed onto the deck, where they "hoisted white sheets and waved white handkerchiefs in token of surrender." Forty-five hundred bushels of corn, enroute to the quartermaster's department at Little Rock, was but part of the sweetening in the spoils Ellet collected. Troops attached to the 17th Texas Cavalry and the 27th Louisiana also were aboard, as well as "a German Jew named Elsasser, who had upon his person $32,000 in Confederate money," and was, Ellet thought, a Rebel quartermaster. With the *Queen;* a coal barge; a captured steamer, the *De Soto* (which mounted a gun and had been provided with iron and cotton bales for protection); and the *Era No. 5,* Ellet moved toward Gordon's Landing.

At sundown the *Queen* rounded the bend four hundred yards from the Rebel fortifications. Bod drew a picture of the setting: "The Red River is here extremely tortuous, so much so that at a point four miles below the fort by river, we were only a mile from it by land. The batteries are entirely concealed from sight by dense forests until we approach within four hundred yards of them, or until the nose of the steamer begins to show around the point on which the Negro cabins are built."

Cautiously the *Queen* crept round the bend and reached the Negro quarters. Downstream rose a "line of dense black smoke moving up the river beyond the fort, indicating the hasty departure of a transport." Ellet bared the bow gun and ordered forward two percussion shells. Then, "whether designedly or otherwise," the pilot misjudged his channel. At the very instant the Rebel batteries opened fire, the *Queen* shuddered and stopped—grounded! "Recollect," Bod explained to readers of the *Tribune,* "we were not four hundred yards from the fort, and immovable. The pilots tried in vain to back her off, but she would not budge an inch. Shots were flying, shells were bursting, and worse than all we could not reply. . . . Your correspondent sought the pilothouse, and thus became an unwilling witness of the terrible affair. Three huge thirty-two-pounder shells exploded upon the deck and between the smokestacks, not twenty feet from our heads."

Fragments of exploding shells filled the air. Below deck the machinery seemed to rock under a shattering blow. Sailors cursed their luck—the lever regulating the engines had been shot away. A second shell ripped loose the escape pipe, another "fractured" the steam chest. The *Queen* shook with a rush of escaping steam. Engineers, firemen, Negroes, prisoners jammed the engine room. Every moment Bod "looked to be launched into eternity."

Still the Rebel shore batteries pounded the *Queen*. Steam, shells, the listing ship enlarged the panic around Bod: "Men crowded to the afterpart of the vessel. Some tumbled cotton bales into the river and, getting astride them, sought to reach the *De Soto*, a mile below." An officer with cocked pistol threatened to kill anyone who tried to enter the yawl tied to the stern. Frightened Negroes, jumping over the rails, screeched and drowned. Shouts raised for Ellet—men scurrying the deck in search of the commander—added to the confusion and anxiety. Ellet seemed to have vanished in the steam. Bod fought for his own life:

. . . I was in the pilothouse when the explosion occurred, and took the precaution to close the trapdoor, thus keeping out a quantity of steam. There was still enough to make breathing almost impossible, that came through the windows in front of us. I had sufficient presence of mind to cram the tail of my coat into my mouth, and thus avoid scalding.

Shortly we discovered that to remain would induce suffocation, and we opened the trapdoor and, blinded by steam, sought the stern of the vessel. Groping about the cabin, tumbling over chairs and Negroes, I sought my berth, seized an overcoat, leaving an entire suit of

clothes, my haversack, and some valuable papers behind, and emerged upon the hurricane deck. The shells
were flying over my head, and here was obviously no
place for me to remain. Looking over, I saw the woolly
pate of a Negro projecting over the stern below me, and
calling to him to catch my coat I swung myself over by
a rope and landed directly upon the rudder. At this
time it was suggested that a boat be sent to hurry up
the *De Soto*, and among those who entered it was your
correspondent. We reached it in about ten minutes,
passing on the way several men on cotton bales, among
them Colonel Ellet and [Joseph B.] McCullagh of [the
Cincinnati] *Commercial*. Almost exhausted, the occupants
remained behind, while another crew was sent to pick
up survivors.

Others beside Ellet and McCullagh who had escaped on
cotton bales were rescued by the yawl. The *Queen* itself
was surrendered. Bod's party pushed on to the *Era No. 5*
and "found her all right"—the one seaworthy remnant of
the fleet Ellet had brought down to Gordon's Landing. The
coal barge leaked miserably. The *De Soto*, both rudders un-
shipped, had become useless and presented the problem of
making certain her gun did not fall into Rebel hands. With
pipes knocked out and live coals spread in her cabin, the
De Soto's days ended. The prow of the *Era No. 5* turned
toward the Mississippi, and again Bod gave readers of the
Tribune a feeling of immediacy in a moment of war:

. . . The night was a terrible one—thunder, lightning,
rain, and fog. I doubt if, under other circumstances,
Red River would be deemed navigable. All hands were
set to work to throw overboard the corn to lighten her
up, and we are slowly crawling down the river. We
know to a certainty that we shall be pursued. The gunboat *Webb* is lying at Alexandria, and we know that
she will start in pursuit of us whenever she learns of

the destruction of the *Queen* and of the escape of a portion of her crew. Our only hope lies in reaching the Mississippi quickly, whence we shall make the best of our way to Vicksburg. The *Webb* is a model of speed, and can make fourteen miles an hour against the current. If we do not get aground, and if our machinery does not break, we hope to outrun her. If I am captured, a visit to Vicksburg will be my portion. We shall see.

2.

At the time young Ellet paced the deck of the *Queen of the West*, debating whether to strike at Gordon's Landing or Harrisonburg, Grant's attention focused on another naval exploit. Idyllic though Bod had found the weather that thirteenth of February, there was little idyllic in the reality confronting Grant. Fighting the river was a slow, discouraging, unrewarding business. Perhaps his whole plan was wrong. "The strategy according to the rule," Grant admitted, "would have been to go back to Memphis; establish that as a base of supplies; fortify it so that the storehouses could be held by a small garrison, and move from there along the line of the railroad, repairing as we advanced, to the Yallabusha, or to Jackson, Mississippi."

But many factors—aside from a growing streak of cussedness in Grant—argued against this plan: war-weariness and a sense of failure pervading the North, the adverse elections of 1862, the draft, the danger that "to make a backward movement as long as that from Vicksburg to Memphis would be interpreted, by many of those yet full of hope for the preservation of the Union, as a defeat." Moreover, Grant feared, "the draft would be resisted, desertions ensue, and the power to capture and punish deserters lost." Despite the Northern "croakers," Grant saw only one acceptable course—"*to go forward to a decisive victory.*"

Part Two: THE MOTH AND THE FLAME

Grant wanted action, Grant wanted results. He wanted to hammer at any vulnerable spot he could reach. The success of the *Queen* in running the batteries at Vicksburg persuaded Grant and Porter—in an effort, the admiral said, "to make matters doubly sure"—to send an ironclad to the support of the *Queen*. The *Indianola*, under the command of one of the heroes of New Orleans, Lieutenant George Brown, represented the newest pride of the Mississippi squadron. Deck flat and just above water, two mighty eleven-inch smoothbores mounted behind armored casement forward, two nine-inch guns between the paddlewheel houses on the quarters, equipped with twin screws in addition to paddles, and fitted with a narrow deckhouse that cleared wide areas for action, the *Indianola* brightened Yankee eyes. In passing the batteries on the night of the thirteenth, the *Indianola* was to carry a coal barge on each side with orders to cut them adrift if she met the Confederate *Webb* on the prowl out of Alexandria.

Commander Brown gave the *Indianola* full steam and passed the batteries at Vicksburg and Warrenton "without being once struck, although eighteen shots were fired, all of which passed over us." Thick shrouds of fog hovered over the Mississippi and until the morning of the sixteenth Brown reported "but slow progress." That morning the *Indianola* approached Natchez.

Confederate telegraph wires meanwhile thrummed with instructions, enemy positions, soundings. Hammers pounded and saws buzzed as the *Queen of the West* was repaired for Rebel service. The *Webb* steamed out of Alexandria. Two Confederate "infantry boats," the *Grand Era* and the *Dr. Beatty*, cruised the Red River. Within a short time this Confederate flotilla would assemble near Gordon's Landing under the command of Major Joseph L. Brent. Dispatches then would place the *Indianola* at a point ninety-five miles away. Bells would sound in engine rooms and the order would be: "Go ahead fast."

8: THE HARES AND THE TORTOISE

At Ellis's Cliffs on the Mississippi, Bod watched the treachery of history repeat itself. The pilot who had run the *Queen* aground at Gordon's Landing now ran the *Era No. 5* aground at Ellis's Cliffs! "Here," Bod informed the readers of the *Tribune*, "we laid for four mortal hours within ten feet of shore, liable to capture at any moment from guerrillas, until our carpenters could go into the woods, select a tree, and fashion a spar to shove us off. To crown our misfortunes, the starboard wheel was dropping to pieces. We had decided that to be captured was our destiny, and Colonel Ellet was discussing the practicability of seizing skiffs and dugouts and attempting to run by the batteries at Port Hudson, fifty miles below."

In time the *Era No. 5* shook loose from the mud. Bod had flung himself on a mattress in the cabin, "in the hope of snatching a moment's rest," when a shout went up: "Gunboat ahead!" One fear dominated Bod, Ellet, and crew— the *Webb* had slipped by in the night and had been lying in wait! Bod rushed to the deck, and at sight of the approaching vessel's smokestacks joy overcame him. A Union gunboat—the *Indianola*! Of that instant, "raised to the heights of exaltation," Bod wrote:

> We are, some of us, hatless, bootless, and coatless. All of us were hungry. We had eaten nothing for the last forty-eight hours but a little stale and sour cornmeal, found in the bottom of a barrel on board the *Era* at the time of her capture. The good people of the *Indianola* acted the part of the good Samaritans; they clothed and fed us, and made us comfortable. Captain Brown invited Colonel Ellet and the two Bohemians [Bod and McCullagh] into his cabin and regaled us with a delicious cup of coffee.

A period of rest until noon also produced a decision: the *Era* would go ahead to scout for the *Webb*. Bod said they had moved about three miles when the lookout sighted her:

Part Two: THE MOTH AND THE FLAME

> . . . All hands were called to quarters, and pre-
> pared for action. . . . The engineers clapped on
> steam, hot-water hose was got ready, and a lively time
> was expected. . . . As we approached the *Webb*, she
> was lying in the eddy directly under Ellis's Cliffs,
> looking for all the world like a frightened racehorse.
> She moved a little, then halted, and then bounded
> away like the wind. At this moment the larboard bow
> gun was fired, and almost simultaneously the star-
> board gun. Both shots lacked elevation, and fell short.
> Long before the smoke cleared away, a long train of
> smoke was moving down the river at the rate of twenty
> miles an hour. This was the last of the *Webb*. . . .

Aboard the *Indianola*, Brown blasted at the *Webb* with
two shots from the eleven-inch guns forward, but these
likewise fell short. Along the banks of the Mississippi the
fog again rose and poured over the water, so that pursuit
became impossible. Brown might well cuss his luck: the
Webb had escaped into the Red River, where he could not
follow with pilots who did not know the stream! The morning of the seventeenth brought two conclusions. The best the
Indianola could do now was maintain a blockade at the
mouth of the Red River and await whatever might turn
up; and the *Era No. 5*, virtually unarmed and loaded with
prisoners, would serve its best purpose if it ran up the river
and communicated with the squadron.

On the eighteenth Ellet set sail—on a journey, Bod said,
that proved the *Era* possessed "a charmed existence." By
nightfall Ellet reached the Old River and anchored at the
Ackley plantation, an example of the personal empire
slavery could build with twenty thousand tillable acres
worked by over a thousand Negroes. At noon on the nineteenth Ellet reached the Jenkins plantation, five miles
above the Old River, and confiscated three hundred bales
of cotton as protection against Rebel sharpshooters.

8: THE HARES AND THE TORTOISE

Another morning brought the *Era* to St. Joseph's, Louisiana, and, seizing Rebel mail, Ellet learned of a new Confederate battery at Grand Gulf. These guns, however, failed to land more than one shot that glanced harmlessly off a cotton bale. New Carthage, Louisiana, twenty miles below Grand Gulf, posed a different threat. An island divided the river here, with the chute nearest New Carthage used the more often. When Ellet turned the point for this island, Bod "saw a white puff of smoke, and at once a Minie ball came whizzing through the cabin. This was followed by others in quick succession. Under almost any other circumstance, we should have thought the main attack was here, but it occurred to us that it was a ruse to drive us near New Carthage. We suspected they had a battery there, and concluded to take the other chute."

For three miles sharpshooters peppered the *Era;* abreast of the island the *Era's* fires gave out and an hour was lost cleaning out and raising steam again; at the upper point of the island a battery of three twelve-pounders opened "most furiously." Ellet came through without losing a man. Darkness and the fact that "the Rebels did not shoot well" helped the *Era* cruise past the batteries at Warrenton. On the morning of the twenty-first the *Era* dropped into the anchorage once occupied by the *Queen of the West.* "One hundred shots for an unarmed steamer within thirty-five miles is no trifle," said Bod, filled with the wonder of the escape.

For Brown aboard the *Indianola* the period from February 18 to the twenty-first produced another brand of harassment. Brown trusted his reports: the *Queen* had been refitted and had joined the *Webb* and "four cotton-clads" to finish off the *Indianola.* Brown left the mouth of the Red River, but he was not running away from a fight; instead, he was after cotton "to fill up the space between the casemate and wheelhouse." By the morning of the twenty-second Brown had his cotton and also a new idea: to keep on up the Mississippi in the belief "that I would meet another boat the morning following, but I was disappointed. I then concluded to communicate with the squadron as soon as possible, thinking that Colonel Ellet had not reached the squadron, or that Admiral Porter would expect me to return when I found that no other boat was sent below."

Brown's decision to run had been too tardy. The bunkers of the *Indianola* were full of coal, and although he could have sunk the barges, he could not relinquish the notion that Porter would send another vessel which would require refueling. Slowed down by the barges, Brown reached Grand Gulf on the twenty-fourth. The batteries opened fire. Brown held his own guns in virtual silence, wanting to hurry on so that he could pass the deadlier batteries at Warrenton before daylight. The night was dark, the time nine thirty o'clock. Out of the gloom came the Confederate hares—the *Webb*, the reconditioned *Queen*, two cotton-clads filled with troops.

Brown braced for the battle:

> The *Queen of the West* was the first to strike us, which she did after passing through the coal barge lashed to our port side, doing us no serious damage.
>
> Next came the *Webb*. I stood for her at full speed; both vessels came together bows on, with a tremendous crash, which knocked nearly everyone down on board both vessels, doing no damage to us, while the *Webb's* bow was cut in at least eight feet, extending from about two feet above the water line to the keelson.

The cotton-clads barked at the *Indianola* with field pieces and small arms. Brown ignored this annoyance—"everything depended on my disabling the ram." The *Webb* struck once more, crushing the starboard barge. Parts hung by the lashings. Shorthanded, the *Indianola* manned only the forward guns at all times, "and fired them whenever I could get a shot at the rams." Darkness prevented effective marksmanship, and the peepholes in the pilothouse were so small that even though the pilots knew the river they could not see enough to help Brown. Five blows from the *Webb* and the *Queen* came forward of the *Indianola's* wheels at angles that loosened the plating where they struck. Doggedly the *Webb* came on for a sixth blow. The *Indianola* rocked, seemed to lift from the water and then to settle back with a palsy of mortal wounds. Checking the damage, Brown's spirit chilled. Starboard wheel crushed. Starboard rudder disabled. Water pouring in through leaks abaft the shaft. With the starboard engine gone, the *Indianola*—"in an almost powerless condition"—waited as the *Webb* bore down once more:

> She struck us fair in the stern [Brown reported] and started the timbers and starboard rudder-box so that the water poured in in large volumes. At this time I knew that the *Indianola* could be of no more service to us, and my desire was to render her useless to the enemy, which I did by keeping her in deep water until there was two and a half feet of water over the floor and the leaks were increasing rapidly as she settled, so as to bring the opening made by the *Webb* under water. Knowing that if either of the rams struck us again in the stern, which they then had excellent opportunities of doing on account of our disabled condition, we would sink so suddenly that few if any lives would be saved, I succeeded in running her bows on shore by starting the screw engines.

The *Indianola* surrendered after a battle that had lasted one hour and twenty-seven minutes. The loss, Porter commented, was "a great disappointment" to Grant, though the admiral took comfort in the fact that the *Indianola* was "blown up next day by a Yankee ruse" and "the Confederates did not benefit by her capture." Whether the

Northern "croakers" whom Grant despised could be so easily mollified over the capture of the *Indianola* within less than a fortnight of the *Queen* remained a moot point.

3.

In official Washington a hard core of resistance to Grant existed. From Shiloh through the unfortunate order expelling Jews from territory controlled by the Department of Tennessee a succession of events had given constant opportunities to opponents of Grant. Secretary of the Navy Welles believed that Grant was not "a special favorite" with either Stanton or Halleck; and an Illinois senator, Orville H. Browning, calling on another Union general and his wife, would hear that "Grant has personal bravery but no capacity" and was "a very small man" who might be considered even less than "the feeblest of the Circuit Judges of Illinois."

Understandably, newspapers were slow in coming down the river to Vicksburg, and many, when they did arrive, were not designed to comfort Grant. Following the now famous—or infamous—order against Jews, the *New York Times* had snapped: "The order, to be sure, was promptly set aside by the President, but the affront to the Israelites, conveyed by its issue, was not so easily effaced. It continues to rankle. . . ." In January the *Times* still barked editorially: Grant remained "stuck in the mud of northern Mississippi, his army of no use to him or to anybody else." The *Cincinnati Commercial* took an equally virulent view. Grant had gained nothing since Iuka and Corinth; he had botched the whole campaign; and, declaimed the *Commercial,* "We want a general who can perfect the organization of forces, improve their discipline, strengthen their confidence in themselves."

Grant was not a profane man—he never used any expletive stronger than "by jinks" or "by lightning"—but this criticism, combined with the loss of the *Queen* and the *Indianola*, must have strained Grant's reticence. A mule-driver, informed of Grant's abhorrence of profanity, replied cynically: "Then thar's one thing sart'in: the old man never druv mules"; and Grant, reading the *Times*, the *Commercial*, and other papers, could be equally sure that their editorial writers had little knowledge of the country around Vicksburg when incessant rains pushed the Mississippi toward flood levels.

The affair at Lake Providence was a further example of the problems Grant faced in trying to get in back of Vicksburg for a crack at Pemberton. On the day after Grant's arrival at Young's Point orders had gone to General Mc-Pherson to cut the levee at Lake Providence (part of the Mississippi's old bed a mile or so from the present channel). If Grant could open navigation here, he could reach the Mississippi through the mouth of the Red River just above Port Hudson and four hundred miles below Vicksburg. Grant did not underestimate, however, the task that confronted McPherson and his corps. Lake Providence was six miles long. Two of its outlets were Bayou Baxter and Bayou Macon, both narrow and tortuous, filled with fallen timber that had been accumulating for years, and with dense forests overhanging the channels. Moreover, as Bayou Baxter reached lower land, it spread out and all but disappeared in a shallow cypress swamp before joining Bayou Macon. Even vessels of the lightest draft could not have navigated these outlets until a passage had been cleared through the timber belt.

Yet in James Birdseye McPherson, Grant relied on a general highly respected. McPherson had been chief engineer of the army at Shiloh, and, like Sherman, had been welded in loyalty to Grant under bitter and galling fire. Sherman believed that Mac, "if he lives," would "outdistance Grant and myself." Born in a log cabin in Ohio, McPherson graduated at the top of his class at West Point.

He was called by fellow officers "a practicing Christian"; Sherman thought of him as "a noble, gallant gentleman, and the best hope for a great soldier."

On the fourth of February Grant went down to Lake Providence for a visit with McPherson. There was not as yet water from the river in the lake, but the troops had managed to tow in a small steamer. During the several days that Grant remained with McPherson this vessel enabled them "to explore the lake and bayou as far as cleared" (which was not very far). The experience was not cheering. The route through Lake Providence back to the Mississippi represented a distance of 470 miles by "the main river"— to Grant, not much as "a practicable route for moving troops through an enemy's country." Insofar as the Confederates could move at will along the Red River, the Washita, and the Tansas, Pemberton easily "could throw small bodies of men to obstruct our passage and pick off our troops with their sharpshooters." If the toil at Lake Providence produced any result, as far as Theodore R. Davis of *Harper's Weekly* could ascertain, that result was illustrated by the

> . . . exploit of one of the Negro soldiers, who went out in company with a small force of soldiers a few days since, shot one Rebel soldier, captured two more, and taking their guns from them, brought the captured twain through the swamp to the party. The name of this bold African is *Jim*—"Union Jim" the soldiers call him—and there are many more like him, brave and ready, who are to be armed and schooled as soldiers. .

Davis pictured the scene of a "constantly recurring event, the coming in of what the soldiers call recruits of color; a stalwart Negro with his little one riding 'pig-a-back' and the family trudging along after."

Although "fizzle" described Lake Providence as a military venture, Grant decided to "let the work go on, believing employment was better than idleness for the men." Obviously here was one more chorus for the croakers in the North to sing. Grant shrugged. The activity at Lake Providence had another use, Grant believed: "It served as a cover for other efforts which gave a better prospect of success."

Grant's reference was to the survey then being made by Lieutenant Colonel James Harrison Wilson, who had gone to Helena, Arkansas, to determine if a passage could be opened through Moon Lake and the Yazoo Pass. Graduate of West Point in the class of 1860, Wilson would emerge as one of the Union's really capable commanders. Wilson joined Grant's staff at La Grange and felt "somewhat disappointed" at Grant's "simple and unmilitary bearing." But Grant's friendly welcome, Wilson confessed (and it was not difficult for Wilson to look down on anyone along his high-bridged nose), "won my heart at once." There were those, like Washington Gladden, who would describe Grant as "a man who could be silent in several languages," but Wilson soon would see him as "a most agreeable companion both on the march and in camp . . . kind and considerate to the officers and men of his staff, and most gentle and sympathetic with the poor people of the country." Wilson looked sharply at Grant for another reason; he had heard the ugly stories and rumors, but Grant gave no indication of the excessive dissipation Wilson presumably had expected to find. Rawlins and Wilson became such fast friends that Wilson one day would write a life of Rawlins. The General did drink, Rawlins confided to Wilson, "but not so bad as the newspapers or one of his ambitious generals made out." Rawlins was keeping his knife sharpened for any thrust at McClernand.

Wilson's mission to Helena focused on an old route through an inlet of the Mississippi into Moon Lake, a mile east of the river. Once steamers had traded with the plantations by branching east from the inlet through Yazoo Pass to the Coldwater, then to the Tallahatchie, and then to the Yallabusha some 250 miles below Moon Lake. A strong levee had been built across the old inlet, however, forcing vessels to go several hundred miles below before finding entry into the region through the mouth of the Yazoo.

4.

On February 3 Wilson was ready to cut the levee across the once-used inlet and see what would happen. Next morning he was writing Rawlins in an exuberant spirit—a river between seventy-five and eighty feet wide had been opened, "the water pouring through like nothing else I ever saw except Niagara." On the seventh Wilson could enter the Pass "with great ease" aboard a gunboat. About a mile inside the levee he entered Moon Lake, and "ran down it about five miles to the point where the Pass leaves it." Here disappointments began to develop. The stream narrowed and grew more undulating; and there were reports that at the mouth of the Coldwater "a force of Rebels (some thirty or forty, with about a hundred Negroes, had been engaged for several days in felling timber across the stream at intervals between its junction with the Coldwater and a point nearly five miles from Moon Lake." Wilson thought then that the logs would not be too great a nuisance, and felt more alarm at the work of cutting the trees overhanging the stream, which, unless cut, would not leave a smokestack standing on any transport. Some of the cottonwoods and sycamores were four feet through at the butt and might weigh thirty-five tons. Through Wilson's letter to Rawlins three days later ran a rising note of irritation: "The country near the stream is overflowed; nowhere is there more than a mere strip of land next the bank, and that only a few inches out of the water."

Pemberton had been more foresighted than Wilson,

Grant, and Rawlins suspected. The Confederate had ordered the Yazoo Pass obstructed two months previously, had repeated these instructions two weeks before Wilson's arrival at Helena, and, with the cutting of the levee, had thrown a party immediately at the task. Still the determined Wilson pushed on, supported by troops from the District of East Arkansas. On the twenty-fourth he told Rawlins: "I am confirmed in the opinions expressed in my previous reports concerning the practicability of this route, during proper stages of water, as a line of military operations." Even if the water should fall four or five feet, this difficulty could be "easily obviated by cutting and pulling inland the trees now partly in the way." After junction with the Pass the Coldwater became "a considerable stream" and boats "180 feet in length" could be sent from the Mississippi to the Tallahatchie in four days. Wilson's optimism rode from February into early March; on the eighth he informed Grant anew of the "suitability of the route."

At Greenwood the Confederates waited patiently. Here the Tallahatchie and the Yallabusha united and the Yazoo also began; here the "bends of the rivers" almost formed an island, where the Rebels had constructed Fort Pemberton. Hardly above water level, the fortification offered no land approach. Close to five thousand troops now had been organized for the Federal expedition against Greenwood, and on March 10 a force of two ironclads, two rams, and six light-draft gunboats, under Lieutenant Commander Watson Smith, arrived opposite Wilson's headquarters at Curtiss's plantation a few miles above the river juncture.

Suddenly the tone of Wilson's letters to Rawlins changed. He hoped Rawlins would understand his communications were intended as "semi-official . . . I should have directed them to the general, perhaps, but upon deliberation thought I could write with more freedom to you, and subserve the same purpose." Also, Wilson might have added, he could write with more bitterness.

Part Two: THE MOTH AND THE FLAME

On the eleventh the gunboat *Chillicothe* opened her batteries upon Fort Pemberton, but retired quickly after a single shot in her left port had killed or wounded fourteen of her crew. Only two guns "of any weight" defended the Rebel position, and the more effective of these was a 6.4-inch bore rifle. On the thirteenth Wilson admitted that he had been "two days and entire nights without sleep, and am almost dead." Then the transformed Wilson leveled at Rawlins a crossfire of invective:

> I'm disgusted with 7, 9, 10, and 11 inch guns; to let one 6½-inch rifle stop our navy. Bah! They ought to go up to 200 yards and "make a spoon or spoil a horn." They are to attack tomorrow, but may not do much. I have no hope of anything great, considering the course followed by the naval forces under direction of their able and efficient Acting Rear Admiral, Commodore, Captain, Lieutenant-Commander Smith. One chance shot will do the work; we may not make it in a thousand. No more troops are needed here till Greenwood is taken. I think we have troops enough to whip all the Rebels in this vicinity if we can only get by the fort. One good gunboat can do the work, and no doubt; the two here are no great shakes.

Two days later, Wilson's mood grew even more snappish:

> We are no nearer Greenwood than when I wrote you night before last. We didn't attack yesterday, because the gunboats had not finished their repairs, and put it off today out of respect for the Sabbath; but tomorrow it is arranged to try it again, though I am not over-sanguine of success, since I can see a disposition on the part of the navy to keep from a close and desperate engagement. I've talked with them all and tried to give them backbone, but they are not confident. Smith, you doubtless have understood by this time, I don't regard as the equal of Lord Nelson. Walker and Foster, of the

De Kalb and *Chillicothe*, are good men, and will cheerfully do what they are ordered, but both think of Commodore Smith just as I do. I don't hesitate to say that, although the Rebels got ahead of us in obstructing the Pass and thereby kept us back ten days, and although we were furnished with miserable old transports and a new element of delay introduced, Commodore Smith is entirely responsible for the detention at this point and the consequent failure of the expedition, and responsible for no other reason than his timid and slow movements. When the ironclads started into the Pass, I urged with all the force I could the absolute necessity of sending them, the rams, and two mosquitoes forward with all possible dispatch. . . . Had this been done, they could have reached the mouth of the Tallahatchie in four days, I think, and even less. I'll bet my life I could have brought them to this point in three days; but grant that it would have required five days, that would have brought them to this place on the first of March, two whole weeks ago, at which time no heavy guns were here. The rifle did not arrive till about ten days ago. This we have from reliable authority.

Wilson writhed at the predicament he faced. As a gunboat, the *Chillicothe* was "an inglorious failure." Her armor was backed by only nine-inch pine that "shivers into pieces every time the plating is struck." Also, "her bolt-work flies off at a terrible rate." Also, "the *De Kalb* stands it well as long as she is square to the front, though her sides do not fare so well." Also, "these gentlemen have ammunition for only two hours' fighting." To support the navy, Wilson had thrown up a shore battery of two thirty-pound Parrotts and an eight-inch ship gun seven hundred yards from the fort—but again "we have only an average of fifty or sixty rounds for them." Wilson could learn nothing definite of the forces inside Pemberton: ". . . the 2nd Texas, 46th and 20th Mississippi [under Generals W. W. Loring and Lloyd Tilghman] are all the troops we have heard of." But snug inside a fortification of cotton bales covered with sand and earth the Rebels sat, a raft across the stream just above them, the steamer *Star of the West* sunk close to the raft, and a second steamer, the *John Walsh*, "either ready to sink or use as a boarding-craft and ram."

Wilson hoped Rawlins would understand that he felt "solicitous for my reputation at headquarters." Perhaps he should have advised sending a heavy detachment down the Pass to Coldwater before starting operations at the levee; on the other hand, he should have been better advised, and his opinion solicited, "either explicitly or implicitly, directly or indirectly," of the organization of an expedition about which "I knew . . . absolutely nothing . . . until I returned to Moon Lake." Wilson, well launched in his Jovian role, tossed Rawlins a final thunderbolt:

> As the thing stands now, without two or three good ironclads are sent very soon, together with a siege train of six or eight eight-inch howitzers and thirty-pounder rifles, or unless fortune should favor us tomorrow, the game is blocked on us here as well as below.
>
> Should it turn out this way, Vicksburg becomes subordinate, our department secondary, and Rosecrans' army our hope in the West. Won't we, in that event, be required to furnish 50,000 or 60,000 men?

Rawlins need never doubt, Wilson warned, that "the Rebels are making great calculations 'to bag us' entire." Then, passion spent, Wilson inquired of the latest gossip at headquarters and thought to add: "Remember me kindly to the general."

By the time Wilson's letter reached Rawlins, events before Fort Pemberton had decided the issue. The unhappy Watson Smith, who had been handsomely commended by

Porter in the action at Fort Hindman, had reached the breaking-point, and, as Porter said, "owing to aberration of mind," resigned from command within a week. The gunboat attack on the thirteenth failed as miserably as the attack on the eleventh. A second cut of the levee was tried six miles above the first "in hope," Grant explained, "of enlisting the elements on our side." Wilson's plan was to "induce" a large volume of water "to take the line of the Coldwater and Tallahatchie and flood the country near both streams," but the twelve-inch rise that Wilson felt certain the Rebels in the fort "could not have withstood" never materialized.

On the twenty-second Wilson started back, the fight at Yazoo Pass ended, as far as he was responsible for it. Old square-jawed General Isaac F. Quimby hated to quit Fort Pemberton without a real scrap, and as he ranked General L. F. Ross, who had been in command, he decided to see for himself whether anything could be accomplished. A simple inspection without an attack convinced Quimby; he "returned but with little delay."

So Grant's failures mounted, his discouragements grew, the fuels of criticism sputtered into brighter flame. Grant only clamped down harder on his half-smoked cigar, giving credence even then to the statement Lincoln would one day make: "It is the dogged pertinacity of Grant that wins." Likely no other quality could explain the new exploit on which Grant already had embarked. In retrospect it would seem more fantastic than any of the schemes yet tried.

9. BATTLE IN THE BAYOUS

By March the quest for dry ground had driven Grant's armies to pitch their camps over a distance of sixty miles. Rains had swollen the tributaries of the Mississippi to depths of seventeen feet, and land lay under flood water where normally the floating of a canoe would have been a major operation. For Porter the country north of Vicksburg had been transformed into an admiral's dream. Great forests had become channels "admitting the passage of large steamers between the trees." Aboard an industrious little tug that puffed and chugged through this wonderland, Porter discovered lanes "where a frigate might have passed."

Porter arranged a novel voyage for Grant. Before reaching Haines' Bluff on the Yazoo, the admiral signaled his helmsman to swing into apparently impenetrable brush. The trees parted and the lead man sang out the sounding—more than fifteen feet. Porter and Grant sailed through an opening that would have permitted two ironclads to move abreast. They were traveling, Porter said, above an old road once used to haul cotton to the river.

Grant listened as Porter, who never lacked for words, talked. A watercourse variously named Cypress Bayou, Steele's Bayou, Black Bayou, and Deer Creek linked the Yazoo with the Rolling Fork. Ironclads drew only seven feet of water; no masts encumbered them and there was "little about their decks that could be swept away by the bushes or the lower branches of the trees." The Rolling Fork led into the Sunflower River, whence an armada could re-enter the Yazoo. Porter's objective made strategic sense: he would come down the Yazoo and take Haines' Bluff in the rear.

Grant had been studying maps for weeks. The Sunflower emptied into the Yazoo one hundred miles below Fort Pemberton and twenty miles above Haines' Bluff. The route, if it could be navigated, was the best anyone yet had suggested. Porter pressed for a chance. In the naval commander's own words, Grant knew there was no point "in sitting down before Vicksburg and simply looking at it." The men grew restive; the loose tongues in Washington sharpened their criticisms. Standing beside Porter, Grant

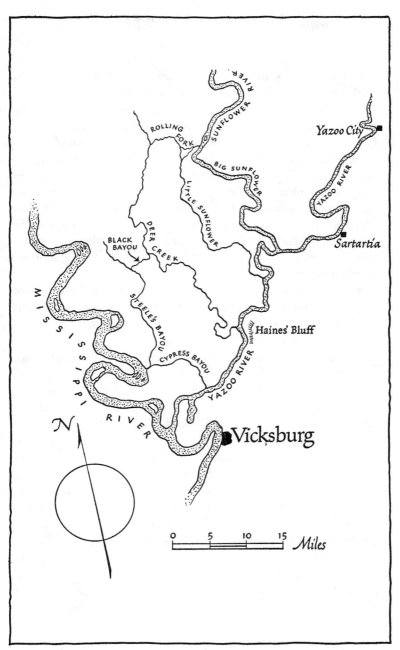

PORTER AND SHERMAN'S BAYOU EXPEDITION

composed a letter to Sherman: "[The Bayous] will be navigable for any class of steamers. . . . Have your pioneer corps, or one regiment of good men for such work, detailed, and at the landing as soon as possible. . . . Take . . . rations, arms, and sufficient camp and garrison equippage for a few days. . . . The 8th Missouri (being many of them boatmen) would be excellent men for the purpose."

A letter to Halleck, giving details of the proposed expedition, found Grant puzzled by the "indication of considerable excitement in Vicksburg." Many troops were being removed, he felt certain, and some were known already to have gone up the Yazoo. Were the others going to Port Hudson? "I have no means of learning anything from below," Grant complained, "except what is occasionally learned through Southern papers."

Halleck replied somewhat crustily; as far as Washington could ascertain, Grant had been a desultory correspondent. "It is very desirable," wrote Halleck, who always had darts in reserve for his verbal blowgun, "that you keep us advised of your operations, in order that proper instructions may be sent to General Banks, General Rosecrans, &c." Old Brains thought the expedition posed dangers—for one, "the danger, on the fall of the water in the Mississippi, of having your steamers caught in the Upper Yazoo, so as to be unable to extricate them." Again, McPherson at Lake Providence could be isolated and attacked. The eyes and hopes of the whole country were on Grant now: "The opening of the Mississippi will be to us of more advantage than the capture of forty Richmonds." In the next letter Halleck wanted some of the steamers on the Mississippi returned: "We cannot otherwise supply our armies in Tennessee and Kentucky." Halleck was obviously irritated and on edge; he was, through a nature that loved gossip, a good barometer of the feeling toward Grant in official Washington.

At Young's Point, Sherman rallied the 8th Missouri and

"some pioneers, with axes, saws, and all the tools necessary." By the sixteenth Porter had assembled a fleet of five ironclads, four tugs, and two light mortar boats "built for the occasion." Grant came down to Young's Point to wish the expedition Godspeed, and Porter felt that he embarked on "one of the most remarkable military and naval expeditions that ever set out in any country." Porter could not disguise his wonder and amusement:

> Here was a dense forest, deeply inundated, so that large steamers could ply among the trees with perfect impunity. They were as much at home as the wild denizens of the forest would be in dry times.
>
> The animals of all kinds had taken to the trees as the only arks of safety. Coons, rats, mice, and wildcats were in the branches, and if they were not a happy family, it was because when they lay down together the smaller animals reposed within the larger ones.
>
> It was a curious sight to see a line of ironclads and mortar boats, tugs and transports, pushing their way through the long, wide lanes in the woods without touching on either side, though sometimes a rude tree would throw Briarean arms around the smokestack of the tinclad *Forest Rose*, or the transport *Molly Miller*, and knock their bonnets sideways.
>
> It all looked as though the world had suddenly got topsy-turvy, or that there was a great camp meeting in the woods on board ironclads and transports.
>
> The difficulty was to preserve quiet, so that our presence might not be detected by the enemy's scouts.

Rebel rams at Yazoo City had been eliminated as a threat on the advice of "a truthful contraband," who told Porter: "Dey has no bottom in, no sides to 'em, an' no top on 'em, sah, an' deir injines is in Richmon'." As the Yankee fleet steamed farther into the forest, Porter's fancies turned to "wood nymphs disporting in their baths." Eight hundred tons of ironclad crashing into trees or knocking down bridges at a velocity of three knots understandably "sent an echo through the woods that would frighten the birds of prey from their perches, whence they were looking down upon the waste of waters, wondering (no doubt) what it all might mean, and whom these mighty buzzards, skimming over the waters and carrying everything before them, could possibly be."

Near Cypress Bayou, about seventy-five miles from the Sunflower, Porter caught up with Sherman's troops. Characteristically, Sherman exuded fussiness and pessimism. Porter's good luck would soon end; he could expect "a devil of a time" now. Insofar as Porter believed that Sherman "knew every stream and bayou in that part of the country better than the oldest inhabitants," images of wood nymphs vanished. But there was comfort in the general's closeness even beyond the protection he offered from Reb sharpshooters. Sherman's army "was no respecter of ducks, chickens, pigs, or turkeys"; obviously in a hungry mood, Porter liked the reputation of one regiment in Sherman's corps that "could catch, scrape, and skin a hog without a soldier leaving the ranks."

A half-mile into Cypress Bayou, Sherman's forecast of impending trouble began to bear discouraging results from the bridge of the *Cincinnati*, where Porter paced.

> . . . We saw the greatest excitement prevailing. Men on horseback were flying in all directions. . . . Pigs were driven by droves to the far woods, and five hundred Negroes were engaged in driving into the fields all the chickens, turkeys, ducks, and geese, and what were a few moments before smiling barnyards were now as bare of poultry as your hand. . . . A mile from the entrance to this bayou there were two piles of cotton containing six thousand bales. . . .

Suddenly I saw two men rush from each side of the
bayou and apply a lighted pine knot to each pile. . . .

"Ring the bell to go ahead fast," shouted Porter.

Tugs pulled mortar boats. "Away we all went, darting
through between the burning bales," Porter said. Crews
manned the fire buckets; boatmen and boats alike were
wet down; the helmsman of the *Cincinnati* covered himself
"with an old flag that lay in the wheelhouse." Paint blistered on the boats; dense columns of smoke set the crews
to hacking and coughing. Along the banks of the levee
Porter felt that the Negroes "looked on with amazement
at the doings of 'Mas' Linkum's gunboats.' " When Porter
caught up with the overseer who had caused the fire, Porter's temper was strained by the colloquy that followed:

"I suppose you are Union, of course? You are all
so when it suits you," I said.

"No, by God, I'm not, and never will be; and as to
the others, I know nothing about them. Find out for
yourself. I'm for Jeff Davis first, last, and all the time.
Do you want any more of me?" he inquired, "for I'm
not a loquacious man at any time."

"No, I want nothing more with you," I replied; "but
I am going to steam into that bridge of yours across
the stream and knock it down. Is it strongly built?"

"You knock it down and be dammed," he said. "It
don't belong to me; and if you want to find out how
strong it is, pitch into it. You'll find a hard nut to
crack; it ain't made of candy."

"You are a Yankee by birth, are you not?" I asked.

"Yes, damn it, I am," he replied; "that's no reason
I should like the institution. I cut it long ago," and he
turned on his heels and walked off.

Porter told the captain: "Ring 'Go ahead fast' . . . we'll
let that fellow see what bridge-smashers we are." At four

knots an hour the boat banged through the bridge "as if it was paper." The overseer, smoking a pipe in the doorway, didn't turn his head to watch. The fellow "was but one remove from a brute"; Porter hoped fervently that Sherman "would pay the apostate Yankee a visit."

For Porter the bedevilments of Cypress Bayou had scarcely begun. "We did nothing but turn upon our course about every twenty minutes," he grumbled. "At one time the vessels all would be steaming on different courses. One would be standing north, another south, another east, and yet another west through the woods. One minute an iron-clad would apparently be leading ahead, and the next minute would as apparently be steering the other way." Logs buried for years in the bayou with one end sunken and the other floating on the surface presented "the appearance of *chevaux-de-frise,* over which we could no more pass than we could fly." Tackles with hook-ropes were used to clear a passage. Next the boats became jammed between trees, and when the ironclads, going no more than half a mile an hour, bullied their way through, "the shock would be so great, the resultant vibration of the tree so violent, that the branches would come crashing on deck, smashing the boats and skylights and all the framework that they reached." Porter felt satisfied—"considering all the impediments"—that by sunset his fleet had made eight miles.

2.

Nightfall multiplied Porter's problems. Ominously through the darkness echoed the thud of axes chopping wood. A tug loaded with a twelve-pound howitzer cruised into the night, searching for the cause. Three shots from the howitzer silenced the wood-chopping, but not before a band of Negroes, impressed into labor by Confederate sympathizers, felled a tree three feet in diameter across the bayou. With lanterns and snatch-blocks, the navy set to clearing the channel while tug and howitzer kept to the quest for signs of further deviltry. Porter tried to see a brighter side to this adversity: "The Confederates . . . forgot the ingenuity of American seamen."

When finally Porter pictured himself sleeping that night "as comfortably as if we had been at the Fifth Avenue Hotel," his mind was scarcely at rest. He was sorry now that he had pushed ahead of Sherman. What would he do if the Rebs blocked up the head of the pass with cotton, turned the channel, and left his ironclads ditched in the mud? Only the image of Sherman seemed to comfort the admiral. He was an unusual ally, Porter thought—"half sailor, half soldier, with a touch of the snapping turtle."

Daylight brought other worries: the men toiled "as men never toiled before"; the vessels looked like wrecks after their quarrel with the tree branches; and again Porter must confess that he had been "rather precipitate" in rushing ahead with the boats. Twelve miles were the best the ironclads could make that second day, and a rising note of urgency prompted the question: *Where was Sherman?* Porter felt encouraged that "there was only one road, so he couldn't have taken the wrong one."

On the third day rafts sunk in the mud, old logs floating treacherously beneath the water, rotten trees overhanging the banks of the levee demonstrated anew that the watercourse had never been intended for craft stouter than the canoes of "a couple of dissipated darkies out on a coon hunt." Porter still endeavored to see his plight good-humoredly:

> Sometimes, when we would strike [a] tree, a multitude of vermin would be shaken out on deck—among them rats, mice, cockroaches, snakes, and lizards, which would be swept overboard by the sailors standing ready with their brooms. Once an old coon landed

on deck, with the life half knocked out of him, but he came to in a short time and fought his way on shore. Even the coons were prejudiced against us, and refused to be comforted on board, though I am sorry to say we found more Union feeling among the bugs of all kinds, which took kindly to the ironclads and would have remained with us indefinitely had they been permitted to do so.

After three days worming through the bayous, Porter lamented: "And no hope of seeing the Sunflower River!" A lieutenant spied an Indian mound—"as old as the deluge"—and urged Porter to fortify it. The admiral assented, but more in the spirit of indulging a whim than of meeting a military necessity. Four boat guns soon crowned the mound. Meanwhile Porter calculated his position philosophically: "We had steamed, or rather bumped, seventy-five miles, and had only six hundred yards to go before getting into the Rolling Fork, where all would be plain sailing; but I waited for all the vessels to come up to repair damages and start together."

Where Porter continued to hope for a successful ending to the expedition, the "half sailor, half soldier, with a touch of the snapping turtle" began to suspect that he had embarked on a military fiasco. Sherman stirred uneasily in his headquarters at the intersection of Black Bayou and Deer Creek. He had watched troops arriving on schedule by transport—the 6th Missouri, part of the 116th Illinois—and had waved as the boats backed out for the return voyage to Eagle Bend, where reinforcements waited.

Sherman had given a day to reconnoitering through the bayous in a tug, and had come back disgusted. The tug had broken her rudder and her smokestack had been carried away. "She is now repaired," Sherman wrote Rawlins, "and will be used in towing an empty coal barge freighted with soldiers as they arrive." Here his patience broke.

Nothing in the bayous fulfilled "any of General Grant's conditions. . . . We cannot reach the Yazoo by land or water." Subsequently Sherman reported that navigation had been "good" five miles up Cypress Bayou; in Muddy Bayou he had found "channel deep but crooked"; the navigation in Steele's Bayou could be considered good "for small boats"; in Black Bayou "wooden boats would be all torn to pieces." Deer Creek remained, and he referred to it with asperity:

> . . . Water deep but channel narrow, crooked, and filled with young willows, which bind the boats and make navigation difficult, and the banks along the whole length are lined with heavy trees and overhanging branches that tear down chimneys and carry away pilothouses, stanchions, and all woodwork.
>
> I did not see the Rolling Fork, but without hesitation I pronounce Black Bayou and Deer Creek useless to us as a military channel.

Three loads of troops reached the foot of Black Bayou by steamboat on the night of March 21. Wearily Sherman faced the duty of transferring the brigades "to the first visible ground above water," conducting them "through the dense canebrake by lighted candles." By morning he could be glad for the arrival of the 13th Regulars, the 113th Illinois, the 83rd Indiana, more of the 116th Illinois, the 54th and 57th Ohio. "In the direction of the fleet," the sound of artillery quickened. Sherman decided that he'd better move.

Six hundred yards short of the Rolling Fork and "plain sailing," Porter scowled at a "large green patch extending all the way across" the bayou. Another of Porter's ever-handy "truthful contrabands" supplied an explanation: "It's nuffin but willers, sah. When de water's out ob de bayou—which it mos' allers is—den we cuts de willers to make baskets wid. You kin go troo dat like an eel."

Porter went into the willows and soon wished that he hadn't. After about thirty yards, the tug

. . . began to go slower and slower, and finally stuck so fast that she could move neither ahead nor astern. I hailed her and told her I would come along and push them through. We started with a full head of steam, and did not even reach the tug. The little withes caught in the rough iron ends of the overhand and held us as if in a vise. I tried to back out, but t'was no use. We could not move an inch, no matter how much steam we put on. . . .

We got large hooks out and led the hook-ropes aft, and tried to break off the little twigs, but we could not move. We got saws, knives, cutlasses, and chisels over the side, with the men handling them sitting on planks, and cut them off, steamed ahead, and only moved three feet. Other withes sprang up from under the water and took a fresher grip on us, so we were worse off than ever.

If ever Porter had felt that the Rebels would permit him to sail unmolested through the "Vicksburg granary," his disillusionment now became complete. After four more hours of toil the ironclad had been budged less than a foot. Then a Rebel steamer was reported coming up the Rolling Fork. Porter planned to "catch that fellow after dark"; the Rebel had his own idea about the situation. Porter, wishing at the moment "ironclads were in Jericho," received a further surprise:

While I was pondering what to do, and the Negroes were looking on in admiration upon the ingenious devices we put into play to get rid of those willow fastenings, wondering to myself if the Confederacy had planted these willows on purpose to keep me out of the Sunflower River, I heard the faint reports of two guns, and directly after the shrill shriek of rifle shot, which came from directions at right angles to each other. The shells burst over the Indian mound where Lieutenant Murphey was studying the strategy of war. They were Whitworth shells. I knew the sound too well to be mistaken. . . . There were two six-gun batteries with a crossfire upon us.

The battle developed quickly. Porter, who hardly ever could resist making estimates, set the number of shells from the enemy's spitfires at fifteen a minute. Pieces of iron and shrapnel, hitting the decks, "rattled like hail." Porter's large guns were below the level of the banks and therefore useless to him; well might he write: "Here was a dilemma." The sailors who had manned the Indian mound fled for the boats. Porter bellowed for them to go back and forget the pounding of the Confederate Whitworths. Most, but not all, obeyed. Then the Yankee mortars unlimbered, and, for a time at least, the crossfire stopped.

But Porter remained stuck in the willows. The Rebels hauled rifle batteries into place. Scouts reported another vessel, filled with reinforcements, steaming down the Rolling Fork. Nor were these diversions the whole of Porter's tribulations: "The stream, for some reason, began to run rapidly, and large logs began to come in from the Rolling Fork and pile up outside of the willows, making an effectual barricade. It was water rushing down through the cut-off and creeks from the opening into the 'Old Yazoo Pass' of the Mississippi River. What was doing good for those fellows was bad for us."

Porter all but embraced the Negro who offered to carry a message through the swamps to Sherman. The spirit of the fellow was in the sassiness with which he replied to Porter: "My name ain't Sambo, sah. My name's Tub, an' I run yer line fer yer half a dollar." Porter scribbled his message:

DEAR SHERMAN: Hurry up, for Heaven's sake. I never knew how helpless an ironclad could be steaming around through the woods without an army to back her.

3.

Tub reached Sherman that night, bringing Porter's message "written on tissue paper" and "concealed in a piece of tobacco." The general, who was "almost alone" on the Hill plantation, jumped into a canoe and paddled down Black Bayou to the gunboat *Price*. There he found that *The Silver Wave* had arrived with another load of soldiers. Sherman, however, didn't dwell on this undeserved luck:

. . . Taking some of the parties who were at work along the bayou into an empty coal barge, we tugged it up by a navy tug, followed by *The Silver Wave*, crashing through the trees, carrying away pilothouse, smokestacks, and everything above deck. . . . The night was absolutely black, and we could only make two and a half of the four miles. We then disembarked, and marched through the cane-brakes, carrying lighted candles in our hands, till we got into the cottonfields at Hill's plantation, where we lay down for a few hours' rest. . . . We had no horses.

On Sunday morning . . . we could hear Porter's guns, and knew that the moments were precious. Being on foot myself, no man could complain, and we generally went at the double-quick, with occasional rests. The road lay along Deer Creek, passing several plantations; and occasionally, at the bends, it crossed the swamp, where the water came above my hips. The smaller drummer boys had to carry their drums on their heads, and most of the men slung their cartridge boxes around their necks. The soldiers generally were glad to have their general and field officers afoot, but we gave them a fair specimen of marching, accomplishing about twenty-one miles by noon. . .

The sounds of the navy guns grew more distinct; still Sherman "could see nothing." A detachment of the 8th Missouri, on picket duty, told Sherman of Porter's situation. Billy sank down on the doorsill of a cabin to rest. A scant ten minutes passed; then, in the woods just ahead,

> . . . not three hundred yards off, I heard quick and rapid firing of musketry. Jumping up, I ran up the road, and found Lieutenant Colonel [Americus W.] Rice [of the 57th Ohio], who said the head of the column had struck a small force of Rebels with a working gang of Negroes, provided with axes, who on the first fire had broken and run back into the swamp. I ordered Rice to deploy his brigade, his left on the road, and extending as far into the swamp as the ground would permit, and then to sweep forward until he uncovered the gunboats. The movement was rapid and well executed, and we soon came to some large cottonfields and could see our gunboats in Deer Creek, occasionally firing a heavy eight-inch gun across the cottonfield into the swamp behind. About that time a Major Kirby . . . galloped down the road . . . and offered me his horse. I got on *bareback*, and rode up the levee, the sailors coming out of their ironclads and cheering most vociferously as I rode by, and as our men swept forward across the cottonfield in full view. I soon found Admiral Porter, who was on the deck of one of his ironclads with a shield made of the section of a smokestack, and I doubt if he was ever more glad to meet a friend than he was to see me. . . .

Sherman minced no words: Why had Porter got "into such an ugly scrape?" Porter arched his brow. Billy grumbled: "This is the most infernal expedition I was ever on: who in thunder proposed such a mad scheme?" But the query was strictly rhetorical. What next—"clean those fellows out" so Porter could go on? "Thank you, no," the admiral said. He was sick of the adventure, and the Confederacy was forewarned of any movement now. Porter wrote: "The game was up, and we bumped on homeward."

The navy boys took a bad ribbing from Sherman's troops on the way back. For three days the crews on the ironclads suffered constant catcalls:

"Halloo, Jack, how do you like playing mud turtle?"

"Where's all your sails and masts, Jack?"

"Johnny Reb's taken their rudders away!"

When a forecastleman could stand the badinage no longer, he'd snap: "We wa'n't half as much used up as you was at Chickasaw Bayou!"

Sylvanus Cadwallader hustled back ahead of the ironclads and the soldiers and scored a three-day beat for the *Chicago Times* in reporting the fiasco in the bayous. The reporter's opinion of Porter added one more drop of acid to the portrait it would ultimately etch: "He absolutely never accomplished anything if unaided. He bombarded Vicksburg for months; threw hundreds of tons of metal into the city; never hit but one house and never killed a man. The Confederates laughed at him."

Grant could not deny that "the fourth attempt to get in rear of Vicksburg" had ended "in failure." Grant "was sadly disappointed," in Sherman's opinion. If Billy's nose appeared to twitch, it was because he had formed by then an instinct for sensing the high- and low-pressure areas of circumstance that could produce storms in Washington, in the press, and usually in both.

10. THE BIG GAMBLE

THE sharp and ofttimes cantankerous mind of Lincoln's Postmaster General, Montgomery Blair, affixed upon Edwin McMasters Stanton the sobriquet "The Black Terrier." This description of Lincoln's second Secretary of War impressed many in official Washington as extraordinarily apt, although it lacked the venom of such other names as "dastard," "betrayer of his country," and "crawling sycophant," which also were applied to Stanton.

Few persons possessed the genius that resided in the thickset, medium-sized Stanton; individuals who were otherwise respectable and placid could be moved to outbursts of rage and profanity at the mere image of Stanton's strong, heavy neck, his long, curling black hair, his large nose and dangerously luminous eyes; the sight of the coarse black whiskers concealing Stanton's jaw and chin sometimes terrorized others who understood the man's strange combination of energy and ambition, his morbid fear and quick-triggered suspicion.

Brilliant at law, pertinacious to the point that he could outlast the almost endless litigation involved in the McCormick reaper case, well versed in history, Stanton strode across the stage of war-stricken Washington as a gladiator whose tongue was his howitzer and his temper his arsenal. Strange stories were told of Stanton—of how once he had insisted that a sweetheart be exhumed from her grave, obsessed with the thought that she had been buried alive; of how, when his firstborn child had died, he had kept her body in a metal casket on the mantelpiece in his bedroom for years; of how, wherever he moved, he carried a dagger in a sheath under his waistcoat. As a child Stanton had sat on the knee of Benjamin Lundy, the father of abolition; he had been weaned on a hatred for slavery, and in part this background of repressed torment and vengeance may have shaped the still inexplicable character of the man who often worked alone at night in the old War Department building while his carriage waited outside.

That February and March of 1863, when in the press and in Washington's most exclusive clubs and salons the dissatisfaction toward Grant erupted in anger and accusations of incompetence, there was small cause for wonder if, during those nighttime vigils in the War building, the brooding fears and suspicions of Stanton focused on Vicksburg. Indicative of the widespread distrust of Grant spreading through capital and nation would be a letter that Lincoln's secretary, John G. Nicolay, wrote to his wife, Therena: "If I were not of a very hopeful disposition I should feel blue about military affairs. Grant's attempt to take Vicksburg looks to me very much like a total failure, with the possible danger that the whole Yazoo expedition may be cut off and captured." Ben Butler insisted that Lincoln had called him to the White House and had suggested that he "might take Grant's command"; but Butler claimed that he replied: "I can see no reason why he should be recalled. He seems to have done well enough, and I do not want to be a party to such another injustice as I suffer." Porter hinted at "some implacable foe, with a corps of reporters at his beck and call," who was "inundating the country with false accounts of Grant's actions," but Sherman minced no words: "We all knew, what was notorious, that General McClernand was still intriguing against General Grant, in hopes to regain the command of the whole expedition."

The course that Stanton pursued in this situation, as should have been expected, was unorthodox and tinged with the undertone of duplicity that distinguished many of his acts; equally provocative was the fact that even war could have produced an attraction between two such strange bedfellows as Stanton and Charles Anderson Dana,

132

an ex-Utopian who liked to roll fine wines around his tongue and pronounce eternal judgments upon them.

Dana had graduated from Harvard at a time when through the rugged intellectual climate of transcendentalist New England swept strong currents of communalism. Into no nostrils did these drafts carry greater sweetness than those of that weary Unitarian apostle George Ripley. Almost at once Ripley regained his wind for life, and at West Roxbury, Massachusetts, fell cheerfully and heartily into the establishment of Brook Farm, where passage into the community of Utopia could be bought for a thousand dollars a share. Margaret Fuller could sniff at the Ripley experiment ("How much nobler stands a man entirely unpledged, unbound"), but Dana, cutting the ties of Harvard, had somewhat less of the individualism of Margaret, or of Emerson. Five happy years at Brook Farm found Dana teaching classes in Greek and German, performing chores in gardening and cookery, and nourishing an æstheticism that would never expire. When at last circumstances forced Dana to leave the boys in their tasseled caps and the girls in their gay muslin dresses at Brook Farm, the literary tastes he had cultivated carried him into journalism. Soon Dana's personal world had become as cluttered with unromantic practicality as the narrow, littered stairs he climbed to his office in the *New York Tribune;* however, to rise to the editorship of Mr. Greeley's fabulous enterprise, and to own twenty magnificent shares in the paper, should have entailed real sacrifices.

Dana was among the stanchest supporters of Stanton as successor to Simon Cameron in Lincoln's Cabinet. Editorially Dana hailed the selection, and Stanton, untroubled in conscience that he actually had drafted the proposal to arm slaves that had catapulted Cameron into the camp of the radicals and out of the confidence of Lincoln, replied in a personal letter: "As soon as I can get the machinery of the office working, the rats cleared out, and the rat holes

stopped, we shall *move*." Soon Dana was suggesting that
Frémont should be given something to do, hearing from
Stanton that "if General Frémont has any fight in him, he
shall (so far as I am concerned) have a chance to show it,"
and taking satisfaction in the subsequent creation out of
parts of Virginia, Kentucky, and Tennessee of a "Mountain
Department" for Frémont to command. However, early
one April morning in 1862 there was less satisfaction for
Dana in a visit from the *Tribune's* advertising manager.
Greeley, whose beard resembled Stanton's and whose idiosyncrasies were equally impressive as far as they went, had
dispatched this functionary to secure Dana's resignation.
The editor was not mystified at the action: "While he was
for peace I was for war, . . . and there was a spirit that
was not his spirit—that he did not like."

Stanton, reading in the press of Dana's break with
Greeley, invited him into the service of the War Department. Dana's first assignment was as a member of a commission to audit unsettled claims against the quartermaster's
department at Cairo, Illinois, and here at a dinner the ex-
Utopian ex-editor had his first meeting with Grant. Dana
found Grant "a man of simple manners, straightforward,
cordial, and unpretending," and was most impressed by
the fact that although Grant "was really under a cloud at
the time because of his operations at Shiloh" no one "would
have suspected it from his manner."

In November Stanton again called Dana to Washington
and offered him the post of Assistant Secretary of War.
When Dana accepted, Stanton said: "All right, consider it
settled." Leaving the old War building, Dana encountered
a former newspaper crony, Major Charles G. Halpine of
the 69th New York Infantry. Dana told Halpine of the appointment, Halpine told others, and by morning the story
was in the New York papers. Stanton raged; he had been
insulted; the appointment was withdrawn, and the Assistant Secretary reverted to a private citizen. However,

when Dana formed a partnership with Roscoe Conkling and George W. Chadwick to buy cotton, a mollified Stanton wrote a letter to be shown to generals in the field: "Mr. Dana is my friend; you can rely upon what he says, and if you can be kind to him in any way you will oblige me."

Dana had invested ten thousand dollars in the venture— a share in Utopia at Brook Farm had cost one tenth as much—and in January 1863 arrived in Memphis. His interest in cotton quickly cooled, and on January 21 he wrote Stanton a bitter letter, decrying the fact that the "mania for sudden fortunes" in cotton had "to an alarming extent corrupted and demoralized the army." Dana pictured every colonel, captain, or quartermaster "in secret partnership with some operator in cotton," while every soldier dreamed "of adding a bale of cotton to his monthly pay." Dana would allow no private purchase of cotton in any part of the occupied region, and he proposed a simple plan by which the government could take over the whole operation. By employing no more than $200,000 to buy up cotton and resell it at public auction, the result, he felt, "would be more than equal to thirty thousand men added to the national armies."

In a postscript Dana added: "I have seen General Grant, who fully agrees with all my statements and suggestions, except that imputing corruption to every officer, which of course I did not intend to be taken literally." Lincoln also agreed, and Dana, who had been twice in and out of the War Department, now was called once more to Washington. By the end of March the President prepared a proclamation declaring unlawful "all commercial intercourse with the states in insurrection," and Stanton issued an order "forbidding officers and all members of the army to have anything to do with the trade."

But Grant more than cotton troubled Stanton. There "were many doubts" about the situation at Vicksburg, he told Dana. Some one must go to Grant's army, Stanton said, "to report daily to him the military proceedings, and to give such information as would enable Mr. Lincoln and himself to settle their minds as to Grant." Would Dana go?

Dana nodded.

"Very well," Stanton said. "The ostensible function I shall give you will be that of a special commissioner of the War Department to investigate the pay service of the Western armies, but your real duty will be to report to me everything you see."

In mid-March Dana started for Memphis. Here he learned little enough, for it was scarcely news that Grant had four schemes in operation to reach high ground behind Vicksburg while maintaining a river base for supplies. Nor was it really news that none of the plans—re-digging the old canal, the routes by Lake Providence and Steele's Bayou, or Wilson's expedition to Yazoo Pass—promised any appreciable success. The rumor at Memphis was rife that Grant had "an entirely new plan of campaign." Dana chafed at being held at Memphis; it was impossible to gather "trustworthy news" here. A telegram to the War Department suggested that he would be "more useful further down the river." Stanton agreed that the dispatches from Dana thus far had been "meager and unsatisfactory"; Dana might go wherever he wanted, being governed "by your own discretion, without any restriction."

Impatiently Dana waited for a boat to carry him down the river to Grant's headquarters at Milliken's Bend.

2.

Somewhere in the War Department there had been a leak, for Grant knew that Dana was coming and why. Colonel William S. Duff, chief of artillery, raged at the staff meeting called to discuss how to deal with Stanton's emissary. Dana was "a government spy," shouted the excitable Duff; moreover he, Duff, would "throw him in the river." Rawlins, who, as Dana would inform Stanton, "never gives himself any indulgence except swearing and scolding," remained calm in this crisis. Dana, insisted Rawlins, was "entitled to as much official recognition as Mr. Stanton, or any other high public functionary." Duff swallowed his temper. The staff had one paramount object, said Cadwallader, who attended the meeting—"to keep Mr. Dana quiet until Grant could work out his campaign." Meanwhile Dana's tent was always to be pitched beside Grant's, sentries were to guard it, orderlies were to be at his service, and a place was to be especially reserved for him at mess.

Unmindful of the storm that had almost broken, Dana reached Milliken's Bend on the sixth of April. Hedges of roses and Osage orange were blooming, the white tents of Grant's army dotted the plains, and the deserted mansions were "enclosed in roses, myrtles, magnolias, oaks, and every sort of beautiful and noble trees." The sensitive youth of Brook Farm responded to a flock of swans that "rose from the water one after the other, and sailed away up the river in long, curving silver lines, bending and floating almost like clouds, and finally disappearing high up in the air above the green woods on the Mississippi shore." He guessed their number at a thousand.

Dana felt pleased that he was not long at Milliken's Bend "before I was on friendly terms with all the generals, big and little." Even Duff, said Cadwallader, acted "deferential," although Dana's private opinion held Duff to be an incompetent who remained on the staff through Grant's "weakness" in being "unwilling to hurt the feelings of a friend." Wilson became an immediate favorite—even if Wilson was "unpopular among all who like to live with little work," Dana would tell Stanton, "he has remarkable talents and uncommon executive power, and will be heard from hereafter"—and Rawlins he rather liked, though not with the affection Grant held for his chief of staff. Brook

Farm and fifteen years on the *Tribune* had left their marks on Dana; peevishly he remarked that Rawlins "can't write the English language correctly without a great deal of careful concentration. Indeed, illiterateness is a general characteristic of Grant's staff, and in fact of Grant's generals and regimental officers of all ranks." Dana thought the prime reason "Grant was always glad to have me with his army" was his distaste for letter-writing, of which he was largely relieved by "my daily dispatches to Mr. Stanton . . . describing every day what was going on in the army."

Among Grant's generals, Dana must admit quickly, he found some who were "very rare men"—especially Sherman, "a man of genius and of the widest intellectual acquisitions." When Dana wrote to Stanton his code word for Vicksburg was "cupid"; and as Dana's admiration grew he might have used that word for Billy. The handsome, dark-eyed, cordial McPherson he also admired—"a man without pretentions, and always . . . a pleasant handshake"—and he felt the fact impressive that Grant, Sherman, and McPherson were all born in Ohio. The "utmost cordiality and confidence" existed among them, Dana testified; "there was no jealousy and bickering, and in their unpretending simplicity they were as alike as three peas." Grant grew in Dana's eyes because of the loyalty and devotion Sherman and McPherson showed him; this camaraderie helped him forget Grant's tolerance for aides-de-camp who often drew such portraits from Dana as "a worthless, whisky-drinking, useless fellow" or "a relative of Mrs. Grant, he has been a stage-driver, and violates English grammar at every phrase."

Despite the hedge roses and blooming Osage orange, nerves tautened at Milliken's Bend. The shape of Grant's new campaign had emerged. Dana heard from Grant that he intended to transfer his army to New Carthage, carry it over the Mississippi, and land "at or about" Grand Gulf;

capturing that point, he intended to operate on the eastern and southern shores of the Big Black River, "threatening at the same time both Vicksburg and Jackson, and confusing the Confederates as to his real objective." In essence, Grant had decided that if he couldn't get at Pemberton inside Vicksburg, then he would force Pemberton to come out and fight him.

Audacity and imagination certainly governed Grant's thinking; this time he gambled his whole neck. But Grant set quietly to the task of opening a passage from Milliken's Bend to New Carthage, so that the army, "with artillery and baggage," might be transported within twenty-four hours. Thirty-five hundred men labored on the canal to the bayou on the west side of the river; Grant hoped to march his army along the bank, but, if necessary, would ship them through the canal on transports. Supplies he would load on steamboats protected by cotton bales and float them past the Vicksburg batteries, for something should be gained from the exploits of the *Queen of the West* and the *Indianola.*

Dana felt drawn to the scheme because "the river men pronounced its success certain." The "one hitch" Dana could see was the fact that "Grant had entrusted the attack on Grand Gulf to McClernand." Both Porter and Sherman, still stinging at the conduct of McClernand in the attack on Arkansas Post, protested the selection, but Grant stood adamant. Dana told Stanton slyly: "I have remonstrated as far as I could properly," and drew a quick reprimand from Stanton: "Allow me to suggest that you carefully avoid giving any advice in respect to commands that may be assigned, as it may lead to misunderstanding and troublesome complications." Dana might act as "the eyes of the army" but not as its voice.

But Billy Sherman could be vocal. He liked so little about Grant's scheme that he must unburden himself in a long letter to Rawlins. Sherman already had stormed into Wilson's tent, sputtering to prove his points from Baron Jomini's *The Political and Military Life of Napoleon*, the redoubtable authority that Halleck had translated from the French. In the main, Sherman argued for some other movement by way of Lake Providence or the Yazoo Pass. The road back to Memphis should be secured and reopened, he thought; a minor force should be left in the present vicinity "to act with the gunboats when the main army is known to be near Vicksburg—Haines' Bluff or Yazoo City"; the "line of the Yalabusha [should] be the base from which to operate against the points where the Mississippi Central crosses the Big Black, above Canton; and, lastly, where the Vicksburg & Jackson Railroad crosses the same river," for then, he was sure, "the capture of Vicksburg would result." Moreover, Sherman wanted a meeting to solicit the opinions of each corps commander, meaning explicitly that he wanted McClernand to go on record now.

Grant's mind, however, in Dana's phrase, was "dead set" on his own plan. Despite Jomini, Sherman was overruled. April 16 was the night when seven transports were to run past the Vicksburg batteries.

If Rawlins's spirits seemed more exuberant as the critical evening approached, the same reason also explained Grant's rising spirits—Julia had come with the children to Milliken's Bend. Julia's amiability, her cheerfulness, her cordial interest made her popular at headquarters. Young Freddy liked to strut around wearing his father's sword hung from a yellow sash at his waist, and those who grimaced could hide their irritation, for Freddy announced that he intended to remain with his father throughout the campaign. Julia visited soldiers who were sick, ate at the regular mess, and sought out the cook to suggest special delicacies. Grant acted quiet and serene with Julia around; in camp as at Galena they were described as "a perfect Darby and Joan." Soon Dana would write that everyone became "more san-

guine that the new project would succeed"; and even
Sherman's mind, he suspected, was "tending to the conclusion of General Grant."

3.

A mass of "black things detached itself from the shore,"
Dana wrote. The time of night was just before ten o'clock.
Soon other dark masses appeared—the squadron, with
Grant's army, had cast loose its moorings. Dana watched
the vessels moving at intervals of about two hundred yards:
"First came seven ironclad turtles and one heavy armed
ram; following these were two side-wheel steamers and one
stern-wheel, having twelve barges in tow. . . . Far astern
of them was the one carrying ammunition. The most of
the gunboats had already doubled the tongue of land which
stretches northeasterly in front of Vicksburg, and they were
immediately under the guns of nearly all the Confederate
batteries. . . ."

Julia held Grant's hand. Flashes came from the upper
forts, and, quickly, Confederate guns were in action along a
four-mile line. Burning tar barrels and a frame building in
front of Vicksburg put to the torch (Porter identified the
blazing building as the railway station) lighted the scene
for the Rebel gunners. The youngest of the Grant children
sat on Wilson's lap. With every roar of the cannon the
frightened child's head pressed against Wilson's chest.

Except for commiseration for the child, whom he ordered
to bed, Grant revealed nothing of his own emotions. Sherman, however, still distrusting the whole venture, had ordered four yawls hauled "across the swamp to the reach
of the river below Vicksburg," and waited "to pick up
any of the disabled wrecks as they floated by." He sat in
one of his yawls as the fleet passed Vicksburg. The scene,
he felt, was "truly sublime":

. . . As soon as the rebel gunners detected the
Benton, which was in the lead, they opened on her,
and on the others in succession, with shot and shell;
houses on the Vicksburg side and on the opposite shore
were set on fire, which lighted up the whole river; and
the roar of cannon, the bursting of shell, and finally the
burning of the *Henry Clay,* [struck in her cotton barri-
cades by an exploding shell and] drifting with the
current, made up a picture of the terrible not often
seen. Each gunboat returned the fire as she passed the
town, while the transports hugged the opposite shore.
When the *Benton* had got abreast of us, I pulled off to
her, boarded, and had a few words with Admiral
Porter, and as she was drifting rapidly toward the
lower batteries at Warrenton, I left, and pulled back
toward the shore, meeting the gunboat *Tuscumbia* towing the transport *Forest Queen* into the bank out of the
range of fire. . . . One of my yawls picked up [the]
pilot [of the *Henry Clay*] floating on a piece of the
wreck. . . . The bulk of her crew escaped in their own
yawl-boat to the shore above.

Sherman saw the *Silver Wave* go by safely and felt the same
tug of relief he did when the *Forest Queen* was out of danger.
One vessel had carried him on the expedition to Steele's
Bayou and the other on the expedition to Arkansas Post.
His attachment to the two boats simply proved that Porter
was right—he was half soldier, half sailor.

By Dana's estimate, the Confederates fired 525 dis-
charges; the cannonade lasted an hour and a half. The
captain and the crew of the *Henry Clay* had abandoned their
ship in panic, but her pilot had ignored the flames and
grounded the steamer before going over the side. The danger to the fleet, in Porter's opinion, was "more apparent
than real."

At 2:30 a.m. the last of the transports dropped anchor at

General Ulysses Simpson Grant. [ABOVE LEFT] *Photograph by Gardner.*

Major General John Alexander McClernand, 1863. [ABOVE RIGHT]

Brigadier General John G. Rawlins. [RIGHT]

Leader of the Mississippi Fleet, Admiral David Dixon Porter, 1866. [ABOVE LEFT] *Photograph by Mathew B. Brady.*

Major General William Tecumseh Sherman, c. 1865. [ABOVE RIGHT]

Major General J. C. Pemberton, CSA. [LEFT]

Vicksburg, the terraced city on the Mississippi. *Engraving by Ed. Willmann, published by Ch. Chardon, Paris.*

Protected by cotton bales, a Yankee tug runs

Yankee gunboats join in the final softening-up of Vicksburg, June 28, 1863. First line of gun-boats from left to right: *Monongahela, Hartford, Winona, Iroquois, Wissahicon,* and *Brooklyn.*

Union transports in the Dixie Bayous, showing, as Sherman said, "their bon-

Major General Logan's headquarters and Union caves and lean-to's immediately behind Fort Hill.

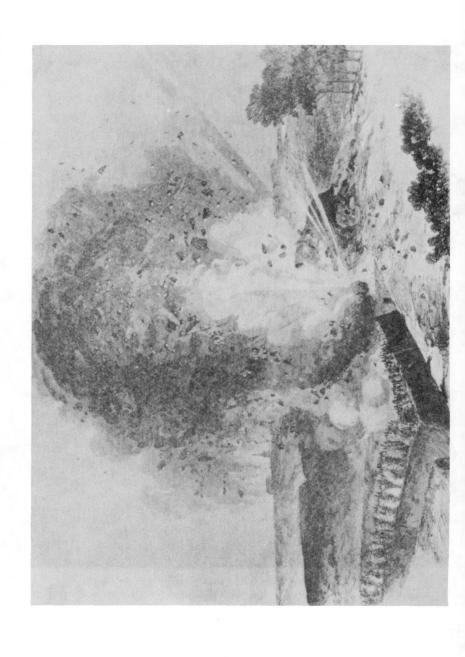

New Carthage. The guns at Vicksburg and Warrenton fell silent. Grant turned to Julia and smiled.

Next morning a restless Grant rode to New Carthage with Dana to review the situation. "We found the squadron there, all in fighting condition," Dana said, "though most of them had been hit. Not a man had been lost." The gambler in Grant bade him ride his luck; he was soon back at Milliken's Bend. Six transport steamers—each loaded with one hundred thousand rations—must be ready to run the batteries by the twenty-second. Grant called for volunteers and got them from Logan's division. "If ten thousand men had been wanted instead of one hundred and fifty," Dana thought, "they would have engaged with zeal in the adventure."

Here was tribute to the *esprit de corps* Johnny Logan inspired among his men, and tribute also to Grant's judgment on that day early in the war when McClernand and Logan had come to Springfield to persuade the militia to volunteer for three-year enlistments. Despite the fact that Duff was one of Logan's closest friends, Dana looked upon Logan as "a man of remarkable qualities." Still, although Dana saw Logan as "heroic and brilliant," he must admit that he was "sometimes unsteady." The affable, profane Logan frankly shocked Sylvanus Cadwallader, who discovered him one night

> . . . with nothing on him in the way of clothing but his hat, shirt, and boots, sitting at a table on which stood a bottle of whisky and a teacup, and playing on a violin for a lot of dark-skinned visitors to dance. When the exercise began to flag, which it generally did at short intervals, in the face of such temptation, potions were indulged in by player and dancers. . . .

Yet, as the night of the twenty-second approached, Logan's boys had done their job well: they were ready, with forty days' coal for each steamer, a barge lashed to each side, bulwarks of hay, cotton, and pork barrels fitted. The ships, Grant told Dana, were "to drop noiselessly down with the current from the mouth of the Yazoo, and not show steam until the enemy's batteries began firing, when the boats were to use all their legs."

Jake Wilkin of the 130th Illinois knew that he would never forget that cloudy night

> . . . as I saw the *Tigress*, followed by her five companies, glide by the *Von Puhl*, and saw standing on the upper deck of his headquarters boat a man of iron, his wife by his side. He seemed to me then the most immovable figure I ever saw. . . . No word escaped his lips, no muscle of his earnest face moved. . . . To say that we were all excited but feebly describes the situation. The excitement and commotion was, however, of that suppressed character which intensifies rather than conceals emotion. Conversations were carried on with bated breath of the deepest anxiety and apprehension for our friends who were floating, as we feared, to certain death. Men were nervously moving about the boat, straining to catch a glimpse of the heroic fleet and the gallant men on board. Grant alone appeared oblivious to what was going on. . . . If those boats failed to reach the army below, it would be without provisions, without forage, and, still worse, without adequate means of crossing the river and gaining the necessary footing on the east side [for the assault on Grand Gulf]. If the boats were sent to the bottom, as the Rebels confidently hoped, thirty thousand men or more would be helpless upon the west bank of the river. . . .

Thirty solid shots through the hull of the *Tigress* saw her break in two and sink, the only transport lost. A few men were wounded. But otherwise the batteries were safely passed; Grant's luck held; the big gamble rode high.

Now, well past midnight, the old river was quiet. Inside Vicksburg a train rattled as its coupling-pin fell into place. Heated guns on the bluffs of the sleepless city began to cool. Troops moved, the moth had seen the flickering of the flame. . . .

Slowly Grant's headquarters boat turned and headed upstream. "I don't remember hearing General Grant speak a word that night," Jake Wilkin said.

11. TENSING FOR THE SPRING

DANA's distrust of McClernand grew from day to day. While Porter, Sherman, Rawlins, and McPherson acted genuinely glad to have Dana around, his presence reminded all of them of how far McClernand's "intrigue" had carried. Grant's attitude seemed almost out of character. In entrusting command of the attack on Grand Gulf to McClernand, Grant justified his decision by insisting that McClernand was "exceedingly desirous of the command," that he was "the senior of the other corps commanders," that he was "an especial favorite of the President," and that "he had entered zealously into the plan from the first, while Sherman had doubted and criticized." McPherson, whom Grant would really have preferred, was away at Lake Providence.

Obviously Grant was temporizing with the rationality rather than the military shrewdness of his selection. At a time when Grant had become a core of political dissension, he seemed, in yielding his main offense to McClernand, to be leaning toward political considerations. The seasoned journalist in Dana detected danger. His training in Greeley's newsroom led him to observe McClernand "narrowly," and to see "a man of a good deal of a certain kind of talent, not of a high order," with the sort of education "a man gets who is in Congress five or six years." He would call McClernand "smart, quick, very active-minded," but without depth to his judgment—in short, a man who "looked after himself a great deal."

Filled with these misgivings, Dana arrived at New Carthage on the morning of the twenty-third. McClernand's XIII Corps, ten thousand strong, was to move next day. McPherson's XVII Corps had left Lake Providence and marched from Milliken's Bend; Sherman's corps, the XV, remained at Young's Point to screen the main movement and confuse the Confederate command at Vicksburg. Grant strained to get across the Mississippi and seize Grand Gulf before Pemberton could reinforce it. Porter, going down the river with his gunboats to test defenses there, returned full of gloom. Grand Gulf was too strong for a direct assault; Porter favored either running its batteries at night or marching the troops down the west bank of the Mississippi to some point where they could be ferried across.

Grant went to Grand Gulf to judge the situation for himself. He was in no sense frightened of the place. Porter overestimated its strength. "The key to the position," Dana reported to Stanton on the twenty-ninth, "is the first bluff approached in descending the Mississippi River. The enemy are fortifying, but have no guns there yet." The attack, Dana thought, would take place "tomorrow or next day," though a further delay was possible through "much apparent confusion in McClernand's command"; and, as a circumstance for Stanton to ponder, a wily Dana added: "McClernand carries his bride along with him." This, too, Dana commented, though it was explicitly ordered that "officers' horses and tents must be left behind"!

McClernand would not be budged, insisting that wherever he went his bride, her servants and baggage also must go. Dana felt "astonished." Arriving at the point of embarkation on the day set for Grant's movement against

Grand Gulf, Dana's credulity was stretched further at finding steamboats and barges "scattered about in the river
and in the bayou as if there was no idea of the imperative
necessity of the promptest movement possible." Aboard
Porter's flagship a nettled Grant sent McClernand an order
to start going.

A thunderstorm threatened. At four o'clock McClernand
reviewed an Illinois brigade, and his friend from Springfield, Governor Yates, made a speech. Despite a directive
that all ammunition was to be conserved, McClernand
rounded off the ceremonies with a salute of artillery.

Darkness descended, neither a man nor a cannon had
been moved, the storm broke, and McClernand retired for
a husbandly evening with his bride. McPherson's corps,
beginning to come up, stood in the rain waiting for Mc-
Clernand's troops to clear out of the way. General Lorenzo
Thomas, organizing Negro troops in Mississippi, told Dana
it looked now as though McPherson's boys might have been
embarked before McClernand's. That night, on Porter's
flagship, Grant composed a scalding letter to his bridegroom-general.

Dana could only hope that at last Grant had come to
the breaking-point with McClernand. Once, as if to placate
the grumbling of the staff, Grant had muttered that he
might take over the command of the XIII Corps in person,
and Dana liked the idea even better now. Lorenzo Thomas
offered to help in any way he could, a not ungenerous offer
as Thomas was suffering miserably with diarrhea. Porter
told of a meeting with Thomas when, the admiral alleged,
the general declared that he had come into Mississippi with
"full authority to remove Grant and place anyone he chose
in command." Whom did Thomas have in mind, Porter
said he asked. Thomas mentioned McClernand. His reply,
Porter said, assured Thomas that if he was seeking a dose
of tar and feathers from both the army and navy he had
hit on a capital way of getting it.

Part Two: THE MOTH AND THE FLAME

Bedeviling though Grant found such undercurrents of suspicion and distrust emanating from Washington, and, as a result, the more infuriating he must have found the current obstinacies of McClernand, problems at least as galling beset his adversary inside Vicksburg. A military precept known to every general taught that "the strength of a position is measured not by the impregnability of the front, but by the security of the flanks," and no one had to tell Pemberton of the danger threatening his left flank!

The forces working against Pemberton within the Confederacy seemed almost to equal those that Grant had unleashed from without. A nation predominantly agricultural and severely drained of its manpower to produce its armies apparently could not manufacture all the guns Pemberton had needed for his river batteries to stand off Porter's gunboats. But a greater calamity for Pemberton was the withdrawal in early January of more than three quarters of his cavalry in order to create a diversion in favor of Bragg. Pemberton's cry for the return of his six thousand mounted troops grew from mild reproval to insistent demand. Then on the morning Porter's fleet moved below Vicksburg, Grant set in motion about a thousand cavalry under Colonel Benjamin H. Grierson, onetime teacher of music and dealer in produce merchandise. Soon all Mississippi was being thrown into a panic. Stations were being destroyed, bridges torn down, railroad tracks ripped up— "part and parcel," Pemberton moaned, "of the formidable invasion preparing under my eyes."

Grierson's raid was disastrous to Pemberton not only for the devastations it wrought within Mississippi, but also for the proof it provided of the schizophrenic character Confederate military operations had acquired in the West. In one breath Jefferson Davis wanted Vicksburg held at any cost, and in the next he wanted Bragg supported in Tennessee, also at any sacrifice. With Grant floundering in his four efforts to get in back of Vicksburg during the winter months of '63 the Confederacy felt secure within its bastion on the Mississippi; at the same time, in Tennessee, Bragg was uncomfortably occupied with fighting Rosecrans.

These two generals clashed in early January at Murfreesboro, a station on the Nashville and Chattanooga Railroad. Here for three days along a sluggish tributary of the Cumberland called Stone River, Union and Rebel armies locked in an exhausting battle that for the number of casualties and indecisiveness of result was another Shiloh. But where Shiloh had decided the fall of Corinth, the bloody slaughter at Stone River had not produced the fall of Chattanooga. Bragg retreated to Shelbyville and Tullahoma, and, catlike, Old Rosy continued to stalk and watch him.

In the field General Joseph E. Johnston, superior in command to both Bragg and Pemberton, tried to balance on his own back this teeterboard of conflicting interests between Tennessee and Mississippi. Over Pemberton's rising protestations he switched the cavalry to the Tennessee operations. Johnston, who distrusted any military thinking that involved Jefferson Davis, had a stubborn streak differing from Bishop Polk's in that Old Joe didn't enlist heaven to silence Richmond; occasions arose when he simply defied both God and man and made his own policy. Out of the delicate balance of these circumstances and personalities had come a moment when a quick, sensitive military mind might see a chance to seize the initiative in the War in the West.

Judged by the Vicksburg campaign, Grant possessed that mind. As long as Joe Johnston remained preoccupied with Bragg in Tennessee, Johnston could not effect with any appreciable speed the concentration of reinforcements needed near Jackson to support Pemberton's defense of Vicksburg. Thus an urgency consumed Grant to drive south and find a spot where he could plunge into the interior of Mississippi before this situation could be corrected. The Grierson raid, designed to help both Old Rosy and himself, was fostered in the hope that through disrupting communications the wedge could be enlarged between Confederate forces in Tennessee and Mississippi.

Seldom has a cavalry raid equaled in brilliance of execution or completeness of result the exploits of the bearded, fierce-eyed, long-nosed Ben Grierson and his Illinois horsemen. Rampaging through Mississippi from the seventeenth of April to the second of May, Grierson's cavalry covered six hundred miles, cut three different railroad lines, destroyed sixty miles of telegraph, and isolated the state capital, Jackson, on the north, south, and west. The raid, said Henry Clayton Forbes, a boy in his late teens riding those six hundred miles through Mississippi, was "essentially a *game* of strategy and speed . . . a strenuous game, rather than a bloody one, intensely exciting, but not necessarily very dangerous."

Intended to confuse, bewilder, and break morale, Grierson's raid spread the blaze of its success across the pages of almost every newspaper in the state. The culprits who had made the raid, mourned the *Columbus Republic* with the admission that "we say it with shame," had escaped without the loss of a man after devastating "the very center of Mississippi." The editor of the *Republic* commented bitterly: "We are almost inclined to believe the words of a correspondent, that the manhood of Mississippi had gone to the wars; women only were left, although some of them wore the garb of men. We do not know where the responsibility rests, but wherever it is, if it is not a fit and proper subject for court-martial, we are afraid there are none."

Understandably, Pemberton despaired. Now he turned a deaf ear upon "the piteous lamentations" of farmers who opposed the impressment of their horses in the midst of the season for planting, plowing, and cultivating. Pemberton faced the sickening reality—his six thousand cavalry were never coming back! If Pemberton wanted more cavalry, he must mount his own infantry!

2.

Alert to the advantage in this situation, with Ben Grierson and his hooting hellions in the tenth day of their raid, the conduct of the bridegroom-general at New Carthage became doubly galling to Grant. The morning of April 27 broke to a continuing heat wave; to Midwestern boys, it was summer in Mississippi. Figs on the trees already were as big as a man's thumb.

Grant came ashore from Porter's flagship with his letter ready for McClernand, then decided not to deliver it. Bridegroom, bride, servants, and baggage actually prepared to embark! As events turned out, the start of the expedition was delayed until the following day. Then, as McClernand's force of ten thousand seemed insufficient for the assault on Grand Gulf, the transports landed across the river at the Louisiana settlement of Hard Times. Here McClernand passed the night while the transports shuttled back for six thousand troops under McPherson.

The principal Confederate bastion at Grand Gulf was Bald Head, perched on a promontory at a bend of the river where its gunners could sight for miles any movement up and down the Mississippi. Centuries of erosion and swirling river eddies had carved a perpendicular wall of over eighty feet. Behind Bald Head hills rising to 350 feet bristled with fieldworks covering the flanks of the battery, and entrenchments linked Bald Head with a line of smaller batteries capable of raking the river with a plunging fire.

Porter set out with seven gunboats at eight o'clock on the morning of the twenty-eighth. Troops were loaded on the transports at Hard Times, poised to dash across the river as soon as the batteries were silenced. Porter felt little relish for the whole enterprise.

From a tug up the river Grant watched through the next five and a half hours a raging duel between gunboats and batteries. Confederate fire lashed the Yankee fleet. In the strong current around the promontory at Bald Head, Porter decided that ironclads were "clumsy vessels at best," and he watched in frowning dissatisfaction as the boats often swung around in the eddies so that the artillerymen on the bluffs could riddle the light armor of their plates with devastating advantage.

Eighty-one times shot and shell struck the *Tuscumbia*, pounding her seams, killing six, and wounding twenty-four; reportedly "shot-proof," the *Tuscumbia* shuddered under one shell that disabled every man at her nine-inch gun; and part of the armor on her forward casement fell overboard. Seventy times the flagship *Benton* was struck, with twelve holes opening in her three-quarter-inch iron and four in her two-inch. The *Lafayette* suffered forty-five direct hits, the *Pittsburgh* thirty-five in her hull.

Aboard the *Benton*, Dana saw her armor pierced repeatedly, her pilothouse wheel smashed by a hundred-pound shot. During the last four hours of the fight the gunboats barked viciously at Bald Head, battling "now at long range, seeking to drop shells within the parapet, now at the very foot of the hill, within about two hundred yards, endeavoring to dismount its guns by direct fire." The boats went at Bald Head in pairs, trying to get under the Confederate guns and "knock off their muzzles." The ironclads, sheering in the eddies, couldn't hold their positions.

Grant called off the attack, less disappointed than might have been expected, for he had reckoned with the possibility that the fleet might fail to silence the guns of Grand Gulf. Grant's revised plan would debark the troops and march them across the peninsula south of Grand Gulf until they were out of reach of the Confederate batteries. Grant plunged into these new preparations, while for Porter "came the melancholy duty of burying the dead, who were followed mournfully to their graves by their messmates and friends."

All of McClernand's corps and three divisions under Mc-

Pherson were at Hard Times, giving Grant a force of about thirty-five thousand. Originally Grant had intended to make the new crossing at Rodney, but an old Negro told him he could save time crossing at Bruinsburg. Riding across the peninsula to De Shroon's plantation, the point of embarkation now, Dana gained an insight into Grant's steadfastness:

> . . . The night was pitch-dark, and, as we rode side by side, Grant's horse suddenly gave a nasty stumble. I expected to see the general go over the animal's head, and I watched intently, not to see if he was hurt, but if he would show any anger. . . . His equanimity was becoming a curious spectacle to me. When I saw his horse lunge my first thought was: "Now he will swear." For an instant his moral status was on trial; but Grant was a tenacious horseman, and instead of going over the animal's head, as I imagined he would, he kept his seat. Pulling up his horse, he rode on, and, to my utter amazement, without a word or sign of impatience.

Apparently awakened to "moral status," Dana closed a letter to Stanton that evening somewhat self-consciously: "I have to report that the paymasters have finished their work and gone, and henceforth any shrewd person can see I am not attending to their transactions."

Bruinsburg, sixty miles south of Vicksburg, fulfilled all the advantages the colored man ascribed to it, not the least of which was a road over dry land leading into the highlands of the interior. The first three divisions crossed on the transports on the thirtieth of April. At De Shroon's, Dana chafed at the orders that reserved every particle of space on the vessels for troops and officers; not until the first of May was Stanton's "eyes" able to report from Bruinsburg. There was little enough to see there, beyond the debris of an army that had passed on. Toward Port

Gibson, sounds of battle were unmistakable. Dana, scrounging a ride in a quartermaster's wagon, reached a field littered with signs of struggle. A small white house with green blinds and vine coverings served as a field hospital. Striding into the yard, Dana stopped suddenly. Before him war seemed nakedly revealed. He looked at "a heap of arms and legs which had been amputated and thrown into a pile outside."

3.

Grant had arrived at Bruinsburg in high spirits. "I felt a degree of relief," he said, "scarcely ever equaled since." The Mississippi and the forts of Vicksburg separated him from his base of supplies, but after almost four dreary months of discouraging trial and error he was at last "on dry land on the same side of the river with the enemy"!

Dispatches reaching Grant at Bruinsburg revealed how well Sherman had executed his part of the general plan. On the day Porter's fleet had fought the batteries at Grand Gulf, Billy slipped up the Yazoo from Young's Point, seeming to indicate Haines' Bluff as his objective. The ruse had proved "eminently" satisfying. About Vicksburg, in the southern phrase, the Confederates were between "hell and Harper's Ferry" trying to decide "our real design." Meanwhile, wheeling around, Sherman drove down the Mississippi with two divisions to support McPherson.

Pemberton's total forces at Grand Gulf, Haines' Bluff, and Jackson, Grant overestimated at sixty thousand, almost double their number, but otherwise Grant's deductions were shrewdly calculated. Obviously the Confederates wouldn't wait in Grand Gulf—somewhere along the road that separated Bruinsburg from the highlands the clash should come. Grant reviewed his situation: "Bayou Pierre enters the Mississippi just above Bruinsburg and, as it is a navigable stream and was high at the time, in order to intercept us [the enemy] had to go by Port Gibson, the nearest point where there was a bridge to cross upon. This more than doubled the distance to the high land back of Bruinsburg."

Supplies, the determinant of any tactical plan, suddenly thwarted Grant's eagerness to race across the bottom land to a solid base. Again the bridegroom-general had fumbled, neglecting to issue rations to his troops before crossing the river. A day was lost in Bruinsburg. Finally, on the thirtieth, McClernand's troops were in motion, reaching the bluffs an hour before sunset. Grant spurred on McClernand toward Bayou Pierre, preaching the sound military gospel that "crossing a stream in the presence of the enemy is always dangerous." At Thompson's plantation, about five miles west of Port Gibson, McClernand's advance contacted the Rebels, although, Grant said, there was "nothing rising to the dignity of a battle until daylight." With morning the Battle of Thompson's Hill could not be sloughed off as a skirmish.

The Rebels that McClernand's advance had flushed were part of the seven thousand troops of the Missouri Brigade and 6th Mississippi Regiment rushed from Grand Gulf by General John S. Bowen. Across the path of the invaders Bowen placed his infantry near a point where the road to Port Gibson divided. On two ridges that were never more than a mile or two apart, Bowen waited, in a country, Grant said, that "stands on edge" with a heavy timber coating on the hills and the ravines a snarl of vines and canebrakes. Bowen's purpose was to hold off the bluecoats until reinforcements could reach him over the forty miles from Jackson or the longer route from Vicksburg.

By covering the fork in the road, Bowen forced McClernand to divide his force with a ravine between the two wings, so that one could reinforce the flank of the other only by marching back to the junction of the roads. Riding down to inspect the ground in person, Grant could imagine more desirable places for a fight. The Federal troops on the right he found commanded by brigadier generals of varying abilities—A. P. Hovey, a lawyer from Indiana, who was quick-witted, energetic, and often irritable; Eugene A. Carr, who, breaking in health and needing a leave to go home, frequently offset personal valor with a lack of energy and initiative; and A. J. Smith, whom, though "intrepid to recklessness," Dana accused of "self-exaggeration." The left flank was commanded by Peter J. Osterhaus, a congenial fellow but an unsteady disciplinarian whose weakness in battle was a failure of "concentrativeness."

The fighting on the right seemed nasty but inconclusive to Grant; if Hovey, Smith, and Carr were not pressing back the Rebels, neither were they being repulsed. On the left, however, Osterhaus wavered and had been thrown back with some loss. The rugged character of the conflict there was understood by Colonel John G. Fonda, commanding the 118th Illinois, who had hammered steadily at the Rebels, first for a cornfield, then for a fence, and then for a point of timber—not much to show for four hours of sweating and bleeding when at last Fonda pulled back his exhausted men to rest. Captain Charles H. Lamphere fought two hours to shove forward the guns of the 7th Michigan Battery a hundred yards, then an hour and a half to advance the next hundred.

Noon came on. The roads were clear of McClernand's troops and Grant brought up two brigades from Logan's division. Throughout the morning McClernand had been requesting reinforcements, and Grant was in rather a huffy mood. He had been over the ground where McClernand fought, and the terrain "did not admit of engaging all the men he had." Osterhaus, on the other hand, did need support. Grant threw one of the new brigades into this sector, seeking to exert pressure that would flank the Rebels out of position.

The fighting at Thompson's Hill stiffened. Toward mid-afternoon the added pressure on the left brought on a climax when Colonel James Keigwin, commanding the 49th Indiana, came out of a ravine to contest for the advantage of a hill behind a farmhouse the enemy had occupied all day. "I gave the order to charge, double-quick, with a yell," Keigwin reported, "and from the noise that was made I am sure that every officer and soldier obeyed the command. We got to the house, and passed to the rear of it, where there was a high fence. Over the fence about thirty yards we found the 6th Missouri (Rebel) Regiment coming up toward us, with bayonets fixed, but we were about one minute too fast for them."

That slim margin proved enough; from the hill Keigwin's boys raked the charging Missourians. The Rebs staggered to a halt, broke, and fled. The 120th Ohio, under Colonel Marcus M. Spiegel, waited in the ravine to which they had retired so that empty cartridge boxes could be replenished from those of comrades killed or wounded. Alertly the 120th Ohio moved to support Keigwin on the hill, but Spiegel found the Rebels fleeing in such confusion that the 120th Ohio "had nothing more to do than to exult, cheer, and be merry, and that I assure you was done."

Union spirit ran high despite the fact that, before the pressure on the left center smashed the Confederate lines at Thompson's Hill, casualties exceeded eight hundred. But a firm foothold had been won on the soil of Mississippi. Grant's boys felt that they were across the river to stay.

4.

On a gunboat in the river twelve-year-old Freddy Grant awoke to find his father gone. Young Freddy rolled out of his berth with a quickening suspicion. His dad had skipped off, with the idea of leaving him behind until Grand Gulf was taken. Freddy hadn't come down to Mississippi to miss any of the fun. Quietly, alone, Freddy slipped ashore at Bruinsburg.

The sounds of the battle searing Thompson's Hill echoed across the bottom land. On foot, Freddy struck out to find the scene of action and soon overtook a crony—Dana trailing Grant's army along the same road. "We tramped and foraged together until the next morning," Dana said, "when some officers who had captured two old horses gave us each one. We got the best bridles and saddles we could and thus made our way into Port Gibson, which the enemy had deserted and where General Grant now had his headquarters."

Grant saw the pair coming—"mounted on two enormous horses, grown white from age, each equipped with dilapidated saddles and bridles." Moving on toward Grand Gulf, Grant reconciled himself to the fact that Freddy intended to stick with him throughout the remainder of the campaign. To those who thought the situation risky, Grant replied that neither Julia nor he felt any anxiety. Fred was at an age that "enabled him to take in all he saw and to retain a recollection of it that would not be possible in more mature years." S. H. M. Byers thought it fine to have the lad with the army. Freddy's brightness, his laughter, his jokes and chatter pleased most soldiers. Many had left youngsters at home not far from Freddy's age, and he seemed to draw the soldiers closer to home ties. Rawlins, too, raised no objection. Freddy's presence was a stabilizing influence on Grant.

The Rebels evacuated Grand Gulf. Grant was glad to escape another fight just then; he hadn't bathed or changed his underclothing in over a week. That night he wrote Halleck a long report, and toward midnight finished his other dispatches. He felt restless, impelled to move on. He sensed the great crisis that was forming. Within hours he must make decisions that could mean bright triumph or failure as utterly abject as his critics predicted. Much would depend on information he received from Banks about an action against Port Hudson.

Before morning Grant had moved his headquarters to the Big Black at Hankinson's Ferry, fifteen miles beyond Port Gibson. He could feel the strength of the initiative he had seized; it must not be lost. The season was right; in spring, since he was a boy in Ohio the age of young Fred, he had always liked to strike out, on his own. Southern newspapers, falling into Grant's hands, testified to how Grierson's raid into central Mississippi was diverting attention from the main movement against Vicksburg. If Johnston and Pemberton worked in concert against him, Grant could be beaten, perhaps disastrously; but he gambled on time—on time to interpose his forces between the armies of Johnston and Pemberton, to beat each in detail, to drive Johnston eastward and to push Pemberton back into Vicksburg.

Word came from Banks on the Red River, and for once Nothing Positive was quite positive—Banks could not cooperate in the reducing of Port Hudson before the tenth of May and could not bring more than twelve thousand troops, a number that must be greatly decimated in fighting-strength by the need to post river guards at high points along a distance of more than three hundred miles. What Halleck would advise—likely with the support of Lincoln and Stanton—was obvious: Grant should establish a base of supplies at Grand Gulf and wait for Banks. But that policy would waste a month! Delay gave the enemy time to fortify positions and call up reinforcements.

What Grant wanted to do, he knew, was without precedent. To move quickly between Johnston and Pemberton, his army must live upon the country, not as Napoleon had done through a regularly organized system of requisitions, but with only the food his men could carry in their haversacks or forage as they marched and fought. Quietly, serenely, Grant came to a decision: "The time it would take to communicate with Washington and get a reply would be so great that I could not be interfered with until it was demonstrated whether my plan was practicable." Doubtless Grant anticipated the protest Sherman would voice on reaching Hankinson's Ferry: "Stop all troops till your army is partially supplied with wagons, and then act as quick as possible." Once more Grant shook his head; Sherman, like Banks, frittered away time. Grant would act on his own hunches at the risk of reversing rules of warfare, ruffling the feelings of Banks, scandalizing the tactical sensitivity of Sherman, and ignoring the authority of Halleck.

At Hankinson's Ferry the weather turned from hot to cold. Wrapped in an overcoat, Dana wrote to a child of what life was like "marching into an enemy's territory" almost two thousand miles from home:

> Away yonder, in the edge of the woods, I hear the drumbeat that calls the soldiers to supper. It is only a little after five o'clock, but they begin the day very early and end it early. Pretty soon after dark they are all asleep, lying in their blankets under the trees, for in a quick march they leave their tents behind. Their guns are all ready by their sides, so that if they are suddenly called at night they can start in a moment. It is strange in the morning before daylight to hear the bugle and drums sound the reveille, which calls the army to wake up. It will begin perhaps at a distance and then run along the whole line, bugle after bugle and drum after drum taking it up, and then it goes from front to rear, farther and farther away, the sweet sounds throbbing and rolling while you lie on the grass with your saddle for a pillow, half awake, or opening your eyes to see that the stars are all bright in the sky, or that there is only a faint flush in the east, where the day is soon to break.

Living in camp is queer business. I get my meals in General Grant's mess, and pay my share of the expenses. The table is a chest with a double cover, which unfolds on the right and left; the dishes, knives and forks, and caster are inside. Sometimes we get good things, but generally we don't. The cook is an old Negro, black and grimy. The cooking is not as clean as it might be, but in war you can't be particular about such things.

If Dana wanted to know what was happening to the ripe strawberries of the Mississippi countryside, young Freddy Grant could have told him that the soldiers gobbled them before the officers had a chance. Down in the camps where Freddy wandered, sights were being set on the plums, peaches, and green pears. These, too, were nearly ripe.

Grant moved his headquarters to Rocky Springs on the seventh of May. Throughout the Union army the movement was like an animal tensing its muscles for a spring. For four days Grant remained at Rocky Springs, judging strength, position, timing. When he uncoiled he expected to bring on a decisive battle within ten days.

Dana wrote diligent reports to Stanton, and at the War Department the attitude toward Grant had begun to soften. The Secretary of War was clearly impressed by Dana's dispatches, and the eyes of "the Black Terrier" snapped at the delay McClernand had caused at New Carthage by being half general, half bridegroom. At his desk in the old War building on May 5 Stanton spoke his mind in a strong note to Dana:

General Grant has full and absolute authority to enforce his own commands, and to remove any person who, by ignorance, inaction, or any cause, interferes with or delays his operations. He has the full confidence of the Government, is expected to enforce his authority, and will be firmly and heartily supported;

but he will be held responsible for any failure to exert
his authority. You may communicate this to him.

This affirmation of faith from the Secretary of War could
not reach Grant at Rocky Springs. Grant read intently the
reports from his own army. McPherson and McClernand
advanced steadily toward the railroad between Vicksburg
and Jackson, and on the eleventh were within ten or twelve
miles of its tracks. Sherman's corps had reached Hankinson's Ferry and supplies had arrived from Milliken's Bend.
Grant, ready to move, sent Sherman orders to destroy the
bridge at Hankinson's Ferry, abandon the rear guards, and
cut communications.

How accurately Grant had guessed Halleck's reactions
was revealed in the orders the general-in-chief wrote on
the very day Grant started the movement from Rocky
Springs. Grant must double back with his army and aim
toward Port Hudson and a co-ordinated operation with
Banks. At that moment, however, Halleck might have
reached Grant from Bagdad as easily as from Washington.
"So complete was our isolation," Dana wrote, "that it was
ten days after we left Rocky Springs, on May 11, before I
was able to get a dispatch to Mr. Stanton."

There was no fun for Dana in the march toward Jackson.
The memories of both Brook Farm and the cluttered office
of the *New York Tribune* seemed filled with the sunshine of
Utopia after all day in the saddle and all night on the
ground in the rain. But the determined Grant pressed on.
The country, to Dana, appeared drained of its youth and
shorn of its spirit. "Slavery is gone," Mississippians along
the road told him, "other property is mainly gone, but,
for God's sake, let us save some relic of our former means
of living."

Grant sent the left wing of his army under McClernand
along the Big Black, and the phrase Grant used was "hug
the river." Sherman, commanding the center, straddled

Fourteen Mile Creek. The right wing under McPherson swung jauntily on Raymond, eighteen miles west of Jackson.

Logan, leading the advance for McPherson on the right, was two miles from Raymond on the afternoon of May 12. The "Gallant Egyptian" wasn't thinking about violins, whisky, and dusky dancers; before a fight, Logan was always eager and full of swagger. Behind Logan came General Marcellus M. Crocker, who had been believed dying of consumption when war was declared and who seemed now to be living by a stubborn resolve to see the Union preserved.

In Grant's opinion, these two gamecocks were division commanders who deserved higher responsibility. That judgment was soon to be tested.

12. GUNS, WHISKY, AND TACTICS

ON MAY 12 Pemberton marched with eighteen thousand troops toward Edward's Station on the Jackson and Vicksburg Railroad. Six thousand Confederate reinforcements had gathered at Jackson, and the five thousand Rebels at Raymond, under Brigadier General John Gregg, consisted of a brigade rushed up from Port Hudson and forces drawn from the Department of South Carolina and Georgia.

Caution had underscored Pemberton's orders to Gregg: "If the enemy advance on you too strong, fall back on Jackson." Gregg felt fretful. His mounted force of scouts did not exceed forty, and were "mostly youths from the neighborhood." Gregg pieced together his dispatches and guessed wrong. McPherson's corps seemed no more than "a brigade on a marauding excursion."

Part Two: THE MOTH AND THE FLAME

A ravine and a branch of Fourteen Mile Creek were the setting of the fighting that quickly opposed Gregg against Logan and Crocker. The banks of the creek, Lieutenant Colonel William P. Davis of the 23rd Indiana reported, were "nearly perpendicular, and covered with dense undergrowth"; Colonel Manning F. Force of the 20th Ohio, halting his brigade at an edge of timber bordering the creek, found a "Rebel battery on a hill beyond the creek throwing shells over the timber into the open field." The instant Crocker realized Logan had been engaged, he came forward through "trees, bush, and vines."

The rallying cry of Logan's troops sprang from a speech the general had delivered in Congress two years previously: "The men of the Northwest will hew their way to the Gulf of Mexico with their swords." The attack opened furiously —"not having time to fix our bayonets," Colonel Davis said, "we attempted to beat them back with our muskets, but, being overpowered by numbers, we were obliged to fall back . . . to the creek." The 20th Ohio could give a good illustration of how "very hot and close" the fire became: "Private [Levi] Donaldson, of F, had his leg shattered by a rifle held within a foot of it."

Along the left and center of the line, where the battle erupted most fiercely, Confederate spirit ran high. Lieutenant Colonel T. W. Beaumont, commanding the 50th Tennessee, watched happily the easy targets the Yankee invaders made struggling along the banks of the creek as "they pulled themselves by the roots of trees and bushes." Beaumont's Tennessee infantrymen held their fire until they had the range on a band of blue-clad cavalry, then Tennessee rifles blazed and the Federals "fled in every direction, many of the horses without riders, and many of the riders without horses, while a considerable number was left dead on the field."

But Gregg had to admit that he had been fooled; the Union strength mounted against him; unless he pulled out quickly for Jackson he would be cut to pieces. The whole Rebel line, Crocker reported, "broke and fled in confusion"; that night both Logan and Crocker camped their troops in the streets, yards, and houses of Raymond.

About sundown Grant was in Sherman's headquarters on Fourteen Mile Creek when the news reached him of the victory over Gregg. The day had been hot, dry, and dusty, but there was a hint of dampness with evening, a threat of rain. The air became heavily scented at such moments with blossoming magnolias and mayflowers, the thickets of blooming black haw and wild plum that clung to the banks of every creek and brook, the sassafras and wild grapevines that crawled along the miles of Virginia rail fence enclosing the plantations. Theodore Davis sat with his pad drawing for readers of *Harper's Weekly* a sketch of Grant on a campstool in the moonlight, dictating dispatches to his subordinates. Since the movement out of Hankinson's Ferry there had been a change, something in the air, that made soldiers and officers break into a grin at the sight of Grant. The old man was all right. He knew what he was doing.

Perhaps in part the high-heartedness around Grant stemmed from the memento that Cadwallader reported Richard J. Oglesby brought on a visit to Hankinson's Ferry —a barrel of whisky. "On leaving," Cadwallader said, "the governor turned over to Colonel Duff and myself all that remained in the barrel with the jocular remark that we seemed to be the only persons who could be trusted with such a valuable commodity. We filled and secreted as many canteens and bottles as we could obtain, and had a small store in reserve when the barrel was finally emptied." The "small store" lasted until May 18.

But other reasons also accounted for the convivial attitude around Grant—and one, surely, was how "foraging upon the enemy was brought to the highest stage of efficiency." Each nightfall the wagons of Grant's army re-

turned "groaning under the weight of impressed supplies";
and "salt, sugar, coffee, and sometimes a small quantity
of 'hardtack' were the only issues then made from our supply trains coming from Grand Gulf." The *New York Tribune*
felt that only the savages of Attila had outstripped Grant's
boys in picking clean the land around them.

Finally, however, as Grant sat in the moonlight with his
staff, the jubilant spirit stemmed from something quite
beyond quenched thirsts and full bellies. Grant had left
Rocky Springs keeping his own counsel; now he could talk
freely. Raymond, Clinton, and Jackson formed a triangle;
Raymond and Clinton, on the line of the railroad, were
one side, but the longest side was from Raymond through
Mississippi Springs to Jackson. Thus Grant drew a visual
image of his position. Pemberton was on his left. Perhaps
Grant chuckled at the thought of a Halleck in Washington
who could not reach him; perhaps his eyes smiled at Sherman; but his decisions were firm and daring:

> . . . A force was also collecting on my right, at
> Jackson, the point where all railroads communicating
> with Vicksburg connect. All the enemy's supplies of
> men and stores would come by that point. As I hoped
> in the end to besiege Vicksburg I must first destroy all
> possibility of aid. I therefore determined to move
> swiftly toward Jackson, destroy or drive any force in
> that direction, and then turn upon Pemberton. But by
> moving against Jackson I uncovered my own com-
> munications. So I finally decided to have none—to cut
> loose altogether from my base and move my whole
> force eastward. I then had no fears for my own com-
> munications, and if I moved quickly enough could turn
> upon Pemberton before he could attack me in the
> rear.

Accordingly, all previous orders given during the
day for movements on the thirteenth were annulled by

new ones. McPherson was ordered at daylight to move on Clinton, ten miles from Jackson; Sherman was notified of my determination to capture Jackson and work from there westward. He was ordered to start at four in the morning and march to Raymond. Mc-Clernand was ordered to march with three divisions by Dillon's to Raymond. One was left to guard the crossing of the Big Black.

Cadwallader retired to his cot in Duff's tent. About midnight he witnessed an unexpected scene when

. . . General Grant came into the tent alone, in the dark, and requested a drink of whisky. Colonel Duff drew a canteen from under his pillow and handed it to him. The General poured a generous potation into an army tin cup and swallowed it with great apparent satisfaction. He complained of extraordinary fatigue and exhaustion as his excuse for needing the stimulant, and took the second, if not the third drink, before retiring. . . . He sat on the edge of Duff's cot, facing mine. . . . Duff did not rise from his cot during Grant's stay that night, but lay stretched out at full length, except when he half rose on one elbow to join the General in his drinks, and to volunteer "success to our campaign, and confusion to the whole Confederacy."

Grant responded without enthusiasm. Cadwallader could not conceal a sense of guilt, as though he had entered into an unholy conspiracy against Rawlins if not the Government. Grant's drinking, Cadwallader rationalized, "was a matter-of-fact procedure," his stay "did not exceed twenty or thirty minutes"; but Duff, too, felt discomfited afterward, and suggested to the reporter that "the affairs of state, as well as my personal interests, might be best promoted by discreet silence." Perhaps Duff knew that Rawlins suspected the chief of artillery of catering to Grant's weakness for whatever advantage the canny Scot gained; it was more than a year later, Cadwallader said, before Rawlins found out for sure about Duff's indiscretions.

2.

Despite boasts of Southern newspapers that Grant represented no real menace, the War Department in Richmond had been badly shaken by recent events in Mississippi. In Tullahoma, Tennessee, on May 9, a telegram from the Secretary of War was delivered to Joe Johnston. "Proceed at once to Mississippi," that message said, "and take command of the forces there, giving to those in the field, as far as practicable, the encouragement and benefit of your personal direction." Johnston should take three thousand of Bragg's troops with him; he would find, moreover, reinforcements from Beauregard's Department of South Carolina and Georgia already on their way to Pemberton, "and many more may be expected."

Old Joe, still troubled with a battle wound, groaned with his aches. "I shall go immediately, although unfit for field service," he wired Richmond. The fine game of cat-and-mouse that Bragg played with Rosecrans hitherto had occupied Johnston's whole interest; he hadn't the least idea of what faced him in this new assignment. Yet few generals excelled Old Joe either in battle record or battle performance; at the outbreak of hostilities he had resigned the highest rank held by any Southerner in the regular army to join the cause of the Confederacy; and not the least of his many services to the South had been the fact that he once had helped to dissuade Stonewall Jackson from quitting the Rebel army.

Johnston caught a train from Tullahoma next morning. Among the factors depressing Old Joe was the news about Earl Van Dorn, leader of the cavalry which in January Johnston had shifted from Pemberton to Bragg. Everything about the Van Dorn case had nasty implications. Van Dorn, writing at his desk, had not seen the irate Dr. Peters enter his rooms, raise a revolver, and shoot at the back of his head. Somewhat obliquely, *Harper's Weekly* reported: "General Van Dorn had never seen the daughter of his murderer but once, and his acquaintance with Mrs. Peters was such as to convince his staff officers, who had every opportunity of knowing, that there was no improper intimacy between them."

Three weary days of travel brought Johnston into Mississippi. A telegram from Pemberton awaited him. Grant moved in force toward Edward's Station, as far as Pemberton could guess. "With my little force," continued Pemberton, striking a tone that might easily irritate Johnston, "I will do all I can to meet him." Reinforcements arrived "very slowly"; his cavalry in Tennessee, a touchy point, should be returned; and, with other troubles, lamented Pemberton, "I am obliged to keep a considerable force on either flank of Vicksburg out of supporting distance."

Johnston hurried on to Jackson to find Gregg's troops falling back from Raymond "after a spirited resistance, considering that it was made by a brigade against a corps." Johnston sniffed at exaggerated Northern reports of the fight at Raymond: "Its effects were trifling." But McPherson now had reached Clinton, and that fact was a bit more than trifling, as this wing of Grant's army had been neatly interposed between Pemberton and Johnston!

Old Joe didn't know quite what to believe. If, as Pemberton suggested, the main body of Grant's army was south of Edward's Station, then Johnston inferred that "McPherson's corps had been *detached* to hold the Confederate line of communication, and prevent the junction of reinforcements with the army." Johnston hastened a message to Pemberton: "If practicable come up on his rear at once. To beat such a detachment would be of immense value.

The troops here could co-operate. All the force you can quickly assemble should be brought. Time is all-important."

At Bovina, near Edward's Station, where Pemberton had drawn his lines to protect the railroad bridge and lower ferries across the Big Black, Johnston's proposed action hit Pemberton as one more bad psychological stroke. Torments arose in almost every quarter to unsettle Pemberton. Clearly he had no notion whatever of Grant's intention. Would Grant strike at Jackson or Vicksburg? Doggedly Pemberton stuck to the theory that he must avoid any step that carried him farther from his base at Vicksburg.

That Johnston's arrival in Mississippi placed an aggrieved Pemberton in a nettlesome mood soon grew apparent. All through the winter months Pemberton had lived with a cosy feeling of security behind his bastions on the river bluffs, and then, like a blow to the stomach collapsing Pemberton's diaphragm, Grant's army appeared below Vicksburg and raced into the interior of the state. Pemberton's confidence shook tipsily; the tart remarks sometimes made ridiculing Jefferson Davis for placing a Northerner in command of a Southern army had seared and scarred Pemberton's sensitive pride; and the latent suspicion that his subordinates watched him covertly in expectation of some act of gross negligence if not of treason did not bolster the general's brittle ego. Pemberton's thin skin likewise might feel pricked by Johnston's behavior; here was Old Joe no more than setting foot in Mississippi and glancing at a couple of scouting reports before acting as though he understood the military situation better than the man who had been in the field for months!

In thirty years of army life Pemberton never had called a council of war, but at Bovina on the fourteenth of May he wanted unity of opinion. To move on the rear of Mc-Pherson's corps at Clinton, as Johnston was suggesting, drew him away from Vicksburg. Also, other scouting information that morning placed Sherman on his right flank. If he went toward Jackson, could he ever get back to Vicksburg? This was the dilemma Pemberton carried into his council of war. "There was not a voice in favor of moving on Clinton," declared Major Jacob Thompson, the Inspector General. General William W. Loring spoke up. Obviously Grant moved on Jackson; why not suppose that he left no more than a single division on the Big Black? Loring's argument, said Thompson, "afterward acquiesced in by all the other officers," insisted that the logical step was "to move next day on the Southern or Raymond road to Dillon's, which was on the main leading road by which the enemy carried on his communications, give battle to the division left in the rear, and thus effectually break up the enemy's communications." In reducing Jackson, Union forces would be "too far removed" to participate in the fight Loring expected. Pemberton liked this plan no better than Johnston's, but he had called the council of war and must abide by its decision if, as Thompson observed, he wanted "any expectation of retaining [his] hold upon the army."

Hopefully, Johnston waited through the night for word from Pemberton that he had moved on Clinton. The threat of rain that for the past few hours had set dry, dusty skies to grumbling unleashed into a downpour. There were new reports for Johnston on the morning of the fourteenth placing Sherman's corps on another road twelve miles from Jackson. Nobody was guessing right.

Sherman, who possessed none of Grant's reticence in damning anything, could well employ a few expletives on the weather that morning. The rain came down in torrents and roads were transformed into quagmires. Sherman sloshed on, determined to time his march with McPherson's in reaching Jackson. About ten o'clock Sherman was within three miles of the state capital; to the left, McPherson's guns started rumbling. The Rebs, the cavalry advance reported, held a bridge at the foot of the ridge along which the road passed.

A brisk battery fire didn't bother Sherman. He pressed forward and soon held enemy entrenchments only a mile and a half from the capital. Grant came up to inspect the action and found Sherman maneuvering to test the Rebel flanks preparatory to an assault. But Johnston had committed no more than a brigade to either road for a delaying action until he could evacuate Jackson. McPherson's advance moved as easily as Sherman's, and at one point, Grant said, Crocker "was so close upon the enemy that they could not move their guns or destroy them."

Mud-spattered Yankees threw off the fatigue of marching and fighting. Cheering and shouting, they entered the capital of Jeff Davis's home state with a heady feeling as satisfying as any the members of Grant's staff obtained from Oglesby's barrel of whisky. Some acts, Sherman admitted, committed by "mischievous soldiers (who could not be detected)" were not "justified by the rules of war." Destruction of the Catholic church and the Confederate Hotel was cited specifically by Sherman, and many other "acts of pillage . . . arising from the effect of some bad rum found concealed in the stores of the town." Sylvanus Cadwallader, hurrying into Jackson with young Fred Grant skipping breathlessly at his side, found the streets "filled with people, white and black, who were carrying away all the stolen goods they could stagger under." Freddy's heart was set on appropriating the large Confederate flag flying on the capitol and raced Cadwallader up the stairs from the garret to the roof. "A ragged, muddy, begrimed cavalryman" met them on the stairs, "the coveted prize under his arm"; for Freddy, half the fun dropped out of capturing Jackson.

Sherman, charged with provost duty in the city, took satisfaction in the ruins of arsenal buildings, the Government foundry, and gun-carriage shop. The penitentiary and a cotton factory also were burned, but, Sherman insisted, these acts were perpetrated by "some convicts who had been set free by the Confederate authorities." Entering the Bowman House, Cadwallader "ran the gauntlet of unfriendly observation," for the hotel's corridors overflowed with "Confederate officers and soldiers, some of whom were wounded and disabled men from convalescent hospitals [and] others . . . were doubtless bummers, skulkers, and deserters who fell out of the Confederate ranks as Johnston's army retreated across the river."

Grant met with Sherman and McPherson at the Bowman House. "Xenophon," reporting for the *New York Tribune,* described the wild cheering among troops at Grant's appearance in Jackson. The quietly smiling "unpronounceable man" who had seemed so little a real general to many of these same soldiers five months ago at Young's Point— and so calamitous a choice for command in Washington only weeks and days ago—had become more than an idol. Grant now appeared to be that rarity among generals that the North had so long sought—a man of success. For all of Grant's dumpiness, soldiers felt his power to act independently, as though the shadow he wore as his own once had belonged to Zach Taylor. The old man seemed to have a nose for smelling out victory.

An intercepted message, falling into McPherson's hands, tipped off Grant as to how Johnston felt Pemberton should deploy his forces to attack the Federal rear. McPherson had better move back twenty miles west of Jackson to Bolton, Grant thought, for that was the nearest point where Johnston could reach the road. Then Grant informed McClernand that Jackson was held, and added: "It is evidently the design of the enemy to get north of us and cross the Big Black and beat us into Vicksburg. We must not allow them to do this. Turn all your forces toward

Bolton station, and make all dispatch in getting there. Move troops by the most direct road from wherever they may be on receipt of this order."

Unworried, Grant slept that night in the room Johnston had occupied the previous evening.

3.

Ten miles out of Jackson, on the Canton road, Johnston established his new headquarters. The reinforcements from Beauregard's Department were on the march under Brigadier Generals Gist and Maxey, promising to raise Johnston's total force to about twelve thousand. These troops under Gist and Maxey, Johnston wrote Pemberton, should prevent Grant from obtaining supplies from the east, and the force now with Johnston on the Canton road should cut off Grant's supplies from the north. Pemberton must complete the encirclement, Old Joe said, by closing Grant's communications with the Mississippi. Johnston added prisoners had informed him that "the force in Jackson constituted half of Grant's army, and that it would decide the campaign to beat it . . . by concentrating, especially when the troops expected from the East should arrive."

At Edward's Station, Pemberton did not receive this letter until "too late to influence his action." Committed by the decision of his council of war, Pemberton prepared stoically for the movement to Dillon's, a settlement situated astride the main road from Raymond to Port Gibson. His object, Pemberton wrote Johnston, would be "to cut the enemy's communications and to force him to attack me, as I do not consider my force sufficient to justify an attack on the enemy in position or to attempt to cut my way to Jackson." Obstacles of man and nature delayed the start of Pemberton's movement, however. He had to await additional rations from Vicksburg, and the rains had so swollen Baker's Creek, which crossed the route from Edward's Station to Dillon's, that a bridge must be built. By ten o'clock on the night of the fifteenth Pemberton succeeded in passing his columns across the creek.

Johnston knew nothing of this movement aimed to cut off Grant's supplies and harass the rear of the Union army. Old Joe's own masterminding on the fourteenth appeared to coincide with the precise course Pemberton followed, for it seemed a great question if Grant could supply his troops from the Mississippi: "Can you not cut him off from it; and, above all, should he be compelled to fall back for want of supplies, beat him?" By the morning of the fifteenth Johnston changed his mind—Pemberton's whole plan was impracticable. "The only mode by which we can unite," Johnston thought, "is by your moving directly to Clinton, informing me, that we may move to that point with about six thousand troops." Johnston complained that he had "no means of estimating" Grant's force at Jackson; Johnston's own officers differed "very widely" on their estimates, and Old Joe feared that Grant would fortify Jackson "if time is left him."

Earlier in the campaign Grant had snorted that two commanding generals on the same field were one too many, and certainly it seemed so now. In this case, too, one general felt unfit for service in the field and the other distrusted his own judgment. Pemberton had his army bivouacked on the route connecting the two roads into Raymond when Johnston's last dispatch reached him. He was headed in exactly the opposite direction from where Johnston wanted him, for Dillon's was away from Clinton. Pemberton's inner sickness required no great imagination. He desperately wanted to unite with Johnston's troops, and now must reverse his column! Supply trains belonging in the rear of his army would be in front! And yet turn back he must over a narrow and treacherously rain-soaked road —back across Baker's Creek, still without any reliable information of what Grant meant to do next. . . .

On the fifteenth of May, Grant awoke after a comfortable night's rest at the Bowman House. The hotel manager and Colonel Wilson were embroiled in an argument as Grant moved off to start his day. What was the amount of the bill for the lodging of the General and his staff, Wilson asked. The proprietor demanded sixty dollars. Cadwallader chuckled at the subsequent scene:

> . . . Lieutenant Colonel Wilson thereupon took out a $100 bill in Confederate paper and handed it to the landlord. The latter seemed thun[der]struck and said that he had expected to be paid in U.S. coin, or greenbacks, or the charges would have been much higher. "Very well," said the Colonel, "charge what you please. We propose to pay you in Confederate money." It was finally settled on the latter basis at ninety dollars. . . .

A cavalier use of Confederate funds inside Rebel lines had become a habit. Cadwallader said of Confederate paper: "I had an abundance of it that cost me nothing." The reporter gave an old Negro a hundred dollars in such currency for a bridle rein. " 'Fore God," shouted the joyful colored man, "dat will buy a mule!"

The fifteenth again brought a disagreeable rain that lasted through the night. Grant and his staff were at Clinton by evening. Carefully Grant reviewed the positions of his army. One division of McClernand's corps, under Hovey, was at Bolton, the two divisions under Carr and Osterhaus were some three miles south "but abreast, facing west," the division under A. J. Smith was north of Raymond with the supply wagons and troops under Blair in his rear. Logan led the head of McPherson's corps and already had reached Hovey and gone into camp. Close on Hovey's rear, on the Clinton road, Crocker had bivouacked. Sherman remained in Jackson with two divisions, tearing down "roads, bridges, and military factories." Early next morning McClernand was to move on Edward's Station, watching for the enemy but under orders not to "bring on an engagement unless he felt very certain of success."

Grant waited. Here was where Johnston had told Pemberton to come. Meanwhile Pemberton, through his council of war, had disregarded these orders and set off to destroy the base of supplies that Grant had abandoned a week before. Then Johnston's new orders had caught up with Pemberton, and he had reversed himself, so that he was coming back to Clinton along the Jackson road, where he could find a good bridge over Baker's Creek. Grant was awakened at five o'clock on the morning of the sixteenth to talk to two men, employed on the Jackson and Vicksburg Railroad, who had passed through Pemberton's army that night. Pemberton—with "eighty regiments of infantry and ten batteries"—still marched east. Grant had him caught, flat-footed, as long as he just kept coming!

Sylvanus Cadwallader passed the evening of the fifteenth at Johnny Logan's headquarters. The whole camp stirred at daylight, "anticipating coming events." With a good reporter's instinct, Cadwallader had picked the right spot:

> Logan's division of McPherson's corps . . . moved out of camp early and briskly, expecting to encounter Pemberton in the forenoon and having the honor of opening the battle which all agreed was now inevitable. Logan and myself were near the head of his column, after an hour or two of marching, when we reached a road coming obliquely into ours from the one on which McClernand's advance was to be made, and Hovey's division of the latter's corps was already half past. Logan was compelled to halt till Hovey had passed this intersection, and then start on squarely in Hovey's rear. I rarely ever witnessed such an exhibition of rage, profanity, and disappointment as Logan then gave. The air was just blue with oaths, till speech was exhausted. McPherson's arrival a few minutes

after was the signal for another outburst. But there was no apparent remedy. Hovey had the road by right of prior occupation, but Logan's division was avenged before nightfall.

McPherson, "the practicing Christian," sent a courier flying to Grant. Pemberton was soon to be caught! Grant and his staff galloped along the road from Clinton at about half past seven and arrived at the Champion plantation. Green with Mississippi springtime was the hill that rolled away from this plantation. Four hours later it would be red with blood.

13. CHAMPION'S HILL

WHILE Logan filled the Mississippi air with Illinois profanity, the former Indiana lawyer Alvin P. Hovey marched testily along the Clinton and Vicksburg road. The ascending sun seemed to bounce the heat in waves. Hovey's column advanced, halted, pressed on, yet despite the jerky pattern of its movement excitement bristled through the lines. To Sergeant Charles L. Longley of the 24th Iowa "the hasty and slender breakfast" that had awaited troops stirred from beds "among the roots" had heralded "a pregnant day." Sometimes the halt in a gully at the bottom of a ravine would last "two solemn hours." The men laughed and joked—"no one is going to blanch and advertise it," Longley said—but Longley wasn't fooled. He sensed the silent prayers, the "mental promises of amendment," the writing of "little notes or memoranda in pathetically covert terms, so that, if possible, they might be saved from the ridiculous in case the future did not permit them to be tragic."

Approaching the middle forties, Hovey had developed the tenacious streak of an old bulldog. "He works with all his might and all his mind," Dana wrote Stanton, "and, unlike most volunteer officers, makes it his business to learn the military profession just as if he expected to spend his life in it." Hovey's mind had much to contemplate that morning. The brigade on his right was commanded by Brigadier General George F. McGinnis, a courageous but excitable fellow who might lose his balance under extreme pressure; and the brigade on his left by Colonel James R. Slack, a poorly educated man who, while deserving in Dana's opinion such adjectives as solid, steady, thorough, and sensible, still would "never set the river afire."

Clearly on edge, Hovey kept to the road between Mc-Ginnis and Slack, "ready for an attack on either flank." The time was about ten o'clock and Hovey approached Champion's Hill, a promontory some sixty or seventy feet "above the common level of the country." Horsemen of the 1st Indiana Cavalry reported a Confederate battery of four guns covering the road. How many of Pemberton's troops had been placed on the crest of the hill Hovey could only guess, and he could guess, too, that dislodging them would involve the sort of nasty, slugging fight that Grant called "the business."

Nothing about the Rebel position on Champion's Hill cheered Hovey. The ridge Pemberton occupied was precipitous, and ended on the east in a ravine that ran north and then west before terminating at Baker's Creek. Large trees and tangled undergrowth filled the ravine and would have made sending troops through it the devil's work if there had not been a Rebel gun within ten miles. To the right and left of the ridge were "undulating fields," and near the summit, where the Bolton and Edward's Station wagon road passed, a narrow belt of timber screened the enemy. Whether Pemberton had selected his position "by accident or design" Grant would not say; but where Grant lacked charity he did not lack comprehension of the risks involved. Pemberton "commanded all the ground in range."

Hovey kept his head, wanting under no circumstances to bring on an action "until we were entirely ready." He rode ahead to check the positions held by McGinnis, ordering that high-strung commander to form his brigade into two lines with three regiments in front and two in reserve. Then he directed Slack to pull his brigade, with two regiments in advance and two in reserve, immediately to the left of McGinnis. Along the front skirmishers crept cautiously forward until they could see the Rebel gunners in their battery.

Hovey still felt hesitant about unleashing the ugly growl of the field guns, and tried to reach Osterhaus, whose troops were coming up a road to his south and left. The messengers, unfamiliar with the country, could not contact Osterhaus; but, while Hovey waited, Grant came up with McPherson. A symbol of Union strength and success, Grant stirred confidence wherever he was seen. Longley, stuck in a ravine with the 24th Iowa, remembered: "Once the imperturbable face of the great commander appears, and a welcome but brief diversion is afforded as General Grant takes a look, asks a question, and moves on."

The time had advanced to perhaps ten thirty. McPherson's troops were being brought up as rapidly as possible, with Logan in front; Grant was posting these forces in the open field, about four hundred yards from the hill, where they touched Hovey's line at right angles and threatened the Confederate flank. Two of Logan's brigades were fanning out westerly, making room for Crocker, who would be up as quickly as he could move over the road. But the chief burden of the fight, at least in the first hours, must fall to Hovey. The Indiana lawyer responded gamely with an order to McGinnis and Slack to press up the hill with the skirmishers and follow with the brigades. Within minutes Hovey's whole line was contesting hotly for the hill.

The Irish blood of George McGinnis roused to the fight. With bayonets fixed, the 11th Indiana and 29th Wisconsin went up the slope in slow, cautious expectation. Rebel gunners waited until the Midwesterners were within seventy-five feet of the battery, then with a fiery roar the guns belched and McGinnis's men dived to the ground. The young, excitable brigadier general waited for the volley of grape and canister to pass over. "The whole line moved forward as one man," McGinnis reported, "and so suddenly and apparently so unexpected to the Rebels was the movement that, after a desperate conflict of five minutes in which bayonets and butts of muskets were freely used, the battery of four guns was in our possession, and a whole brigade in support was fleeing before us, and a large number of them taken prisoner."

To Hovey, "gallantly" described the drive that carried the 11th Indiana and 29th Wisconsin six hundred yards up Champion's Hill. Meanwhile, on the right of the road the 46th Indiana routed the Confederates from two guns; and on the left the "brave and eager" 24th Iowa killed gunners and horses as it slashed through a battery of six guns.

Heartening though these early successes were to Hovey, he knew that they were in no sense conclusive. His gain was not in ground, but in time for Logan and Crocker, Osterhaus and McClernand, to bring up relief. The Confederates, as Hovey expected, rallied gamely. A cover of woods gave them a natural vantage point to break out with a ringing Rebel yell and pour down the hill and into the road.

For Hovey, the battle entered a phase in which he must keep his fingers crossed hopefully. More and more he must throw his reserves into the breaches the Rebs opened, knowing that both his men and ammunition were limited. McGinnis, pushed back, pleaded for permission to throw part of the 16th Ohio into the battle. Hovey consented, persuaded largely by McGinnis's eagerness to regain every inch of the sloping ground he had held moments before.

Rebel yells rose shrilly, the fighting increased in bitterness, the dead, the dying, the pitiably wounded mushroomed in little heaps upon the hillside. Hovey stood grim and stolid. Before his eyes his division seemed to be melting under the intense Mississippi sun. Grudgingly he moved up still others of his dwindling reserves.

Yet Hovey could take pride in the spirit of his boys—gallant heroes every one of them, in Hovey's eyes—boys like Sergeant Longley of the 24th Iowa, whose tedious halt in a ravine suddenly ended:

> . . . The grim chorus of battle has been nearing, rising and swelling on the air until its angry roar seems to have filled the earth; then, at a little after twelve comes the dreaded and impatiently expected command, "Fall in." . . . The lines are formed and dressed with an absolute sense of relief. See them now, stretching away to the length of nine companies of about forty-five men each, and prolonged by the rest of the brigade on the right. Now we are advancing over rough ground, but steadily touching elbows, while the warming blood begins to be felt bounding through the veins and throbbing at the temples. Now we pass through the first brigade, lying at the foot of the long wooded hill, and for the first time begin to hear the wicked *zipping* of the hostile lead. Soon it tells its errand—the first man falls. . . .
>
> Onward and upward you go; thicker and faster falls the hissing hail. At last the timber grows larger and you begin to locate the flaming line whence the trouble comes. Suddenly the added elevation brings into view a battery, and at the same instant the horrid howling of grape and canister is about us. A halt is made and the Enfields of the 24th add their clamor to the hell of sound, and their missiles to the many that make the

very air writhe. The more accustomed eye now detects
here and there a gray-clad enemy marking their line
at but a few rods distant. You note one, perhaps, striv-
ing to find shelter behind a slender tree—he is reload-
ing, and, hastily withdrawing his rammer, uncovers
the upper part of his body—instantly you aim and
fire, and when he falls backward, throwing the useless
gun over his head, you forget that other bullets than
your own have sped and scream aloud in the very
frenzy of self-congratulation.

At this moment, while every human instinct is
carried away by a torrent of passion, while kill, *kill*,
KILL, seems to fill your heart and be written over the
face of all nature—at this instant you hear a command (it may have come from the clouds above, you
know not) to "Fix bayonets, forward, charge!" and
away you go with a wild yell in which all mouths join.

From the sunken road along the ridge, then almost at
shoe-tip, a line of gray rises to confront Sergeant Longley:

. . . Their backs are toward you—they fly—the
line becomes a crowd—you pause only to fire—from
one end of the regiment to the other the leaden hail
converges upon that fated band; you see them plunging down in all directions, and shout with unnatural
glee. They pass through the Rebel battery, and that
too is swept with the besom of destruction. As it runs
parallel with the line, a full artillery team catches the
eye just long enough to see a leader fall and the six
horses almost stand on end as they go over and down in
struggling confusion—now the battery itself is ours,
and fairly won, and cheer follows cheer!

What next? Alas, there is no leader. Wilds is
wounded, and so is Wright. . . . You had seen no
one fall but enemies since your own work began. But
so it is; they, with brave Carbee, Johnson, Lawrence,

and many more. Confusion reigns. . . . There comes a new line of gray. Its head of column is already in our rear. See that orderly sergeant in advance making the ins and outs of the fence he is following. Shoot at him? Yes; and all the rest while you may, for now they halt, front, and enfilade that road with a fire that patters in the dust like the big drops of a summer shower and makes the wounded wretches lying there writhe again in impotent agony and terror. . . .

For McGinnis the battle on Champion's Hill must be called "one of the most obstinant and murderous conflicts of the war." How else could he describe it except to say that "for half an hour each side took their turn in driving and being driven"? Hovey, however, could see only threatening disaster in the bloody struggle that raged around him. The section of the 16th Ohio that he had permitted McGinnis to rush up the hill had been hurled back within minutes.

Hovey looked around for Grant, but Grant was gone. Across the open fields on the right flank Logan's troops handled the Rebels "roughly," but, more alone than ever in the responsibility of command, Hovey still wallowed in the thick of battle with the Rebs driving down the road determined to hack Hovey's brigades to bits! McGinnis begged for help. He was fighting outnumbered, gaining and losing the same ground, filling his cartridge boxes from those of the dead and wounded.

Hovey ordered the captured guns pulled down the hill. The insistent gluttony of war challenged him squarely: for over an hour and a half his front lines, his reserves, had been nibbled and chewed in a ravenous blood-letting. What hope for support existed must come from other commands. Fresh troops of the ailing Quimby, under Crocker's command, were near. Hovey pleaded for reserves.

A curious delay followed. The officers on Quimby's staff

didn't know Hovey. They did nothing. Minutes of bitter, heart-burning waiting became half an hour. Hovey saw his forces yielding, "contesting with death every inch of the field they had won." In desperation, Hovey appealed to Grant.

2.

Until noon Grant watched the struggle on the left, sensing that the tide had swung against Hovey and easily could overwhelm him. Grant sent an order to Crocker to speed a brigade to Hovey's support. McPherson pulled two batteries to a point where they "nearly enfiladed" the Rebels. "They did good execution," Grant said.

But Grant's attention focused on Logan. "A direct forward movement," Grant noted, "carried him over the open fields, in rear of the enemy and in line with them." Logan struck the Rebels through the belt of woods covering a short part of the west slope of the hill. Grant wheeled on his horse, leaving Hovey to fend for himself, while he rode to Logan.

On the edge of a meadow sloping toward the woods on the west of the hill stood S. H. M. Byers, serving in one of the brigades under Blair that had been drawn from Sherman's command at Jackson. Rebs still were concealed in the belt of timber, steadily firing upon the brigade in the meadow. To Byers

> . . . We were in that most trying position of soldiers, for regulars even—being fired on without permission to return the shots. We were standing two files deep, bearing as patiently as we could not a heavy, but a steady fire from infantry, while an occasional cannon ball tore up the turf in front or behind us. A good many men were falling, and the wounded were being borne to the rear of the brigade, close to an old well, whose

wooden curb seemed to offer the only protection from bullets on the exposed line.

"Colonel, move your men a little by the left flank," said a quiet, though commanding voice. On looking round, I saw immediately behind us Grant, the commander-in-chief, mounted on a beautiful bay mare, and followed by perhaps half a dozen of his staff. For some reason he dismounted, and most of his officers were sent off, bearing orders, probably, to other quarters of the field. It was Grant under fire. The rattling musketry increased on our front, and grew louder, too, on the left flank. Grant had led his horse to the left, and thus kept near the company to which I belonged.

He now stood leaning complacently against his favorite steed, smoking—as seemed habitual with him —the stump of a cigar. His was the only horse near the line, and must, naturally, have attracted some of the enemy's fire. . . . I am sure everyone who recognized him wished him away; but there he stood— clear, calm, and immovable. I was close enough to see his features. Earnest they were; but sign of inward movement there was none. It was the same cool, calculating face I had seen before . . . the same careful, half-cynical face I afterward saw busied with affairs of state.

Across the meadow, where Byers stood watching and admiring the commander-in-chief, dashed an orderly. Hastily Grant read the communication. The picture of battle formed in Grant's mind had missed one main point: "Hovey, reinforced by two brigades from McPherson's command, confronted the enemy's left; Crocker, with two brigades, covered their left flank; McClernand two hours before had been within two miles and a half of their center with two divisions, and the two divisions, Blair's and A. J.

Smith's, were confronting the Rebel right; Ramson, with a brigade, . . . had crossed the river at Grand Gulf a few days before and was coming up on their right flank." But what Grant missed was the fact that Logan, square across the road leading down to Baker's Creek, cut the only route by which the Confederates could retreat! Now Hovey's orderly was back, asking for more reinforcements. "There were none to spare," Grant said crisply. Yet, justified by the necessity, though it cost the chance to trap Pemberton's force on the ridge of Champion's Hill, Grant called for a rapid movement by the left flank around to Hovey.

Byers, caught up in this quick flanking movement, suddenly found the air "too hot to be borne." Then:

. . . "Forward!" came a second order, all along the line—"Forward! double quick!" Everybody shouted "double quick," as the noise was becoming terrific. We had forgotten to fix bayonets . . . and again the screaming was: "Fix bayonets! fix bayonets!" I had been selected by the colonel, just as we entered the road, to act as sergeant major, and I now ran along the line, shouting at the top of my voice: "Fix bayonets!" The orders were not heard, and we were charging the enemy's position with bare muskets. A moment more and we were at the top of the ascent, and among thinner wood and larger trees. The enemy had fallen back a few rods, forming a solid line parallel with our own; and . . . for half an hour we poured the hot lead into each other's faces. We had forty rounds each in our cartridge boxes, and, probably, nine tenths of them were fired in that half-hour.

For me it was the first real "stand up and fight," as the boys called it. . . . I tried to keep cool, and determined to fire no shot without taking aim; but a slight wound in hand ended my coolness, and the smoke of the battle soon made aim-taking mere guessing. One Rebel officer I noticed, through the smoke, directly in front of me on horseback. That was my mark, and I must have fired twenty times at him before his own form disappeared. I remember how, in the midst of it all, a young lad—he could not have been more than sixteen—came running up to me and, weeping, cried: "My regiment—my regiment is gone—has run! What shall I do?"

"Here's the place," I said, "pitch in!" and pitch in he did. He was of metal, that boy, and kept his place with the bravest veteran in the line. Hotter and hotter grew the fight, and soon this same boy cried: "Look— look behind us," and, sure enough, the regiment to our left had disappeared, and we were flanked.

Byers and his young friend heard a hundred Rebel voices yelling: "Stop! Halt! Surrender!" The boy didn't wait to argue the matter, nor did Byers:

. . . We ran, and ran manfully. It was terribly hot, a hot afternoon under a Mississippi sun, and an enemy on flank and rear, shouting and firing. The grass, the stones, the bushes, seemed melting under the shower of bullets. . . . We tried to halt, and tried to form. It was no use. Again we ran, and harder, and farther, and faster. We passed over the very spot where, half an hour before, we left Grant leaning on his bay mare and smoking his cigar. Thank God! he was gone. The dead were still there, and the wounded called pitiably to us to halt and help them as we ran headlong to the rear.

Like ten thousand howling wolves the enemy pursued, closer and closer, and we scarcely dared look back to face the fate that seemed certain. Grant had seen it all, and in less time than I can tell it a line of cannon had been thrown across our path, which, as soon as we had passed, belched grapeshot and canister into the faces of our pursuers. They stopped, they turned, and they, too, ran, and left their dead side by side with our own. . . .

The time now was after three in the afternoon. Across the hill Hovey braced, supported by the reserves sent at Grant's orders. The third brigade from Quimby's division, under Colonel George B. Boomer, had been followed quickly by two small regiments, the 10th Missouri and 17th Iowa, under Colonel Samuel A. Holmes. Boomer and Holmes had rushed into the conflict, but the Confederate forces, Hovey reported, "slowly pressed our whole line with reinforcements backward to a point near the brow of the hill." Step by step, Hovey's soldiers, with help from Boomer and Holmes, dug stubbornly for a foothold on the hill. "I never saw fighting like this," Hovey said. Colonel Slack, sharing the command of Hovey's brigades with McGinnis, cited a major "wounded in the abdomen, immediately after which he captured a stalwart Rebel prisoner and made him carry him off the field."

Amid shrieking grape, canister, and rifle fire, clashing bayonets and musket butts, screams of the wounded, the terrified stomping of horses, the climax loomed. It was felt by Byers on the right and Longley on the left, these men in the ranks who fired and ran and tasted fear, who snatched ammunition from the dead and fired at gray blurs through the smoke on the field. A battle was a vast, uncertain teeterboard, wobbling between victory and disaster.

The minutes ticked on toward four o'clock. On the ridge, where the Confederates wheeled, deployed, and threw their forces at Grant's massed forces, fearful decisions also must be faced.

3·

Pemberton's long day, beginning at about six thirty in the morning, had posed many problems. First he had endured hours of gnawing indecision—would Grant throw his main attack left or right? Pemberton perched his head-quarters to the left of the center of the line, not sure which way he should turn. Lieutenant J. C. Taylor, one of the general's trusted aides, sent forward to determine where Grant's concentrations were the heaviest, returned with a report that certainly brought little cheer. Grant's skirmish-ers, Taylor thought, were pegging away with equal violence on either side of the ridge.

At ten o'clock, or thereabouts, the heavy action on Pemberton's left became unmistakable. Here he had posted three brigades in the division under a hard-bitten veteran Confederate general, C. L. Stevenson. In immediate sup-port of Stevenson, in the center, were the two brigades of Bowen's division, and on the right were three brigades under the command of Major General W. W. Loring. The Union dead and wounded on the slope of Champion's Hill attested to the vigor and effectiveness with which Stevenson and Bowen fought off the assaults of morning and early afternoon: Hovey's casualties especially were running high (nightfall would find that they had been one in three).

Noon came on, the harassed Hovey appealed to Grant for reserves, and Grant sent a brigade. As a result, the pressure exerted on Stevenson's left flank spread justifiable alarm among the Confederates. Pemberton responded intelli-gently. No matter what the risk, he must draw strength from Bowen's forces in the center and Loring's forces on the right. Bowen already had supported handsomely, but Pemberton still waited for a sign from Loring that he in-tended to follow an order already given to make a similar move. Now "several staff officers in rapid succession" were dispatched to implore Loring to hurry up. The kindest re-mark that Pemberton could make for Loring afterward was that he had been "inert" and "ill" at Champion's Hill.

William Wing Loring was a vain man with a sharp

tongue, austere like the red hills and silent pines that dominated the North Carolina country where he was born, and aggressive like many professional soldiers without a West Point background. He had fought the Seminoles, served in the War with Mexico, and, at the outbreak of the present conflict, had held the rank of colonel in the United States Mounted.

"Loring is like a scared turkey and so is his command," said Confederate Major John A. Harman, giving a clue to the sort of difficulties that arose between Loring and his superior officers. Lee had found him a troublesome subordinate, and only the previous year Stonewall Jackson had felt that Loring's "conduct subversive of good order and military discipline" should see him "cashiered." Such was the spirit of Loring's command at the time his troops jested openly that Jackson was insane.

At Champion's Hill Loring's easily offended nature and delicately balanced judgment were under constant strain. His report could not disguise his huffiness when in the morning, he said, "I received an order to retire, also one to advance, both of which were countermanded." Clearly he feared the strength of the enemy before him; they occupied a series of wooded ridges, he wrote—"a very strong if not impregnable position." The firing he heard on the left he described as "desultory"; then, he said, Bowen was "summarily ordered in that direction," without "warning" to himself.

Loring, ordered soon afterward also to send a brigade to the left, declared that it arrived sooner than expected and saved a battery the Yankees had overrun. Loring said that he hurried in person to the part of the field where the fighting had grown the bitterest, and: "I found the whole country, on both sides of the road, covered with the fleeing of our army, in many cases in large squads, and as there was no one endeavoring to rally or direct them, I at once placed my escort under an efficient officer of my staff, with orders to gather up the stragglers and those in retreat away from the road."

From information obtained at this time, Loring felt that "by an attack upon the enemy's right during the panic which had befallen his center [where McGinnis fought] we could overwhelm it, retrieve the day, certainly cut him off from the bridge on our extreme left (of which it was highly important we should hold possession), and save our scattered forces."

Loring launched his attack, only to receive orders from Pemberton in the heat of the engagement that the movement must not be made. Moreover, Loring must "order a retreat and bring up the rear," a galling command at best to his fiery temperament. Loring's usefulness for the day seemed to have ended there. Retire he did—"on a road we did not know to the left," reported Jacob Thompson, Pemberton's Inspector-General, after a frantic, time-consuming search along the ridge for Loring.

The afternoon wore on and Grant's flanking movement in support of Hovey mounted its pressure against Stevenson and Bowen. "Where's Loring?" Pemberton kept asking. The gap opening between Bowen and Stevenson grew perilous. Again Pemberton demanded: "Where's Loring?" Grant threw his full force then, turning Pemberton's left.

And Loring? The North Carolinian marched to the south. Darkness approached, and, Loring reported, "by a well-concerted movement we eluded the enemy upon three sides, and to his astonishment made our flank march from between his forces across the fields to a given point in the woods skirting Baker's Creek." Doubtless to Pemberton's astonishment also, fleeing with a routed army as best he could toward Vicksburg. Meanwhile Loring made for Canton to join Johnston.

Yet generals apparently are often born under strange stars. Pemberton might well writhe at Loring's disobedience, but Grant, too, could complain bitterly: "McClernand, with two divisions, was within a few miles of the battlefield long before noon, and in easy hearing. I sent him repeated orders by staff officers fully competent to explain to him the situation. These traversed the wood separating us, without escort, and directed him to push forward; but he did not come. It is true, in front of McClernand there was a small force of the enemy and posted in a good position behind a ravine obstructing his advance; but if he had moved to the right by the road my staff officers had followed, the enemy must either have fallen back or been cut off. Instead of this he sent orders to Hovey, who belonged to his corps, to join on to his right flank. Hovey was bearing the brunt of the battle at the time. To obey the order he would have had to pull out from the front of the enemy and march back as far as McClernand had to advance to get into battle, and substantially over the same ground. Of course I did not permit Hovey to obey the order of his immediate superior."

Charles Dana likewise discovered that generals—even the best generals—developed unpredictable traits. Riding with Rawlins across fields silent after four hours of carnage, Dana reached Logan's command:

. . . We found him greatly excited. He declared the day was lost, and that he would soon be swept from his· position. I contested the point with him. "Why, general," I said, "we have gained the day."

He could not see it. "Don't you hear the cannon over there?" he answered. "They will be down on us right away! In an hour I will have twenty thousand men to fight."

I found afterward that this was simply a curious idiosyncrasy of Logan's. In the beginning of a fight he was one of the bravest men that could be, saw no danger, went right on fighting until the battle was over. Then, after the battle was won, his mind gained an immovable conviction that it was lost. . . . It was merely an intellectual peculiarity. It did not in the least impair his value as a soldier or commanding officer. He never made any mistake on account of it.

But starkly real to Wilbur Crummer of the 45th Illinois was the Union victory, and the price it had cost. Engaged all day in battle, the Illinois troops halted and "rested" on the battlefield. The scene, Crummer said, made "a horrible picture":

> . . . All around us lay the dead and dying, amid the groans and cries of the wounded. Our surgeons came up quickly, and, taking possession of a farmhouse, converted it into a hospital, and we began to carry ours and the enemy's wounded to the surgeons. There they lay, the blue and the gray intermingled; the same rich, young American blood flowing out in little rivulets of crimson; each thinking he was in the right. . . . The blue and the gray took their turn before the surgeon's knife . . . with no anesthetic to soothe the agony, but, gritting their teeth, they bore the pain of the knife and saw, while arms and legs were being severed from their bodies. There was just one case that was an exception. . . . He was a fine-looking officer and colonel of some Louisiana regiment of the Confederate army. He had been shot through the leg and was making a great ado about it. Dr. Kittoe, of our regiment, examined it and said it must be amputated; the poor fellow cried and howled: "Oh, I never can go home to my wife on one leg. . . ." "Well," said the gruff old surgeon, "that, or not go home at all." The colonel finally said yes, and in a few minutes he was in a condition (if he got well) to wear a wooden leg when he went home.

A Confederate, dying, called piteously: "For God's sake, gentlemen, is there a Mason among you?" Rawlins, who was a Mason, knelt down and comforted the man in his last moments. Grant set the number of his troops "absolutely engaged" at Champion's Hill at fifteen thousand, his casualties at about twenty-five hundred, with almost half of the killed, missing, and wounded in Hovey's division. If Loring's three brigades were included, Pemberton reported the number of Confederates engaged at 17,400, his casualties at 3,624.

But Byers stated the cost of Champion's Hill more eloquently: "Our mess had three that night instead of the six who had shared our rations in the morning at reveille." And Sergeant Charles Longley of the 24th Iowa—one of those who still lived in Hovey's division and, as Grant said, "remained on the field where they had fought so bravely and bled so freely"—watched the sun go, the twilight flickering its last tints across the sky. It was time for assembling the colors: "The report of those present finally cuts off the hope that any more will come that night, and the roll is called. The orderly's memory is too true. Name after name is called to which there is no response. . . ."

4.

But Champion's Hill otherwise animated Grant. "We were now assured of our position between Johnston and Pemberton," he said, "without a possibility of a junction of their forces." Yet Grant based this statement upon the hypothesis that Pemberton would not yield Vicksburg except after further battle on the bluffs of the Mississippi. Throughout the night Grant could not be sure—Pemberton still could march to the Big Black, cross the river, and join Johnston, precisely as Loring had decided to do and as Grant, had he faced Pemberton's dilemma, would have acted. In this situation Sherman became a vital factor.

While Hovey, with gallant support from Logan, Crocker, and McPherson, wrested victory at Champion's Hill, Sherman put the finishing touches to devastating anything of military importance in Jackson and started for Bolton, some twenty miles west of the capital. It was a fine day for marching, despite the blistering sun, and Sherman rode into Bolten in high spirits. Here Billy came into possession of a rare memento of the war:

> Just beyond Bolton there was a small hewn-log house, standing back in a yard, in which was a well; at this some of our soldiers were drawing water. I rode in to get a drink, and, seeing a book on the ground, asked some soldier to hand it to me. It was a volume of the Constitution of the United States, and on the title page was written the name of Jefferson Davis. On inquiry of a Negro, I learned that the place belonged to the then President of the Southern Confederation. His brother Joe Davis's plantation was not far off; one of my staff officers went there, with a few soldiers, and took a pair of carriage horses, without my knowledge at the time. He found Joe Davis at home, an old man, attended by a young and affectionate niece; but they were overwhelmed with grief to see their country over-run and swarming with Federal troops.

Near dusk, on the sixteenth of May, a staff officer from Grant reached Sherman at Bolton. Grant's orders turned Billy to the right, sending him toward Vicksburg along the upper Jackson road, which crossed the Big Black at Bridge-port. Toward this point also Grant dispatched Blair's division from Champion's Hill, hoping to bring all of Sherman's corps together there next morning so that it could "flank the enemy out of his position in our front, thus opening a crossing for the remainder of the army." Meanwhile Pemberton's army fled for Vicksburg along the Edward's Station road.

The divisions of Carr and Osterhaus and McPherson's corps pursued steadily. When Pemberton was found next morning, he had taken refuge in previously constructed trenches near the railroad bridge. Here field artillery supported a line of pits for nearly a mile north and south. A bayou followed the railroad and protected the pits; to the north the bayou abutted the river and to the south ran into a cypress brake.

Grant, coming up, again admitted Pemberton's position seemed formidable. That there was but a foot or two of water in the bayou hardly helped. Cotton bales from a near-by plantation gave the Rebels a satisfactory parapet along the inner bank of the bayou; a height west of the river commanded the whole area.

Grant drew his forces into uncleared land at the upper end of the bayou. Carr's division held the right and Osterhaus the left, while "McPherson was in column on the road, the head close by, ready to come in whenever he could be of assistance." To the brigade on the extreme right would fall the opening of the attack, and its leader was a two-hundred-and-fifty-pound Douglas Democrat from Shawneetown, Illinois, Michael K. Lawler. "He is as brave as a lion," Dana told Stanton, "and has about as much brains." Once Lawler had hung a man for murdering a comrade, but Dana couldn't remember whether it was before or after the hanging that Lawler failed to report the deed to his commanding general. Yet Dana drew a balance in the general's favor: "Grant has two or three times gently reprimanded him for indiscretions, but is pretty sure to go and thank him after a battle." Grant, waiting for Lawler to attack, found his attention suddenly diverted:

> . . . An officer from Banks' staff came up and presented me with a letter from General Halleck, dated 11th of May. It had been sent by way of New Orleans to Banks to be forwarded to me. It ordered me to co-operate from there with Banks against Port Hudson, and then to return with our combined forces to besiege Vicksburg. I told the officer that the order had come

too late, and that Halleck would not give it now if he knew our position. The bearer of the dispatch insisted that I ought to obey the order, and was giving arguments to support his position when I heard great cheering to the right of our line and, looking in that direction, saw Lawler in his shirt sleeves leading a charge upon the enemy. I immediately mounted my horse and rode in the direction of the charge, and saw no more of the officer who delivered the dispatch.

Lawler, with two hundred and fifty pounds of muscular power and Roman Catholic faith, dealt Pemberton his second stunning blow. The Rebels were conditioned now more to flee than to resist. With the railroad bridge flaming, isolating their men and guns on the east side, Pemberton's troops high-tailed for Vicksburg. Eighteen guns and 1,751 prisoners were left behind against Grant's losses of thirty-nine killed, two hundred and thirty-seven wounded, and three missing. Pemberton could not disguise his despair and dejection. To Major Samuel H. Lockett, chief engineer, Pemberton spoke broken-heartedly: "Just thirty years ago I began my military career . . . and today—the same date—that career is ended in disaster and disgrace."

Grant pushed on to Bridgeport, where Sherman had joined Blair. A pontoon bridge had been built across the Big Black, and that night, with the whole river lit up with pitch-pine fires, Sherman and Grant "sat on a log, looking at the passage of the troops by the light of those fires" as the bridge "swayed to and fro under the passing feet." The scene, Billy felt, "made a fine war picture."

At daybreak Sherman's columns were across the river, ascending the ridge and stretching out along the Benton road so that he held command of the peninsula between the Yazoo and the Big Black. By nightfall on the eighteenth, when Grant joined Sherman again at his headquarters, they had reached the Walnut Hills above Vicksburg. "Sher-

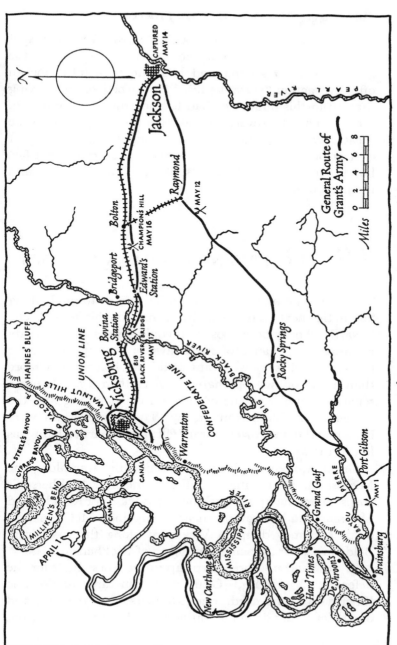

GRANT'S ROUTE TO VICTORY

man had the pleasure of looking down from the spot coveted so much by him the December before on the ground where his command had lain so helpless for an offensive action," Grant said. "He turned to me, saying that up to this minute he had felt no positive assurance of success. This, however, he said, was the end of one of the greatest campaigns in history and I ought to make a report of it at once." Perhaps Dana would not go quite that far, but his dispatch to Stanton spoke of Grant's "great and momentous victory."

14. McCLERNAND CLAIMS A VICTORY

WHEN Grant moved he seemed to pitch along "as if the next step would bring him on his nose." The inward intensity of purpose that could propel Grant's body in apparent defiance of fixed laws of gravity must have become manifest now. Grant could not believe that more than a day or two—perhaps no more than a few hours— separated him from the occupation of Vicksburg and the surrender of Pemberton's army. The Confederates were beaten and demoralized, Grant felt; little heart or fight was left in them.

Grant wanted no delay in finishing the war along the Mississippi. By nightfall on the eighteenth, McPherson's corps had come up the Jackson and Vicksburg road behind Sherman and had camped near enemy lines. McClernand's corps had moved up to Vicksburg along the road from Baldwin's Ferry, placing him south of McPherson.

"I now had my three corps up to the works built for the defense of Vicksburg," Grant said, "on three roads—one [Sherman] to the north, one [McPherson] to the east, and one [McClernand] to the southeast of the city." When, hot and muggy, the morning of the nineteenth arrived, Grant saw his investment "as complete as my limited number of troops would allow."

The quick battle that Grant wanted, however, posed peculiar problems. Captains Frederick E. Prime and Cyrus B. Comstock, of Grant's engineers corps, could attest to how well nature aided Pemberton. Country that once must have constituted a plateau reaching the Mississippi at an elevation of from two hundred to three hundred feet had become eroded through long decades into "an intricate network of ravines and ridges." Soil cut vertically remained so for years, and, reported Prime and Comstock, "for this reason the sides of the smaller and newer ravines were often so deep that their ascent was difficult to a footman unless he aided himself with his hands." Wooded slopes and felled trees formed "in many places entanglements which under fire were absolutely impassable." Furthermore,

the enemy's line of defense, leaving the river on the north side of the city where the bluff strikes the river, was generally on a dividing ridge, this ridge being as high or higher than the ground in its vicinity; [and] in two places the line crossed the valleys of small streams, reaching the river bluff again two miles below the city, at a point where the bluff has receded to a distance of one mile from the river, and then following the bluff up the river for a mile, to give fire toward the river or any troops that might attempt an attack from the south by moving up between the bluff and the river along the river bottom. This line was well located for seeing the ravines in its front, and consisted of small works on commanding points, necessarily irregular from the shape of the ridges on which they were situated; in only one case (that of a redoubt 30 yards square) closed at the gorge; of weak profile; placed at distances varying from 75 to 500 yards from each other, and connected by lines of simple trench or rifle pit.

Vicksburg was, then, rather an entrenched camp than a fortified place, owing much of its strength to the difficult ground, obstructed by fallen trees in its front, which rendered rapidity of movement and *ensemble* in an assault impossible.

Still convinced that the Rebels "would not make much effort to hold Vicksburg," Grant ordered the skirmishers pressed forward in preparation for an attack on the nineteenth. The "omnipresent eye and quick judgment" that Dana ascribed to Sherman would be needed now, for the honor of "opening the ball," to use the phrase of the infantryman, belonged principally to Billy.

Colonel Thomas Kilby Smith, commanding the second brigade of the 54th Ohio, faced the typical problems of Sherman's subordinates that morning. At daybreak, on Billy's orders, Smith threw forward his pickets and advanced his brigade in battle line along the Graveyard Road. The Ohioans aimed for a "sally port in the fortifications," and came to a hill about five hundred yards from the Confederates' works. It was perhaps nine in the morning when Company A fired five shots "to get range"; almost immediately the fire along the line opened vigorously, and skirmishers and sharpshooters poured in "most destructive volleys from sheltered points along the range of hills and close under the parapets." Two hours later an order came from Grant: "Corps commanders will push forward carefully, and gain as close position as possible to the enemy's works, until 2 p.m.; at that hour they will fire three volleys of artillery from all the pieces in position. This will be the signal for a general charge of all the army corps along the whole line. When the works are carried, guards will be placed by all division commanders to prevent their men from straggling from their companies."

By one o'clock reconnaissance had convinced Smith of his ticklish situation. "It would be impossible to advance my whole brigade in line of battle," he wrote, "the hills and knobs being exceedingly precipitous, intersected by ravines in three directions, the bottom treacherous [and] filled with sink holes concealed by dried grass and cane." At the point of intersection of the Graveyard Road and the Rebel fortifications an embankment rose some eighteen feet. At two o'clock the expected signal was given; Smith commanded his brigade forward, and saw his troops advance "gallantly and without hesitation." But the subsequent passages in Smith's official report could not disguise the anguish that grew in him:

. . . It was almost vain to essay a line, owing to the nature of the ground, yet three times, under a most galling and destructive fire, did these regiments halt and dress upon their colors. . . . Having advanced some four hundred yards, I discovered that the men were thoroughly exhausted, and halted the left wing under the crest of a hill, from sixty-five to seventy-five yards from the ditch and parapet, and where they were comparatively sheltered from the small arms of the enemy. Returning to reconnoiter the position of my right wing, hid from my view by the embankment of the road, I perceived their colors advanced to the very base of the parapet, and also that my brigade was alone, unsupported on the left or right, save by a portion of the 13th Regulars, who had advanced to a position under the parapet, near the 83rd Indiana and 127th Illinois.

To the left, as far as I could see (and from an elevated point I had great range), not a soldier [was] to be seen, and only an occasional puff of smoke from the rifle of a sharpshooter, concealed far away among the hills, revealed the fact that we had friends near us outside of our division. Therefore I determined to halt my command, report, and wait for further orders, especially as . . . the sharpshooters of the enemy . . . were picking off our officers with devilish skill.

Smith's "further orders," coming from an optimistic Sherman, urged him to press up to the parapet as closely as possible and "be ready to jump in when they began to yield." McPherson was well engaged, Sherman assured Smith; Grant was on the ground; and "the artillery of the enemy, which began to enfilade us, would be silenced." Smith ordered his troops to cease firing, to fix bayonets, to stand ready for the charge; but he would never give the order: "A few men could have been got over by the aid of a ladder of bayonets or digging holes in the embankment, but these would have gone to destruction."

The hard fact was that Confederate morale had not been shattered, as Grant believed. Days of marching under confused orders, of piecemeal fighting at Port Gibson, Raymond, Jackson, Champion's Hill, and Big Black River, where surprise and uncertainty had been Grant's constant ally, of galling retreat with disrupted communications on every side, found the back of Johnny Reb stiffening as he fell into the prepared defenses around Vicksburg. Grant had to come and get him now in a frontal attack, the meanest sort of fight there was. Pemberton's troops understood the shift of strategical position. They still possessed a lot of nastiness that they were eager to reveal.

After four charges, blue-clad officers and infantrymen were willing to admit the scrap was tougher than they had expected. Report after report from the Union command told a story similar to Smith's. "After advancing two hundred yards, with severe loss, to the first line, I found the ravine in my front, which I had not had time to reconnoiter, impassable for troops," Brigadier General Thomas E. G. Ransom told McPherson's headquarters. Major General

Frank P. Blair, Jr., could make no lodgment in the Rebel works, he reported to Sherman: "The enemy, who, not being pressed in any other quarter, were strongly reinforced in our front."

With the coming of evening Sherman had to confess his failure. His troops had "reached the top of the parapet, but could not cross over." Moreover, "the enemy fought hard and well" and several of Billy's regiments were "pretty badly cut up." With nightfall Sherman drew back his troops a short distance, and ordered them to counter-trench. On the Graveyard Road, Billy estimated that less than fifty yards separated his parapet from the Rebel ditch.

Pemberton, breathing easier as the assaults on the nineteenth ended, telegraphed Jefferson Davis in hardly an optimistic mood, however: "We are occupying the trenches around Vicksburg. The enemy is investing it, and will probably attempt an assault. Our men have considerably recovered their *morale*, but unless a large force is sent at once to relieve it, Vicksburg before long must fall. I have used every effort to prevent all this, but in vain."

The assaults on the nineteenth cost Grant casualties of 942—157 killed, 777 wounded, 8 captured or missing. Porter's gunboats controlled the Mississippi and the Yazoo. Pemberton was in a trap; he *couldn't* hold out much longer. Grant called McPherson, McClernand, and Sherman to his headquarters next day. Notes were compared, Billy said; and agreement was reached that the failure of the previous day's assault had resulted "by reason of the natural strength of the position, and because we were forced by the nature of the ground to limit our attack to the strongest parts of the enemy's lines." The meeting in no sense constituted a council of war, Sherman insisted, but was "a mere consultation, resulting in orders from General Grant for us to make all possible preparations for a renewed assault on the twenty-second, simultaneously, at 10 a.m."

2.

On the twenty-first, passing along the Union line, Grant heard a soldier mutter: "Hard tack." Soon all along the line the cry was taken up: "Hard tack! Hard tack!" Grant kept his temper. Every effort, he told the troops, was being made to build a road over which they could be supplied, and "the cry was instantly changed to cheers." That night before the second assault on Vicksburg the men ate well, testified Wilbur Crummer of the 45th Illinois, "if hard tack, sow bacon, beans, and coffee can be called a square meal."

Three considerations led Grant to press the second assault, first among them the fact that "the troops believed they could carry the works in their front." Also, Johnston was being reinforced, according to all the reports that reached Grant's headquarters, and should Old Joe come to Pemberton's assistance "he might defeat my anticipations of capturing the garrison if, indeed, he did not prevent the capture of the city." Finally, Grant reasoned, "the immediate capture of Vicksburg would save sending me the reinforcements which were so much wanted elsewhere, and would set free the army under me to drive Johnston from the state."

Wilbur Crummer, approaching the fatal hour of ten on the morning of the twenty-second, felt with his comrades in the 45th Illinois that "we could whip any armed force that opposed us." The battle opened furiously. "Every piece of artillery was brought to bear on the works," Crummer remembered. "Sharpshooters at the same time began their part, [and] nothing could be heard but the continual shrieking of shells, the booming of cannon, and the sharp whiz of the Minié ball."

Crummer's company had bivouacked on the road from Jackson to Vicksburg. For perhaps five hundred yards the road had been cut through a ridge "to a depth of a man's head"; then the ridge sloped and the road opened into "plain view of the forts of the enemy not two hundred yards distant." At this point the 45th Illinois were to deploy to the left along the slope, then "by the right flank, charge" go over the Rebel works. The major commanding the 45th gave the order and "fell at the first volley from the enemy, having only taken a step or two." Reeling under that first "awful volley of shot and shell," Crummer realized that

. . . there was no one to give the command to halt, or right face and charge; the major was killed and the ranking captain didn't know it. We went as far in that hail of death as we thought would be sufficient for the regiment to form in line of battle, and then we dropped flat on the ground. Being first sergeant of Company A of my regiment, I was at the head of the regiment with Major Cowan when we started across that deadly piece of open ground, the major falling by my side, but I kept right on at the head of my regiment until space enough was given to the regiment to form in line under the brow of the hill. The ground sloped downhill from the enemy's parapet, and by flattening one's self about as flat as a hard tack, he was comparatively safe from the musketry fire of the enemy.

The regiment came through, but the dead and wounded lay thick over that stretch of two hundred yards. The order to charge the works was, after a short time, given by the ranking captain, and we started up the hill, to be met by a sweeping volley of musketry at short range which mowed the men down in bunches. We could not return the fire, for the enemy was safe behind their breastworks. Some of our men reached the top of the parapet, but fell as fast as they climbed up. No troops could face such a destructive fire from a protected enemy. . . .

Hugging the hillside "as flat as a hard tack," Crummer

realized that only one ally really could save his regiment—
darkness.

On the morning of the twenty-second Sherman recon-
noitered his front in person. He would make his real attack,
he decided, at the right flank of the bastion where the
Graveyard Road entered the Rebel entrenchments and also
at a point "in the curtain" a hundred yards or so to his
left. Simultaneously he intended to throw Steele's division,
a mile on his right, in a strong demonstration toward the
river. At ten o'clock, when the big guns began to roar,
Sherman's troops "sprang to the assault."

> . . . A small party, that might be called a forlorn
> hope, provided with plank to cross the ditch, advanced
> at a run, up to the very ditch; the lines of infantry
> sprang from cover and advanced rapidly in line of
> battle. I took a position within two hundred yards of
> the Rebel parapet, on the off slope of a spur of ground,
> where by advancing two or three steps I could see
> everything. The Rebel line, concealed by the parapet,
> showed no sign of unusual activity, but as our troops
> came in fair view, the enemy rose behind their parapet
> and poured a furious fire upon our lines; and for about
> two hours we had a severe and bloody battle, but at
> every point we were repulsed. In the very midst of this,
> when shell and shot fell furious and fast, occurred that
> little episode which has been celebrated in song and
> story, of the boy Orion P. Howe, badly wounded,
> bearing me a message for cartridges, caliber 54. . . .

But young Howe's heroism could not alter the reality of
the situation when Grant came up to join Sherman on the
off slope of the spur. Sherman's boys had been "badly
beaten back"; the assault had failed. The sickness of having
twice guessed wrong on the breaking-point of Confederate
morale, the responsibility for the futile Union blood-letting
that had resulted, were Grant's to bear—in customary si-

lence, presumably. Grant admitted that McPherson fared no better. McClernand, too, he believed had been beaten. There the assault would have ended, except for the surprising dispatches McClernand had begun to write from the field.

3.

At 11:15 that morning McClernand scribbled a message in pencil to Grant:

> General,
>
> I am hotly engaged with the enemy. He is massing on me from the right and left. A vigorous blow by McPherson would make a diversion in my favor.

At 11:50 a.m. Grant replied to McClernand:

> If your advance is weak, strengthen it by drawing from your reserves or other parts of the lines.

At 12:00 noon a courier carried a second message from McClernand to Grant:

> General,
>
> We are hotly engaged with the enemy. We have part possession of two forts, and the stars and stripes are floating over them. A vigorous push ought to be made all along the line.

Clearly, McClernand approached the battle on the twenty-second as one impelled by his star of destiny. Like Grant, McClernand believed that Confederate morale was ready to crumble, and to Brigadier General John McArthur, "a shrewd, steady Scotsman" who commanded the sixth division in McPherson's corps and whose troops had been ordered up from Warrenton, McClernand wrote, in part, as the assault roared around him: "I hope circumstances will justify you in immediately joining me with your whole division. I can greatly add to its efficiency here by supplying you with artillery. With your assistance I have no doubt I will be able to force the enemy center and reach Vicksburg tomorrow."

To separate the reality from the delusion in the messages between McClernand and Grant in the hour before noon— a delusion that would produce tragic consequences—the elusive intangibles in the personality of McClernand at least deserve conjecture. In heart, had he ever surrendered the supreme command to Grant? He had promised Lincoln, Stanton, his bride, the victory of Vicksburg; had he still a sense that he alone should win the day?

McClernand has left in the manuscript of an unpublished "authorized biography" his account of events till the writing of his noontide claim to near-victory:

> Five minutes before ten o'clock the bugle sounded the charge, and at ten o'clock my columns of attack moved forward, and within fifteen minutes Lawler's and Lauman's brigades had carried the ditch, slope, and bastion of a fort. Some of the men . . . rushed into the fort, finding a piece of artillery, and in trying to seize the men who had been serving and supporting it, stayed behind the inner defense, commanding the interior of the former.
>
> All this daring and heroic party was shot down except one, who, recovering from the stunning effect of a shot, seized his musket and captured and brought away thirteen Rebels who had returned and fired their guns. The captor was Sergeant Joseph Griffith of the 22nd Iowa, who, I am happy to say, has since been promoted. The colors of the 130th Illinois were planted upon the counterscarp of the ditch, while those of the 48th Ohio and the 77th Illinois waved over the bastion.
>
> Within fifteen minutes after Lawler's and Lauman's success, Benton's and Burbridge's brigades, fired by example, rushed forward and carried the ditch and slope of a heavy earthwork and planted their colors on

the latter. Crowning this brilliant feat with a parallel
to Sergeant Grifith's daring, Captain White of the
Chicago Mercantile Battery carried forward one of his
pieces by hand, quite to the ditch, and, double-shoot-
ing it, fired into an embrasure, disabling a gun in it
ready to be discharged, and scattering death among
the Rebel cannoneers. . . .

Alarmed for his safety, and the assault of the corps
on my left having failed, the enemy early hastened to
mass large numbers from the right and left on my front.
Thus reinforced, he renewed his efforts with increased
effect. All my forces were now engaged. Failure and
loss of my hard-won advantages became imminent.

Advising General McArthur . . . of the state of
affairs, I requested reinforcements, and notified Maj.
Gen. Grant of the fact. At eleven o'clock a.m. I also
informed him that I was hotly engaged; that the enemy
was massing upon me from right and left, and that a
vigorous blow would make a diversion in my favor.
Again at 12:00 m. that I was in partial possession of
two forts, and suggested whether a vigorous push
ought not to be made all along our line.

Where did reality end and delusion begin? That morning
Sylvanus Cadwallader remembered riding

. . . to a point between McClernand's and McPherson's corps that promised reasonable protection, but
was soon compelled to take refuge in a canyon, or
gully, near by. From this I had a fair view of the movement, but I could not see much of the field across
which his advance was made. The cannonading from
both sides was terrific. The air was filled with hollow
shot, percussion shells, and about every kind of missile
ever thrown from heavy guns. At this time we were
using many Hotchkiss shells having wooden bases
fastened to metal points with wires and strips of tin.

These were so imperfectly manufactured that the wooden base was blown off a larger proportion of them before they reached the enemy. When fired over the heads of our advancing columns, it was a common remark that they killed more of our own men by flying to pieces prematurely than the killed and wounded of the enemy combined. . . .

As McClernand's advance neared the Rebel works, it came into plain view from my place of shelter. It had been so mercilessly torn to pieces by Confederate shot and shell that it had lost nearly all resemblance to a line of battle or the formation of a storming column. Officers and men were rushing ahead pell-mell without much attention to alignment. The small number in sight could no longer be mown down by artillery, as the guns of the fort could not be depressed sufficiently. When they crossed the deep ditch in front of the earthworks and began to ascend the glacis, they were out of musketry range for the same reason, excepting from one or two salients within reach. A struggling line, continually growing thinner and weaker, finally reached the summit, when all who were not instantly shot down were literally pulled over the Rebel breastworks as prisoners. One stand of our colors was planted halfway up the embankment and remained there until a dreary Confederate ventured over and carried it back inside. Many stragglers took refuge in the ditch outside the earthworks and remained there till they could crawl away covered by darkness. . . .

Grant stood with Sherman. An orderly arrived from McClernand, begging that Grant order McPherson and Sherman to press their attacks, "lest the enemy should concentrate on him." McClernand repeated his claims, Sherman said—"his troops had captured the Rebel parapet in his front . . . the flag of the Union waved over the stronghold of Vicksburg."

14: MCCLERNAND CLAIMS A VICTORY

"I don't believe a word of it," Grant said.

Sherman remonstrated. The note was official; it must be credited. He offered to renew his own assault.

Grant remained skeptical. He would ride down the line to McClernand's front. If Sherman did not receive orders to the contrary by three o'clock, he "might try it again."

At half past two McClernand received a message from Grant, stating in part:

> McPherson is directed to send Quimby's division to you if he cannot effect a lodgment where he is. Quimby is next to your right, and you will be aided as much by his penetrating into the enemy's line as by having him to support the columns you have already got.
>
> Sherman is getting on well.

McClernand's heart lifted at "this welcome intelligence." He replied that he had "lost no ground" and that he had learned from prisoners "the works in which I had made my lodgment were commanded by strong defenses in their rear, but that with a division I doubted not that I should force my way through the hostile lines."

The conflict between reality and delusion rode high in McClernand; bitterly his story turned on "obstacles" that prevented his great victory:

> . . . Cols. Boomer's and Sandborn's brigades of Quimby's division, moving in direction of my position, and in view of the enemy, prompted the latter to concentrate additional forces on my front, and to make a sortie which was promptly repelled. Coming up late in the evening and much exhausted, their services were not available, and night set in and terminated the struggle before either of these brigades could be fully applied; and indeed before one of them was entirely formed.

But this story did not jibe with the scene that Cadwallader recreated:

. . . Instead of using Quimby as a support to his own troops, McClernand ordered them to the front in the forlorn hope of retrieving the fortunes of the day, and attempted to make a second assault, with some of his own demoralized troops on Quimby's flank. One of his colonels flatly refused to obey this order, and declared that he would take the consequences of his disobedience other than lead his men to certain death. Colonel Joseph Mower, in command of the brigade sent, looked the ground over with the eye of an able commander, and exclaimed: "Good God! No man can return from this charge alive!" He accordingly took off his watch and handed it, and what money he had, to a personal friend who remained behind, requesting him to forward all to his wife. He led his men gallantly into action and fell dead at the first fire. The whole affair was miserable and inexcusable to a point beyond endurance. . . .

Promptly at three o'clock Sherman renewed his assault, and found it "a repetition of the first, equally unsuccessful and bloody." McPherson did no better. Sherman suspected the worst: "that General McClernand, instead of having taken any single point of the Rebel main parapet, had only taken one or two small outlying lunettes open to the rear, where his men were at the mercy of the Rebels behind their main parapet."

Rather sparse was Grant's comment on the outcome of McClernand's demand for renewed assault: "This last attack only served to increase our casualties without giving any benefit whatever." The day's losses would be an aggregate of 3,199 for Grant, his bloodiest day. His dead would include 37 officers and 465 enlisted men, his wounded 173 officers and 2,377 enlisted men, his captured or missing one officer and 146 enlisted men.

Grimly, as night ended the tragic day, Cadwallader set

out to find Grant and Rawlins. He meant to tell them the brutal truth: "that I was within plain view of the Rebel earthworks—that McClernand never gained a footing inside of them—and that the small number of his men who actually reached the crest, or scrambled over it, was there yet as prisoners." Here, felt an angry Cadwallader, "was a fair sample of General McClernand's victories."

PART THREE

✶✶✶✶✶✶✶✶✶✶✶✶✶✶✶✶✶✶✶✶✶✶✶✶✶✶✶✶✶✶✶✶✶✶✶✶✶✶✶

City of Caves

15. LIFE IN THE DITCHES

GRANT's growing restlessness sharpened the temper of Rawlins. The General's manservant, Bill, had been caught slipping Grant a drink, and Rawlins, ordering the Negro strung up by the thumbs, threatened to blow out the wretch's brains if the incident were repeated. So Bill sulked, Rawlins glowered, and Grant, determined "to out-camp the enemy," chewed an unlighted cigar.

Everyone knew the failure of the bloody assaults on May 22 rankled in the old man's mind. McClernand had been proved worse than a vain, reckless fool; McClernand amounted to an outright liar. Cadwallader's testimony demonstrated that fact beyond dispute, even to a cautious Rawlins. The burst of indignation from Rawlins at the evidence of McClernand's "duplicity" the reporter had found "fearful," and Grant's "usually placid countenance" had filled with a "grim, glowering look of disappointment and disgust." Writing to Stanton on the twenty-third of May, Dana admitted that Grant had been on the point of firing McClernand, then had changed his mind, deciding to wait until the siege of Vicksburg ended, when Grant would "induce McClernand to ask for leave of absence." Dana obviously approved Grant's decision to place "no reliance" in any of McClernand's reports "unless otherwise corroborated." Dana told Stanton: "McClernand has not the qualities necessary for a good commander, even of a regiment."

With husbandly cynicism Sherman wrote his wife: "Grant is now deservedly the hero . . . belabored with praise by those who a month ago accused him of all the

sins in the calendar." After a Cabinet meeting Secretary of
the Navy Welles noted that "confidence is expressed in
Grant," and on May 26 the *New York Times* asked: "Why
has Gen. Grant thus at last distanced every other general?
In natural brilliancy he is probably surpassed by many of
them; in science he certainly is. It all lies simply in the fact
that he is *a man of success.*" In twenty days, after crossing
the river at Bruinsburg, Grant's troops had fought and won
five battles. Perhaps, as the *Times* felt, there was little of
"natural brilliancy" in the victories at Port Gibson, Raymond, Jackson, Champion's Hill, and the Big Black, but
Grant's *Memoirs* stressed the fact that the Confederates
"were in their own country, where no rear guards were
necessary. The country is admirable for defense, but difficult
for the conduct of an offensive campaign." Perhaps, as the
Times suggested, there was even less "science" in the
Union's achievements under Grant, but the General could
reply: "All their troops had to be met. We were fortunate,
to say the least, in meeting them in detail." The *New York
Tribune* drew another estimate of the role in which Grant
had emerged: "The soldiery . . . look upon Grant as in-
vincible and matchless for strategy and vigilance." Next
week, Sherman remarked to his wife, many who praised
Grant would again turn against him "if so blows the popular breeze."

A poet once called Vicksburg "the Sky Parlor," but
Grant's smile would have twisted at that pretty allusion.
To his practical mind, a siege possessed one thoroughly
unimaginative purpose: to demonstrate that hungry bellies
could accomplish what bullets could not. As long as the
Union forces kept Pemberton locked on land with his back
against a river floating with Yankee gunboats, the "Defender of Vicksburg" must survive on his present supplies
of food, men, and munitions. Grant didn't doubt that
Pemberton would exert "the most strenuous efforts" to es-

cape from this trap; the Confederates must take any risk to avoid capture or annihilation within Vicksburg.

Grant calculated his own risks, the odds that could easily turn against him. Rosecrans wasn't pinning down Bragg the way he should in Tennessee; almost every scouting report reaching Grant's headquarters told of more of Bragg's troops arriving along the Big Black to reinforce Confederate positions there. Grant couldn't ignore the enemy at Canton and Jackson; irked, he threw up a rear line of defense and drew from his cavalry to watch every ford of the Big Black over which the wily Johnston might lunge. At the same time Grant's frontal line, extending from Haines' Bluff to Vicksburg and then on to Warrenton, covered fifteen miles, whereas Pemberton's line could be squeezed into seven. Densely wooded ravines and gullies carved into the land by centuries of rain and erosion protected the Rebel batteries and breastworks defending the city. Moreover, Pemberton's engineers had exhibited cunning. What was the sense of entrenching each of these spurs? Pemberton's line needed simply to jump from one gully head to the next, and a triangular outer work at these juncture points required a minimum number of men to command the approaches to the main line.

On the twenty-fifth of May, Pemberton sent a flag of truce, asking for a respite in the sniping between lines to bury the Federals killed in the assault of three days previously. The blue-clad casualties, "lying in every attitude of agony, on the open fields, in the trenches and ditches, and among the slashed trees," Pemberton found "a hard ordeal even for their Confederate enemies." To Stanton, Dana wrote that the dead Yankees "evidently caused . . . great annoyance by their odor," and added cynically that Pemberton "probably also hoped to gain information." But Grant played the same game. While hostilities halted and the dead were buried, said Union Major Andrew Hickenlooper, Grant's chief engineer "closely inspect[ed] the ground to be passed over, fixing the salient points in his mind and determining upon the general directions of the various sections of sap." Thereafter Grant kept his boys digging steadily behind their sap-rollers; why charge the Rebel forts when, once they could be tunneled under, dynamite would do the work of a regiment? To anyone who wished a description of a sap-roller, Wilbur Crummer of the 45th Illinois answered laconically: "A bullet-stopper," and explained: "Suppose we take two empty barrels and lash them together, one on top of the other, then wrap them round and round with willow saplings, fill them with earth, put a cover on, lay them down, and you have a sap-roller." Pushing a sap-roller before them, two men could dig without fear of Minié balls.

But sap-rolling was slow work; it was like all the operations that went into a siege—ill-suited to Grant's nature or temperament. If Rawlins frowned those late May days, it was because he understood Grant, perhaps better than anyone else. Despite Grant's sedentary appearance, despite his stubby legs, his mood wouldn't long sustain standing still, waiting, playing at cat-and-mouse. Grant clung all through life to one boyhood superstition—never take a step backward. Scarcely into his teens, he had driven alone on a seventy-mile journey, and thereafter a need for movement dominated his life. He rode horses, head up, glad to feel the wind whipping against his face. While Sherman virtually sweated away his life's blood at the thought of cutting loose from a base of supplies, Grant shrugged and moved on . . . on to Port Gibson and Raymond and now to the shadowy hills of Vicksburg. But here he had stalled. Here patience and caution and executive ability must replace movement. In a way, Grant had chosen to oppose his own disposition. How long could *he* hold out? Rawlins, knowing Grant, must have wondered if a blow-up came, what form it might take.

The siege ended its first week. Corn-fed lads from Indiana

and Illinois, Iowa and Missouri, began to feel at home in their "ditches." Their letters told the real story of how events were shaping—told it plainly and honestly and intimately, told it better than the reports of the journalists who too often hung around the sutler's boats at the river landings. Those letters described Grant as quiet and composed, confident and determined. Time would win for them, their pencil scrawls said—and, they hinted, maybe not too much time either, for the itch to move had been ingrained into Grant's army. Private Francis W. Tupper of the 15th Illinois Cavalry wrote his parents: "The Rebels don't starve with success. I think that if I had nothing to eat I'd starve better than they do." At some points, Tupper said, Yank and Reb lines ran so close that men from the two armies hooted at one another, mixing profanity with good-natured derision and often with nothing more belligerent than gossipy curiosity. "The army is a great place for jokes," Tupper added; the Yankee 6th Missouri Regiment faced the Confederate 6th Missouri and "the boys call them 'the bogus six' to distinguish them from ours."

To the men in the ditches, there was ever present a personal enemy—the sharpshooter. Both individuals and areas of the front lines acquired a kind of ghoulish renown. Staff artist Theodore R. Davis told readers of *Harper's Weekly* about "the Dead Hole," where seventeen Rebels were killed. "A favorite amusement of the soldiers," Major Hickenlooper said, "was to place a cap on the end of a ramrod and to raise it just above the head-logs, betting on the number of bullets which would pass through it within a given time."

Confederates and Yankees indulged in this sport, rolling over on their backs and chortling with glee at the number of bullets the enemy had wasted, but a scrapy edge crept into their cackling. Sharpshooting was a nasty, deadly business. At night, out digging behind a sap-roller, a man felt comforted by the darkness; in daylight "not even a hand could be safely raised above the parapets; and heavy rope shields, or aprons, were hung in front of the gunners while they were sighting their pieces."

Cavalryman Tupper thought he'd like a lick at sharp-shooting, and with the zeal of the raw recruit volunteered for "an advance place where no one went." His letter home was somewhat less enthusiastic:

> One of the boys gave me his gun, but I couldn't see any heads in sight above their works, yet I could hear the balls whistle over, every minute, and some of them very close. At last we discovered that they had a hole through the embankment about two feet from the top, and by knowing where it was, and looking sharp, you could see the sky beyond it. I fired a few times to get the range. The boys told me where my shots struck. After that every time we couldn't see through the hole we would all fire, and the firing from the hole soon ceased. There are several such places along the line, and I am told that at one of them the Rebs have had over a dozen men killed. We also have a lookout and sharpshooter post, on the highest point of the ridge; the lookout is twenty or twenty-five feet high, and is built of heavy timber and protects a man on three sides. . . . An ingenious plan was devised to watch [enemy] oper-ations and not be exposed. . . . A looking-glass was put on top, and to the back side of the tower. You could just stand in the tower and look into the glass and see all that was to be seen of their operations. They soon discovered this and commenced firing at it and broke it all to smash after about a hundred rounds had been fired at it.

The toast of Yankee sharpshooters was "Coonskin" Henry C. Foster of the 22nd Indiana Volunteers. Coonskin's cap and gun were known everywhere along the lines, for Coonskin took to sharpshooting the way Grant and Duff had

cottoned to the barrel of whisky left behind earlier in the
month by Oglesby. One night Coonskin crept out toward
the Confederate defenses, dug a burrow in the ground, and
fashioned a peephole in it. He liked the place so well that
he and his racoon fur hat would share the hole for several
days at a stretch. Coonskin's mind was never idle, even
though, occasionally, he rested his gun arm. What was the
sense, Coonskin asked, of wasting all those rails and cross-
ties where the Jackson and Vicksburg Railroad had been
torn up for several miles? Well tutored in the lore of the
backwoodsman, Coonskin reckoned it wouldn't be much
of a job building a tower "genuine pioneer log-cabin style."
He could build it in the dark.

Each night Coonskin's tower rose higher until, climbing
aloft one morning, he winked with satisfaction. He could
see real pretty—right over the Confederate parapets. There
Coonskin stationed himself, aiming through the chinks,
mowing down the Rebs, and thumbing his nose at a Confederate battery in his front already silenced by Union guns.
The musket balls fired by the Rebs were no worse than
fleabites to Coonskin. Bullets whistled around the corners
of the tower or buried themselves in the logs while Coonskin
flipped the tail of his cap out of his eyes and drew a bead
on his harried assailants.

But the Confederates, in other quarters of the front, gave
as much or more than they took. The main road from
Grant's headquarters to Logan's crossed a ravine leading up
to a salient in the Rebel works. "They killed so many men
and horses," Cadwallader said, that the road "was abandoned by teams and trains, but single horsemen would often
ride quietly to the edge of the timber coat and then, putting
spurs to their animals, dash across the open ravine . . . at
full speed." One day Cadwallader watched an orderly
whose horse was not equal to the test. The shots came
"woozing and zipping." A bullet cut the orderly's bladder;
urine oozed out through the wound. The lad felt that he

suffered only from shock and rode on to headquarters. He was buried next morning.

2.

The second week of siege set in. It was June now—hot, muggy, enervating. Grant's batteries covered the eight roads leading into Vicksburg, and the big guns rocked and roared almost constantly. Before the siege ended, Federal guns in position numbered 220, and among the heavy weapons listed by Captain Cyrus Comstock of the Engineers Corps would be ten-, twenty-, and thirty-pound Parrotts, twelve- and twenty-four-pound Howitzers, twelve-pound smoothbores, a single Napoleon, a pair of nine-inch Dahlgrens, and a pair of thirty-two-pound siege guns, but the majority of the field pieces would be six-pounders, both rifled and smoothbore. Parrotts and Howitzers, generally six- and twelve-pounders, supplied the bulk of Confederate fire power.

Lieutenant Cyrus E. Dickey of the XVII Corps's 6th Division found the fact "astonishing that these [Rebel] missiles do no more execution." Dickey was present one evening when Logan was visited at his siege guns by some fifty officers. A Reb eleven-inch mortar shell "fell in the center of the group, sunk three feet into the ground, and exploded, completely burying Major Walden and scattering the dirt over the whole party, but not a man was hurt." Half an hour later another shell exploded near an officer's tent, "tearing it all to pieces and scattering his furniture over five acres of ground." Union batteries, Cadwallader thought, fired two shells to one for the Confederates, and the confidence felt by Pemberton's gunners in holding and calling their shots must be explained by the careful planning and construction of the Rebel forts. Even when heavy, concentrated fire from Union guns ripped away the face or crest of an earthwork, darkness found the Rebels toiling on repairs and "the morning sun would show a dazzling array of white gunny sacks filled with dirt and sand in the breaches made the day before." Powder-grimed Yankee artillerymen, spotting those white sacks, went along the lines taking wagers on the number of shots they would require to dislodge one. "The second or third shot would generally hit the mark," Cadwallader said.

The pattern of siege that Grant unfolded at Vicksburg was as old, in a sense, as man's will to attack fortifications. To be successful, a siege followed five steps: the investment, the artillery attack, the construction of parallels and approaches, breaching by artillery or mines, the final assault. And to be successful, the spirit of a siege remains impersonal. It fights guns, it fights forts, it fights brick and mortar composing the city, it fights time and space and the elements. Almost incidentally, it also fights people, both the armed and the unarmed, the lame and the able-bodied, the rich and the poor, the young and the aged.

Inside Vicksburg the sight became one that Edward S. Gregory would never forget. Standing amid the rubble of the city, where now only the fragments of houses remained, scarred, half-burned, seeming in the encroaching dusk to be like misshapen old men about to totter and fall, Gregory wondered from where next Grant's guns would hurl destruction. Federal artillery encircled Vicksburg, for even across the Mississippi eleven- and thirteen-inch mortars had been placed where "these preachers of the Union" could be trained "directly on the homes of the people."

Gregory watched the shells "rising steadily and shiningly in great parabolic curves, descending with ever-increasing swiftness, and falling with deafening shriek and explosion." The "ponderous fragments" flew everywhere. How many shells came and burst in a single day no one knew. Toward late June the estimate of the number falling in a day would be 150,000, doubtless an exaggeration. But even now, in only the second week of siege, one fact remained incontestable. The shells spared nothing. Homes, churches, libraries, stores, factories crumbled under the wrath from Grant's guns. The "Sky Parlor" had become the "City of Caves."

Mrs. James M. Loughborough, who had come to Vicksburg to be with her soldier husband, asked a friend: "How is it possible you live here?"

"After one is accustomed to the change," her friend answered, "we do not mind it. But becoming accustomed—that is the trial."

Mrs. Loughborough turned away, reminded of the question a traveler had put to the inhabitant of an infected area: "How do you live here?"

"Sir, we die," the other had replied.

If, as Gregory contended, the shelling "became at last such an ordinary occurrence of daily life that I have seen ladies walk quietly along the streets while the shells burst above them, their heads protected meanwhile by a parasol held between them and the sun," Mrs. W. W. Lord could not share this nonchalance. She had heard that Johnston had evacuated Jackson, that Pemberton's army was "advancing along toward Big Black," and she had seen the two movements as "parts of a great plan . . . to surround Grant's army." Then the shells from Grant's guns, blasting everything above ground, blasted hope also. "I was sadly undeceived," Mrs. Lord wept bitterly to her journal. "We have been terribly whipped." She could not describe her feelings—"as if I almost believed Pemberton was a traitor."

Mrs. Loughborough also felt the undercurrent of resentment against Pemberton. A Confederate straggler—"an awkward, long-limbed, weary-looking man"—told her harshly, after the retreat on the seventeenth of May:

"It's all Pem's fault. We would ha' fit well, but General Pemberton came up and said: 'Stand your ground, boys! Your General Pemberton is with you!' And then, bless you, lady, the next we seed of him, he was sitting on his horse behind a house! And when we seed that, we though 'tain't no use."

But when the shells began to fall, there was no point in blaming anyone—Grant or Pemberton, Lincoln or Jeff Davis. Mrs. Lord, with her four children huddled near her, thought then only of "the horrible shells roaring and bursting all around us and the concussion making our heads feel like they would burst." Eight families, "besides other single families," shared Mrs. Lord's cave. "The whole hill shook," she wrote; she had not "undressed now for nearly two weeks." Pity touched Mrs. Lord's heart when she glanced across at "poor Mrs. Gunn, with her little baby only ten days old"; and terror returned at the memory of a day when "a large piece of earth fell upon Mrs. McRoas's little daughter and almost killed her." But, Mrs. Lord added proudly, the children behaved "like little heroes"; at night, "when the balls began to fly like pigeons over our tent," and she called to them to flee to the caves, "they spring up, even to little Loulie, like soldiers, slip on their shoes without a word, and run up the hill." One infant was born during the siege. At mid-life he delighted in autographing his photograph: "I was born twelve feet under ground."

Another woman, who in later years would permit herself to be identified only as "a young lady of New Orleans," lamented: "We are utterly cut off from the world, surrounded by a circle of fire." And she wondered: "Would it be wise like the scorpion to sting ourselves to death?" Life inside the beleaguered city stretched before her bleakly:

. . . The fiery shower of shells goes on day and night. H——'s occupation, of course, is gone, his office closed. Every man has to carry a pass in his pocket. People do nothing but eat what they can get, sleep when they can, and dodge the shells. There are three intervals when the shelling stops, either for the

guns to cool or for the gunners' meals, I suppose—
about eight in the morning, the same in the evening,
and at noon. In that time we have both to prepare
and eat ours. Clothing cannot be washed or anything
else done. On the nineteenth and twenty-second, when
the assaults were made on our lines, I watched the
soldiers cooking on the green opposite. The half-spent
balls, coming all the way from those lines, were flying
so thick that they were obliged to dodge at every turn.
At all the caves I could see from my high perch, people
were sitting, eating their poor suppers at the cave
doors, ready to plunge in again. As the first shell flew
again they dived, and not a human being was visible.
Mrs. Loughborough could understand why:

. . . The room that I had so lately slept in had been
struck and a large hole made in the ceiling. Terror-
stricken, we remained crouched in the cave while shell
after shell followed one another in quick succession.
My heart stood still as we would hear the reports from
the guns and the rushing and fearful sound of the shell
as it came toward us. As it neared, the noise became
more deafening; the air was full of the rushing sound;
pains darted through my temples; my ears were bursting. And as it exploded, the report flashed through my
brain like an electric shock, leaving me in a quiet state
of terror.

Even the dogs seemed to share the general fear. They
would be seen in the midst of the noise to gallop up
the street, and then to return, as if fear had maddened
them. On hearing the descent of a shell, they would
dart aside—then, as it exploded, sit down and howl in a
pitiful manner.

But in time neither a dog nor a cat could be found in
the streets of Vicksburg. "I think all . . . must be killed
or starved," the "young lady of New Orleans" decided.

15: LIFE IN THE DITCHES

In the loose, friable soil of the slopes around Vicksburg, two men, working a week, could dig a cave. The charge in March had been thirty dollars, but as May saw Grant draw closer to Vicksburg, as June brought a ring of Yankee siege guns around the city, cave-diggers, if they could be found at all, hiked their prices—to one hundred dollars, to one hundred and fifty, to two hundred. Mrs. Lord described her cave:

> . . . Imagine to yourself in the first place a good-sized parapet, about six feet high, a path cut through, and then the entrance to the cave. . . . Secured strongly with boards, it is dug the height of a man and about forty feet under the hill. It communicates with the other cave which is about the same length opening out on the other side of the hill—this gives us a good circulation of air. . . . I have a little closet dug for provisions, and niches for flowers, lights, and books —inside just by the little walk is our eating-table with an arbor over it and back of that our fireplace and kitchen with table, &c. In the valley beneath is our tent and back of it the tents of the generals. This is quite picturesque to look at, but Oh! how wearisome to live!

Pillars and wooden joists usually strengthened the caves; beds and furniture were jammed in as best the circumstances permitted. All semblance of privacy disappeared, Gregory declared, so that "home was a den shared with others, perhaps with strangers." The air, another witness said, became so foul in the overcrowded caves "you could not have made a candle burn."

Derisively, the Yankees renamed Vicksburg "the prairie dog's village."

16. ON FANNING A GENERAL TO SLEEP

RAWLINS should have been forewarned. Grant's increasing restlessness foretold an impending eruption. The General even ignored the rumors, uncomfortably persistent during those early June days, that Johnston was advancing across the Big Black to raise the siege of Vicksburg.

In two weeks Grant had grown more assured as he heard the pounding of his big guns, saw the Federal lines dug in deeper, received encouraging reports of the progress made by the night diggers behind their sap-rollers. Word came from General Frank Blair that he had marched his troops fifty miles up the peninsula, had made a reconnaissance in force, and had found the spiders and mosquitoes "Godawful." Kimball arrived from Memphis with a brigade, received support from a cavalry detachment, and pushed a dozen miles northeast of Haines' Bluff, tearing up bridges, obstructing roads, and stripping the neighborhood of food, grain, and livestock. For a hundred miles up the Yazoo—from Chickasaw Bayou to the landing at Satartia—Porter claimed free water for his light-draft transports and dispatch boats.

"The siege is being pressed with all possible vigor," an almost jubilant Dana wrote Stanton on the thirtieth of May. Sherman had pushed a breaching battery of four thirty-pound Parrotts within eighty yards of the chief fort in his front, and McPherson's approaches—with a battery "all ready for three similar guns"—were within fifty yards. If intercepted messages could be trusted, Dana reported, Vicksburg couldn't hold out later than mid-June. A conversation with Blair next day increased Dana's optimism. Johnston's forces, previously estimated at forty-five thousand, did not exceed eighteen thousand, Blair thought. In five days Blair had marched ninety miles to reach Haines' Bluff; Blair's troops, once thrown on the extreme left, "will render the investment total." What if Johnston, "finding all lost at Vicksburg," should dash at Memphis? Dana answered easily that Grant would rely "on the vigilance of Hurlbut's cavalry and the rapidity of his own transport steamers to get reinforcements there in season." On June 3, appraising the situation at Vicksburg for Stanton, Dana added another cheerful note: "All the roads by which the enemy can approach are being filled by every practicable obstruction. Of this last work much already has been well done."

Grant should have been content. His headquarters were pleasantly situated on an elevation about five miles from Vicksburg. A strip of timber shaded the General from the sun; a brook close by had been cleared of any pollution. Sherman and McPherson were within easy reach, and Logan, a stout friend of Duff's, appeared almost nightly. But convivial companions couldn't change the fact that it had been some time since Grant had seen Julia. An old moodiness, tinged with melancholy, usually returned at such periods. His legs grew itchy.

And so one day Grant disappeared.

At about this time Cadwallader decided to go up the Yazoo and ascertain what he should be telling readers of the *Chicago Times* about the situation along the river. Well installed now at Grant's headquarters—Cadwallader messed at the same table with Rawlins and shared a tent with Duff—he found no trouble in engaging passage aboard the steamboat *Diligence* under Captain Harry McDougall. The trip proved a disappointment. Cadwallader could sum up in three words the gist of that experience: "Everything was quiet." What happened afterward prudently remained unreported in the *Times*.

Next morning the *Diligence* started back to Chickasaw Bayou. Around a bend in the Yazoo appeared a second steamer and its flag signaled the *Diligence* to drop anchor. Grant, who had come up the river on the other steamer, had recognized the *Diligence* as a craft of superior speed on which he had once sailed. Grant insisted on transferring to the *Diligence* with his cavalry escort. From a dozen yards away it was obvious that Grant had been drinking heavily; moreover, he had no intention of stopping. Several quick trips to the barroom of the *Diligence* hardly improved his condition. Cadwallader could only describe him as "stupid in speech and staggering in gait."

For Cadwallader this side of Grant was entirely new: "I was greatly alarmed by his condition, which was fast becoming coarse." But the reporter's affection for Grant remained unshaken and he possessed but one purpose—to shove the General into a stateroom where he couldn't be seen. The only staff officer aboard was Towner, the acting adjutant, a virtual youngster still self-consciously proud of his new stripes as a lieutenant. Towner responded timidly when Cadwallader sought his help. Wasn't Grant able to judge his own behavior? McDougall seemed even less inclined to co-operate. Wasn't Grant the Department commander "with full power to do what he pleased with the boat and all it contained"?

Cadwallader refused to back down. If McDougall wished to get ahead in the Department, then let him not underestimate the vindictive feelings of Rawlins toward those who supplied Grant with liquor. McDougall could either close the barroom and lose the key until Grant was safely ashore, or Cadwallader would see the captain "sent out of the Department in irons." The bedeviled McDougall capitulated, but only on the promise that Cadwallader would assume responsibility for the key. In triumph, the reporter sought out Grant, "took the General in hand, . . . enticed him into his stateroom, . . . and commenced throwing bottles of whisky which stood on the table, over the guards, into the river."

Grant's blurred mind reacted violently. That was good

whisky. Get out, Grant roared at Cadwallader—get out of his room. The General rattled the door, found it locked, and burst into a new fury. He wanted that key, his key. Cadwallader stood his ground: "I said to him that I was the best friend he had in the Army of the Tennessee; that I was doing for him what I hoped someone would do for me, should I ever be in his condition; that he was not capable in this case of judging for himself; and that he must for the present act upon my better judgment and be governed by my advice."

The day grew hotter, the stateroom almost suffocating. Cadwallader helped Grant take off coat, vest, and boots. He coaxed the General to lie down on one of the berths.

Then Cadwallader "fanned" the General to sleep.

The *Diligence* reached Satartia before Grant roused from his stupor. The General awoke as one startled, leaped from his berth, and demanded his clothes. Certainly he wished to go ashore. He wanted the escort men and horses disembarked. Osband, captain of the escort, looked sick. Grant's orders were absurd—in Cadwallader's estimation, really "suicidal," if Grant intended to land at night "in such a miserable little hamlet filled with desperadoes and Rebel sympathizers." Only a handful of troops under Osband could protect him.

Cadwallader could well believe that Grant's mind remained completely befogged if he were thinking of returning overland to Vicksburg "through a section of the country as hostile as any in the Confederacy, and without any knowledge whatever of the roads traversing it." Nothing less than a miracle could save Grant from capture. Osband had no grounds for disobeying Grant's orders, but Cadwallader could come to his aid "by promising to take . . . the responsibility of shooting or hamstringing every horse on the vessel."

Delay, discussion found Grant wavering. In the midst of the altercation the General kicked off his boots and went back to sleep.

Part Three: CITY OF CAVES

The boat docked at Haines' Bluff in the morning. The danger seemed passed. Grant acted sober and rational in ordering the escort to Kimball's camp for news. Cadwallader relaxed and watched Grant wander ashore. When the General reappeared, he was as staggering drunk as the day before.

The escort returned from Kimball's camp and Grant decided to proceed at once to Chickasaw Bayou. Cadwallader felt treed at last. The *Diligence* would reach the bayou in midafternoon "when the landing would [be] alive with officers, men, and train from all parts of the army." Grant faced "utter disgrace and ruin." McDougall agreed. Under Cadwallader's urging, almost two hours were wasted on the pretext that the steamboat had been loaded with low-fired green wood. Grant, striding the deck, presumably resembled a blowfish. When at length McDougall decided that he could sail, a bargain had been struck with Cadwallader "to look out for a safe sandbar or beach to stick on for a while." Through sundry forms of connivance the arrival of the *Diligence* at Chickasaw Bayou was delayed until sundown.

The devil, clearly on Grant's side, proved an insistent adversary. Moored at the landing was the headquarters sutler boat belonging to "Wash" Graham.

Cadwallader knew Wash. If a slave could be a rascally "nigger," Wash had the taint of a rascally white. The sutler kept open house on his boat for officers: free liquor and cigars were dispensed generously. The attraction of Wash's boat was especially understandable in the South after the winter of '62 when whisky grew scarce and often was labeled "rifle knock-knee" and "spill skull," and the mellowing of a concoction of about thirty per cent good alcohol mixed with vitriol, water, and coloring matter became one of the best-guarded secrets of the war.[1]

---

[1] Usually veal or young fowl were soaked in the mixture to give it "smoothness." Cf. Bell Irvin Wiley: *The Life of Johnny Reb* (Indianapolis: 1952).

But Cadwallader wasn't thinking of the quality of Wash's liquor when he slipped over the guards in search of the sutler. Whether Wash served good whisky or rotgut, Grant already had drunk enough. Solemnly Wash promised that the General should not have a drop on his boat. Meanwhile Osband had unloaded the horses. All stood ready for the ride back to headquarters. All but Grant.

Cadwallader stalked into Wash Graham's office on the bow of the sutler's boat. There was no sign of Wash. A boom of conversation and laughter emerged from a room opening off the ladies' cabin. Officers filled the place. Wash stood in front of a table "covered with bottled whisky and baskets of champagne." Beside the sutler lounged Grant, swallowing a glass of whisky.

Grant didn't disguise his annoyance at the interruption Cadwallader created. Stifly he strode out of the cabin ahead of the reporter. The General had brought with him a horse called Kangaroo, an animal noted for his habit of rearing on his hind feet and plunging forward when mounted. Grant leaped into the saddle, put his spurs to Kangaroo, and left a startled escort gaping after him. A road crooked and tortuous, following the firmest ground between shoals and bayous and bridged in several places, didn't faze Grant; nor the guards stationed at each bridge to prevent fast riding; nor camps and crowds as he went full speed and "literally tore through and over everything in his way." By the time the escort was mounted, Grant was "out of sight in the gloaming" with the air "full of dust, ashes, and embers from campfires, and shouts and curses from those he rode down in his race."

The chase ended abruptly. Three quarters of a mile from the landing, across the last bayou bridge, Grant jogged along at a leisurely gait. Cadwallader, riding up, seized his bridle.

Grant felt dizzy and pitched in the saddle. The escort was nowhere in sight. Cadwallader resolved to get Grant off the road, and selected as a spot of refuge a thicket near the foot of the bluff. Grant needed help in dismounting, and Cadwallader left him swaying blearily while he stripped the saddle from Kangaroo. After some little time the reporter persuaded Grant to stretch out on the grass with the saddle for a pillow.

The General slept almost instantly.

Across the bottom land for an area of half a mile Cadwallader heard the escort circling about, hallooing as they searched for their commander and expecting at any instant to come upon Grant's lifeless body. Luck brought one of the party within hailing distance and Cadwallader ordered the fellow "to proceed directly to headquarters and to report to Rawlins—and to no one else—and to say . . . that I wanted an ambulance with a careful driver."

Darkness closed in. Grant slept fretfully, stirred, sat up. What was he doing here? Cadwallader stalled for time, took Grant's arm, walked him along the foot of the bluff, and kept up "a lively, one-sided conversation" until the ambulance arrived.

Grant balked. He'd reach headquarters under his own power. But again Cadwallader won his way by offering to ride in an ambulance with the General while an orderly brought their horses.

Remorse smote Grant. Cadwallader had saved him from disgrace. Henceforth the reporter should consider himself a staff officer entitled to give any necessary order in Grant's name. The pair reached headquarters at about midnight. Rawlins and Colonel John Riggin waited anxiously at the driveway. Cadwallader stepped first from the ambulance. Then Grant appeared:

> . . . He shrugged his shoulders, pulled down his vest, shook himself together as one just rising from a nap, and seeing Rawlins and Riggin, bid them good night in a natural tone and manner, and started to his tent as steadily as he ever walked in his life.

17. "A JACKASS IN THE ORIGINAL PACKAGE"

OVERNIGHT Cadwallader became installed as one of Grant's favorites. Even Rawlins discussed military matters "of the most confidential nature" when he met Cadwallader at mess. Special facilities were provided "for instant communication with the General and staff at any hour of the day or night," and Cadwallader had contact with all of Grant's personal movements, knew first when news was received from all parts of the line, and learned instantly when couriers arrived and departed. "If I was a trifle too late in depositing my correspondence in the General's mail pouch," the reporter recalled, "or if a courier were hurriedly and unexpectedly started with dispatches up the river or elsewhere, my arrangement was such that when he was mounted and had received his final instructions, he came past my tent and took everything I had in readiness." Thus Cadwallader was "enabled . . . to keep from one to two days ahead of my less fortunate competitors."

Rawlins, hacking with a consumptive cough that in only a few years would prove fatal, felt sickened at the risk Grant had run in his spree in Satartia. Rawlins, when he grew excited, invariably orated rather than talked: his tones became stentorian, his gesticulations vehement, his expletives numerous and pointed. The scene between Rawlins and Grant next morning found Rawlins "impetuous and stormy." How many times had Grant promised him not to drink and then violated those pledges? If Grant "had no more regard for his own reputation," if such dissipation came before "the lives of the men he commanded," then Rawlins desired to have his resignation accepted immediately, for Rawlins "would no longer be a party to further concealment but would retire from his official position while he could at least maintain his own self-respect."

Grant replied "with the utmost good humor." He had quit drinking, he told Rawlins, and "so disarmed Rawlins by his confessions, his open sincerity, and promises of amendment, that the latter was induced to pass over the matter for that time." Rawlins drew from Cadwallader a promise to discuss the incident with no one; and once, during the interview with the reporter, Rawlins muttered through clenched teeth: "I know him, I know him!" Cadwallader wrote also of "one or two trunks filled with valuable papers and documents" that "mysteriously disappeared" when Rawlins died; and in one of these trunks, the journalist claimed, "was a copy of a letter sent by Rawlins to Grant, dated June 6, 1863, protesting in his usual vigorous manner against the General's drinking."

Grant didn't appear to take any of his mail seriously. Two days previously McClernand had penned Grant a letter. McClernand believed that "a systematic effort" existed "to destroy my usefulness and character as a commander." He told Grant: "It is reported, among other things, as I understand, that I attacked on the twenty-second ultimo without authority; again, that I attacked too late; again, that I am responsible for your failure and losses; again, that I am arrested and being sent North; again, that my command is turned over to another officer; and, again, that you have personally assumed command of it." These reports, "finding their way from the landings up the river," unsettled McClernand; and it remained for Grant "to determine whether truth, justice, and generosity do not call on you for such a declaration as will be conclusive in the matter." Grant, if he read the letter, determined to ignore the whole incident.

Meanwhile Rawlins brooded over another problem, and, in all probablity, believed that he walked on eggshells during the next few days whenever he caught a glimpse of Joseph B. McCullogh. The *Cincinnati Commercial* was Mc-

Cullogh's paper, and peppery, influential Murat Halstead, editor and proprietor of the *Commercial*, stood among Grant's severest critics. As intense as Rawlins in devotion to Grant, and in this instance almost as fluttery, Cadwallader provided scant solace. McCullogh, in Cadwallader's opinion, most certainly would send Halstead "some account of Grant's intemperance," and with almost equal certainty Cadwallader believed that Halstead would write another of his sulphurous letters to Salmon P. Chase, Secretary of the Treasury, proving anew that "the foolish, drunken, stupid Grant" couldn't "organize or control or fight an army." At least one of the letters Halstead sent Chase was forwarded to Lincoln, and likely was a good example of the "many such letters" that Cadwallader declared were written by Halstead in an impassioned one-man crusade to oust Grant and save "our noble army of the Mississippi." In the letter known to have passed from Chase to Lincoln, Halstead wrote in part:

> Well, now, for God's sake say that Genl Grant, entrusted with our greatest army, is a jackass in the original package. . . . He is a poor stick sober, and he is most of the time more than half drunk, and much of the time idiotically drunk. . . .
> Grant will fail miserably, hopelessly, eternally. You may look for and calculate his failures, in every position in which he may be placed, as a perfect certainty.

Lincoln didn't believe that Grant had failed. In late May, with the siege of Vicksburg ending its first week, the President answered a demand from Congressman Isaac N. Arnold that Halleck be dismissed. In a letter marked "private and confidential," Lincoln stated:

> . . . And now my good friend, let me turn your eyes upon another point. Whether Gen. Grant shall or shall not consummate the capture of Vicksburg, his

campaign from the beginning of this month up to the twenty-second day of it is one of the most brilliant in the world. His corps commanders, & division commanders, in part, are McClernand, McPherson, Sherman, Steele, Hovey, Blair, & Logan. And yet taking Gen. Grant & these seven of his generals, and you can scarcely name one of them that has not been constantly denounced by the same men who are now so anxious to get Halleck out, and Frémont & Butler & Sigel in. . . . I am compelled to take a more impartial and unprejudiced view of things. . . . My position enables me to understand my duty in all these matters better than you possibly can. . . .

Rawlins, dealing with a flesh-and-blood Grant, could not know that his chief was protected from the worst McCullogh or Halstead could say against him by a Lincoln who had grown to feel confidence in his own ability as a commander-in-chief. From the distance of Washington, never having met Grant in person, Lincoln judged simply by the record. Surely the daily reports that the astute Dana sent to Stanton had not diminished Grant's reputation, and there were others—principally Galena's own congressman, E. B. Washburne, and William P. Mellen, United States Treasury supervisor for the Mississippi Valley—who strengthened the chorus in support of Grant. But Lincoln, rarely awed by a top dog and invariably drawn to an underdog, responded likewise to the very commonness, the very unpretentiousness of Grant—to that quality that led one observer to describe the General as "the unpronounceable man." Drunk or sober, from Belmont on, Grant had kept coming—confounding not only his critics, but also Lincoln himself. Lincoln at least could see the humor in the situation; he would have agreed with the English military authority Colin Ballard in appraising Grant, that to get four aces once required good luck, but to get them five or six times in the same game called for good dealing.

17: "A JACKASS IN THE ORIGINAL PACKAGE"

But Rawlins contended with the Grant of mood and fancy, and Rawlins remained fretful despite the fact that much had transpired at Vicksburg to make Grant feel more cheerful. Hurlbut's command sent a full division under General Sooy Smith that arrived on June 8; on the eleventh, General Francis J. Herron appeared with a strong division from the Department of the Missouri; and on the fourteenth, General John J. Parke of Burnside's corps brought two more divisions. Grant now commanded an army of approximately seventy-one thousand men. More than half of these troops were "disposed" across the peninsula, between the Yazoo at Haines' Bluff and the Big Black. Further south and west, from the crossing of the Jackson road to below Baldwin's Ferry, Grant had sent a division under Osterhaus to watch the crossings of the Big Black.

2.

There were sour notes, however, and Dana's letters to Stanton grew less ebullient. On June 5 the Secretary of War was informed of "a deplorable lack of engineer officers" that hampered the siege, and Dana felt that the fortifications at Haines' Bluff "advance with exceeding slowness for want of engineers and laborers." Grant toyed with the idea of sudden attack in great force on the south, "where there are no siege lines and where [the] enemy expect nothing"—wishful thinking, at best, both on the part of Dana and Grant. Minor skirmishes at Mechanicsburg, Milliken's Bend, and Young's Point filled most of Dana's letter for June 6–8; and he mentioned a cryptic report from Banks at Port Hudson that "if he had ten thousand troops more he could reduce the place in a few days, but we have not facts enough to understand the grounds of this opinion" (nor would it ever be understood). Gloomily Dana reported that "the siege has not yet reached a decisive point." On the eleventh, Dana's missive to Stanton ended testily: "It is my duty to report that the Marine Brigade, with its seven large steamers and its varied apparatus of artillery, infantry, and cavalry, is a very useless as well as a very costly institution."

Grant's personal attention to detail doubtless filled his mind and eased his conscience whenever he encountered the accusing glance of Rawlins. Cadwallader believed the communication of June 6 that mysteriously disappeared from Rawlins's trunk had dealt with the affair at Satartia. In truth, it had been concerned with another incident:

> . . . Tonight when you should, because of the condition of your health if nothing else, have been in bed, I find you where the wine bottle has just been emptied, in company with those who drink and urge you to do likewise, and the lack of your usual promptness of decision and clearness in expressing yourself in writing tended to confirm my suspicions.

All day, virtually all night, prowling the camps, trying to keep Grant in check . . . Rawlins coughed and swore; damn liquor, damn Grant, damn Dr. McMillan at Sherman's headquarters, offering the chief the glass of wine that set him off again!

To shy away from Rawlins, Grant always could visit the front lines, and Davis of *Harper's Weekly*, tagging along with his sketch pad, observed that "to dislodge our men, the Rebels send over ever and anon a shell thrown by hand. Some of these grenades are seized by our men as they come rolling and fizzing into the trench, and [are] hurled back to explode on the heads of their senders." It was not unusual when forces were within "talking-voice distance" to hear "some of our men request an Alabama or Carolina friend to raise his head 'just a leetle higher' above the Rebel works, in order to have a fair shot."

Grant grew short-tempered at the type of explosive musket ball the Confederate sharpshooters employed. No doubt, Grant conceded, the Rebels felt that these balls "bursting over our men in their trenches . . . would do some execution"; Grant couldn't recall "a single case where a man was injured by a piece of one of these shells"; but the fact remained that the use of such ammunition was "barbarous" and could only produce "increased suffering without any corresponding advantage to those using them." Stiffly, Grant grumbled: "A solid ball would have hit as well."

For Grant trouble brewed in another quarter. Jealousy now had begun to turn acid in McClernand's mouth; distrust for the whole West Point crowd had assumed the deeper, more sinister proportions of persecution; the prairie politician began to hear in the brooding chambers of his mind the voices of intrigue that went with the smoke-filled room. Sulking in his tent with no word of comfort from Grant, McClernand composed many documents to justify his behavior in the assaults of May 19 and 22.

McClernand's correspondence grew vigorous and sometimes curious; from Henry C. Warmoth, a former aide-de-camp, came a letter in early June telling of a meeting in St. Louis with a group of political and military leaders, among them "a brother of Gen. Sherman." Wrote Warmoth: "I took it upon myself to drop a flea in his ear as to who was the hero of this campaign." The purpose of Warmoth's letter was to assure McClernand that "public sentiment is pretty thoroughly formed in your favor"; and he asked for copies of McClernand's reports on the battles of Port Gibson, Champion's Hill, and Black River Bridge, as "my friends desire to use them for me and such other reports as you may think proper to send, and I will have them published in each of the papers at St. Louis, Cincinnati, and Chicago and New York."

Unknown to Grant, on the twenty-eighth of May, McClernand had written a letter to Richard Yates, Governor of Illinois, in which McClernand had summarized precisely the type of material that Warmoth sought; and to Yates McClernand stated what to him now seemed an inescapable necessity: " 'Let justice be done'—if need be, let there be an investigation of the whole campaign, in all its parts and policy and [with] regard to all its officials, from Milliken's Bend to this place be made by competent authority and the truth declared." Days, nights of tormented inward whisperings had led McClernand to decide that he must fight fire with fire. Halleck he despised, Sherman and McPherson he disparaged, Grant he distrusted—and, the letter to Yates said flatly, rumors that would fix upon himself responsibility for the failure of the assault of the twenty-second were "senseless and mendacious . . . the spawn of petty, prejudiced partisans." What fault existed for failure, he assured his old political friend in Springfield, "was not with me." With whom, then? With Sherman? With McPherson? With Grant, who had ignored McClernand's advice when "I only asked what, in massing our forces on a single and shaken point, would have materially conduced to the success of the attack"? McClernand gave Yates no margin for questioning who the blunderers had been, and who, in Warmoth's phrase, was "the hero of this campaign."

But Grant, ignoring all forewarnings, settled into the pattern of tedium blended with danger that life in the ditches before Vicksburg had become. In letters home men frequently complained of the almost constant headache they suffered from the ceaseless cannonading. A mule-driver, caught beating his animal, was ordered strung up by his thumbs, not because the teamster answered profanely —"I could defend myself," Grant said—but because "the poor dumb animal could say or do nothing for its own protection." Bewildered Aus Griffin of the 130th Illinois, appropriating the furnishings from a near-by church for Grant's headquarters, found that he must carry them all back—proof to a fellow Illinoisan that Grant was "a man of cruel war with a Christian heart and reverence for sacred things." By mid-June the men in the trenches felt with Grant that the ring around Vicksburg had tightened and soon "Old Pem" must capitulate. To hang around doing nothing imposed an unbearable strain on nerves. Sometimes, Davis said, when a man ran out of ammunition he seized a clod of dirt and hurled that across the lines.

The balm that soothed every soldier's bruises of body and spirit was his right to grumble—about his food, his pay, his generals, the weather. But a gift for grousing also had been well developed by Brigadier General William Ward Orme, who led a brigade in the division that Herron brought to Vicksburg on the eleventh. "The water here is very bad," one letter told Orme's wife. In another Orme complained of the oppressive heat: "I perspire very freely and so much that it makes me feel very weak sometimes." In the next letter Orme not only referred to an attack of bilious diarrhea the day before, but also spoke feelingly of another annoyance:

> I am now suffering terribly from the effects of mosquitos & other bugs—I am full of bites all over. There is a small insect about the size of a pin's point which bites its way into the flesh & makes a very sore place— this insect is called a "chiger" or "jigger" [chigger]. We are all suffering from its depredation. They are much worse than the "wood tick"—I have to stop every sentence I write to scratch myself & drive off the bugs.

Anyone, Orme said later, who saw him without a collar, wearing "a loose linen coat & my old white hat," would hardly "guess that I was an officer." Orme shrugged: "I must be comfortable even at the expense of my military etiquette."

Part Three: CITY OF CAVES

3.

Orme's discomfiture remained slight beside the aggrava-
tion that on June 17 caused the dark eyes of Billy Sherman
to flash angrily above his red beard. Through Frank Blair,
Sherman had received a copy of the *Memphis Evening Bul-
letin* for four days previous. There he discovered an item
entitled "Congratulatory Order of General McClernand."

"If the order be a genuine production and not a for-
gery," Sherman informed Rawlins in a scalding letter, "it
is manifestly addressed not to an army, but to a constituency
in Illinois, far distant from the scene of the events attempted
to be described, who might be innocently induced to think
General McClernand the sagacious leader and bold hero
he so complacently paints himself." McClernand's order to
his army, Sherman snorted, "orders nothing, but is in the
nature of an address to soldiers, manifestly designed for
publication for ulterior political purposes." McClernand's
order, Sherman charged, "perverts the truth to the ends
of flattery and self-glorification, and contains many un-
truths, among which is one monstrous falsehood. It substantially accuses General McPherson and myself with
disobeying orders of General Grant in not assaulting on
May 19 and 22, and allowing on the latter day the enemy
to mass his forces against the XIII Army Corps alone."

McPherson could answer for himself, an angry Sherman
said; as for the part played by the troops he had commanded on May 19 and 22, "tens of thousands of living
witnesses beheld and participated in the attack." Mc-
Clernand, three miles off, never saw those lines; if the truth
must be told, McClernand's "mere buncombe communication" when he claimed that "he had carried three of the
enemy's forts, and that the flag of the Union waved over
the stronghold of Vicksburg," had proved a "mischievous
message whereby we lost, needlessly, many of our best
officers and men." Stung to the quick, Sherman informed

Rawlins: "In cases of repulse and failure, congratulatory addresses by subordinate commanders are not common, and are only resorted to by weak and vain men to shift the burden of responsibility from their own to the shoulders of others. I never have made a practice of speaking or writing of others, but during our assault of the nineteenth several of my brigade commanders were under the impression that McClernand's corps did not even attempt an assault."

McPherson read McClernand's address in the *Missouri Democrat*, and found it, he wrote Grant, "ungenerous." Then McPherson's Scotch-Irish temper exploded:

. . . There is a vaingloriousness about this order, an ingenious attempt to write himself down the hero, the mastermind, giving life and direction to military operations in this quarter inconsistent with the high-toned principles of the soldier, *sans peur et sans reproche*. Though born a warrior, as he himself stated, he has evidently forgotten one of the most essential qualities, viz, that elevated, refined sense of honor which, while guarding his own rights with zealous care, at all times renders justice to others.

Grant secured a copy of the order to which Sherman and McPherson referred, and which McClernand had published without Grant's knowledge. "As your commander," McClernand exhorted his troops, "I am proud to congratulate you upon your constancy, valor, and successes. . . . Your victories have followed in such rapid succession that their echoes have not yet reached the country." For every Union victory since Milliken's Bend, McClernand did more than claim credit; he had opened the way, he hinted, "to redeem previous disappointments." The charges resented by Sherman and McPherson were clearly implied by a McClernand who placed himself and his soldiers "with the honored martyrs of Monmouth and Bunker Hill."

Grant no longer procrastinated. On the eighteenth

Rawlins wrote out the order relieving McClernand of command, freeing him to "proceed to any point . . . in the state of Illinois," and placing the XIII Corps under Major General E. O. C. Ord. Huffily, McClernand responded: "Having been appointed by the President, . . . I might challenge your authority in the premises, but forbear to do so at present." The congratulatory order, Dana confided to Stanton, "is the occasion of McClernand's removal, [but] not the cause." McClernand's "repeated disobedience of important orders, his general insubordinate disposition, and his palpable incompetence for the duties of the position" had all contributed to his undoing, but still another reason had decided the matter, Dana said. If Grant were disabled, the chief command would devolve upon McClernand—with, in Grant's opinion, the "most pernicious consequences to the cause." .

Murky-eyed, arrogantly confident that Lincoln and Stanton must intervene, McClernand returned to Springfield, where he could solicit support from Yates in person, and persuaded the Governor to suggest to Lincoln that "if General McClernand, with some Western troops, was put in command of Pennsylvania, it would inspire great hope and confidence in the Northwest, and perhaps throughout the country." Meanwhile the tenor of McClernand's own communications with Washington was indicated by his official biographer (presumaby Adolph Schwarz of the 2nd Illinois Artillery, McClernand's onetime chief-of-staff), who believed that "a mysterious combination of circumstances which could not all be *fortuitous*," and which doubtless reflected "the combined machinations and conspiracy of Gens. Grant and Halleck," had worked to deprive McClernand "of the original command which had been expressly conferred upon him by the President and Mr. Stanton."

With all the tactfulness and compassion that Lincoln could muster for a fellow townsman, the President at last faced the crisis that McClernand forced upon him: ". . . It is a case, as appears to me, in which I could do nothing without doing harm." If he were to "magnify the breach" between Grant and McClernand, Lincoln said, that act "could not but be of evil effect." Leave the issue, the President advised, "where the law of the case has placed it. . . . This is now your case, which, as I have before said, pains me, not less than it does you."

McClernand reacted badly; if his official biographer reflected his judgment, the President and Stanton revealed "a yielding weakness which was highly censorable if it is not actually criminal."

Throughout all these days of travail, McClernand could be certain of one fact. No tears were shed by Grant.

18. A SADISTIC WIDOW

To A friend who asked how the siege of Vicksburg was progressing, Lincoln replied: "We are pegging away, and shall continue to peg away until our work is done."

Editorially, in mid-June, *Harper's Weekly* eulogized "The Western Boys":

> . . . They stand beside the river which is their river. They fight not only for the great and general cause of the Government and of civil order which inspires all our troops, but they strike for a palpable, present object, the control of the river, which is the life-current of their prosperity, which is the natural highway to the sea of ten millions of free men between the Alleghenies and the Rocky Mountains, the vast central basin of the continent, the valley of the imperishable empire.

Part Three: CITY OF CAVES

Perhaps in less florid prose, but surely with greater prescience, Cavalryman Francis W. Tupper could understand why the situation remained obscure for anyone not on the scene at Vicksburg. The reason, Tupper asserted, rested with the reporters, who "stay mostly on the boats at the landings, eight or ten miles off" and "fill a whole column and have it headed with large type about something no one here would cross the road to see." These journalists, Tupper commented cynically, would send "any report they may hear without ascertaining whether it is true or not," and that was why "Vicksburg and other places come to be captured so often." However, studying a sketch in *Frank Leslie's Illustrated Weekly* of the manner in which "the Secesh ladies make their appearance at our office to get an order on the commissary for rations," the cavalryman must admit that the drawing was "a facsimile of the scene." Tupper wrote his parents:

. . . When we came here we had nothing to eat and the soldiers ate up everything the folks had for ten miles around. They are now of necessity compelled to come here and ask for something to live upon, and they have also discovered that they have the best success when the youngest and best-looking one in the family comes to plead their case, and they have some very handsome women here. They were well educated and were rich before their niggers ran away. If I was to meet them in Illinois I should think that they were born and brought up there. . . .

The Negroes who "ran away" brought Grant one of his most difficult problems. From the moment the General approached Vicksburg, the contrabands "came swarming into our lines by hundreds." Cadwallader's pen captured the picture they made:

. . . They were of all ages, sexes, and conditions; and came on foot, on horses and mules, and in all manner of vehicles, from the typical Southern cart to elegant state carriages and barouches. Straw collars and rope harness alternated with silver plate equipments, till the moving, living panorama became ludicrous beyond description. The runaway darkies who had made sudden and forcible requisition upon their old masters for these varied means of transportation generally loaded their wagons and carriages with the finest furniture left in the mansions when their owner had abandoned them. . . . Feather beds and tapestried upholstery seemed to possess a peculiar charm and value to the dusky runaways. . . .

Existence at Grant's headquarters was made more congenial by the body servants staff officers appropriated from among the contrabands. Rawlins's boy, Jerry, was a lad of fourteen who remained with Rawlins after the war, received "quite a fair education," and, Cadwallader added, Rawlins "had no more sincere mourner at his funeral than this faithful black boy Jerry."

But Duff drew the prize; Grant's chief of artillery had a knack for coming off with the best, whether the stakes were contrabands or Oglesby's barrel of whisky. Duff's colored boy was Willis, who stayed with the officer until the end of his army service at City Point, Virginia, attached himself afterward for a time to Cadwallader, and then, during a visit of Grand Duke Alexis's retinue to the United States, captured the fancy of Count Saldatankoff. "Dat Count Saldat'nkoff," Willis said, "was a mitey nice man." Willis accompanied the Count on his return to Russia, but presently grew homesick and pined to see "his 'Ole Mammy' in Arkansas." And so Willis reappeared in New York "as a full-fledged marine on a Russian war vessel," secured a three-month furlough to visit his Mammy, and "is presumably a loyal subject of the Czar, as I write this [1894]."

In contrast to Jerry and Willis, a Negro named Gordon, who, the story ran, had escaped from a Mississippi plantation and found his way into the Federal lines at Baton Rouge, inflamed Yankee tempers when he arrived at Vicksburg. Davis made several sketches of Gordon for *Harper's Weekly*, based on photographs supplied by McPherson. First Gordon was depicted in the ragged condition in which he had been found "covered with mud and dirt from his long race through the swamps and bayous"; then with back stripped to show the brutal welts remaining there from "a whipping administered on Christmas Day last"; and finally in the natty attire of the U.S. Army. Stories were told of Gordon's intelligence in rubbing himself with onions after crossing each creek to throw the bloodhounds off his scent. The evidence given of the "cruelties" Gordon had suffered—captured at one time by the Rebels, the Negro claimed that he was tied to a tree, beaten, and left for dead—not only found ready retelling in the Union trenches before Vicksburg but also set off a chain of Negro atrocity stories in Northern journals.

For sheer sadism, one tale outstripped all the others, and seemed, in a sense, to belong to the miasmic swamp fogs, the steaming bayou shores, the hot, quivering night darkness of the Vicksburg countryside. From "Mrs. Gillespie's estate on the Black River" came the stories told by "refugees" of floggings with leather straps, of "paddling the body with a handsaw until the skin is a mass of blisters," of burning with dry cornhusk brands. Slaves who ran away from the Gillespie plantation, one correspondent wrote to the *New York Times*, were stripped naked, placed in a hole squatting or lying down, and then covered with a "grating" of green sticks. "Upon this," the account continued, "a quick fire is built, and the live embers sifted through upon the naked flesh of the slave until his body is blistered and swollen almost to bursting. With just enough life to enable him to crawl, the slave is then allowed to recover from his wounds if he can, or to end his suffering by death."

For those not too squeamish to read on, additional evidence of the inhuman practices of the "Widow Gillespie" was provided. In one instance, when a young Negro mother failed to wean her baby as promptly as Mrs. Gillespie ordered, the widow, it was alleged, attempted to pluck off the nipples of the offending breasts with a pair of hot tongs. "The writhing of the mother," the correspondent said, "foiled her purpose." On another occasion a slave girl who dissatisfied the widow was stripped and bound to a table and—the italics belong to the correspondent—a heated poker "was applied to *the most tender part of her body.*" Quoting from several "refugees" interviewed, the account in the *New York Times* concluded: "It was a very common thing to see a slave carried by force to the bedroom or shed-room of Madame, for punishment. She would order him to undress, and with her own hands apply the lash until she became exhausted."

A dispassionate reader might have questioned Widow Gillespie's treatment of property as valuable as a slave. Frederick Law Olmsted's work *The Cotton Kingdom*, appearing the year before, had emphasized how Southerners often indulged their Negroes, even to the extent of hiring Irish day labor for work judged too hazardous to risk the limbs or life of the slave. Yet, appending a footnote to a later chapter of *The Cotton Kingdom*, and after visiting some of the larger plantations in central Mississippi, Olmsted asked: "How can men retain the most essential quality of true manhood who daily, without remonstrance or interference, see men beaten, whose position renders effective resistance totally impracticable—and not only men, but women, too!" In Olmsted's estimation, of all the influences of slavery, such behavior was "as baneful to us nationally as any other"; and he cited the case of two Southern white men he witnessed fighting a duel: when a shot felled one, the other "drew a bowie knife and deliberately butchered him" without objection from the bystanders.

At Vicksburg the stories of Gordon and the Widow Gillespie undoubtedly received credence. They were tales to tell and retell as Grant's boys sweated in the ditches, tired of waiting and digging. The Yankees now could best be described, one observer thought, as "an army without tents." Hillsides, protected from enemy fire, were used for encampments. "A place was dug against the hill," Wilbur Crummer said, "and in many cases, into it, forming a sort of cave. Poles were put up and covered with oil cloths, blankets, or cane rods, of which an abundant supply was near at hand. For fuel, the farm fences were laid under contribution."

Lieutenant Cyrus E. Dickey wrote his sister: "This is a queer phase of war to us all. . . . The excitement . . . has worn away, and we have settled down to our work as quietly and as regularly as if we were hoeing corn or drawing bills in chancery." On the terraced slopes around Dickey's shelter were the caves dug by comrades in the XVII Corps. "The timid boys who have not dug caves for themselves try to buy out others who have dug their holes," Dickey said. Tonight, however, "since the line has become quiet," business was not very brisk. Captain Henry S. Nourse of the 55th Illinois related an incident of the picket line:

. . . A Mississippian one night inquired for the whereabouts of the 54th Ohio, and being told that the 54th men were our particular friends and near neighbors, asked that Sergeant —— of that regiment, if alive, might be notified to come to the picket line at a certain hour the next night, where he would recover something of great value to him. The sergeant was found, and, appearing as requested, received from the

Southerner a letter enclosing the likeness of his sweet-heart, which he had somehow lost during the Battle of Shiloh. . . .

Thus the days and nights dragged on, while, in Crummer's phrase, the "work of slaughter and destruction" continued. Along the river every breeze carried the echo of cannon and musketry. No matter how dismal life in the ditches became to the Yankees, even a phlegmatic imagination could conceive of how much worse it must be inside the "prairie dog's village."

19. "RATS AND OTHER SMALL DEER"

MID-JUNE. Hunger crept silently up the hills and into the caves of Vicksburg, stretching tight the flesh over the ribs of children, signaling its persistent threat in an infant's pitiful whimper, driving hard-eyed mothers, like Mrs. Lord and Mrs. Loughborough, to the canebrakes below the city for tender sprouts to cook in the hope that this pallid concoction might provide a soothing taste if not much nourishment.

"How these people subsisted was another wonder," Edward S. Gregory declared. After the tenth day of siege, the Confederate fighting-man lived on half-rations, which, Mrs. Loughborough reported, "many of them ate all at once and the next day fasted, preferring, as they said, to have one good meal." But the ragged Reb soldier with his quarter-pound of bacon, his half-pound of beef, his five-eighths quart of meal, his allowance of peas, rice, sugar, and molasses (while such provisions existed), was better off than the civilians. Certainly they must have had less, Gregory thought, "and where they got that from was a mystery." One night across the picket line a Confederate threw Wilbur Crummer a note:

> We are pretty hungry and dreadful dry. Old Pemberton has taken all the whisky for the hospitals and our Southern Confederacy is so small just now we are not in the manufacturing business. Give our compliments to Gen. Grant and say to him that grub would be acceptable, but we will feel under particular obligations if he will send us a few bottles of good whisky.

Bread, however, was the staple that haunted the woman in the cave. As long as cornmeal lasted, it could be mixed with ground field peas and, after a fashion, baked into what might be called bread. When the cornmeal disappeared, rice was ground for a substitute. Tree buds simmered in a little water gave a bit of flavor on the side. Again, imagination helped.

Like a grim horseman riding beside hunger through the wretched streets of Vicksburg emerged the extortioner—a symbolic figure to Gregory, fulfilling "the prophecy of Jerusalem's undoing." The *Vicksburg Daily Citizen* reported flour selling at five dollars a pound, molasses at ten dollars a gallon, corn at ten dollars a bushel. An outraged editor wrote bristling sentences:

> If aught would appeal to the heart of stone of the extortioner with success, the present necessities of our citizens would do so. It is needless to attempt to disguise from the enemy of our people that our wants are great. . . . We are satisfied that there are numerous persons within our city who have bread secreted, and are doling it out, at exorbitant prices, to those who had not the foresight or means at their command to provide for the exigencies now upon us. . . . We have not as yet proved the facts upon the parties accused, but this illusion may induce some of our citizens

to ascertain whether such prices have been paid, and to whom; and if so, may a brand not only be placed upon their brow, but seared into their very brains, that humanity may scorn and shun them as they would the portals of hell.

Worse than such charges, Gregory thought, were "the two later facts—that nobody had the money and then nobody had the flour."

Early in the siege General M. L. Smith sent a circular to his brigade, suggesting that "the experiment of horse meat be tried to piece out supplies." At one of the regimental headquarters Gregory saw some of the Rebs "cutting a steak out of a horse that had been shot that day beneath them. All tasted a little—most, a very little—and found that the flesh was coarse." Nobody hungered for any more, except some Louisianians, who, being French, were likely to enjoy anything, "not to speak of rats and other small deer" which they were reputed "to prepare in many elegant styles for the table." Upon another occasion Gregory found that Pemberton "had half a dozen fellows, men who looked like Mexicans or Indians, cutting mule meat at the old depot of the Southern Railroad, and jerking it over slow fires to make it handy and ready. One morning, for trial, I bought a pound of mule meat at this market, and had it served at breakfast for the mess. There was no need to try again."

Not until July did Major George S. Gillespie, chief of subsistence at Vicksburg, release his order: "The issue of meat tomorrow will be one half ($\frac{1}{2}$) pound of mule to the ration. Please report to me the am[oun]t you require for your command so that I may have it prepared." The commissary officer of Moore's brigade believed that 5,106 pounds of mule would serve his men very nicely. After two meals, the officer felt that mule was "passable"; a Texan who joined him still preferred beef-pie.

Louisiana rum, "the poison that once had been so abundant," had disappeared from the city; and the cistern water upon which the inhabitants in their "troglodyte existence" slaked their thirst seemed no healthier. Confederate reports characterized the water as "muddy and warm" and ascribed to it "many of the disorders which prevailed with effects so fatal." A little ice might have made it more palatable, but no one in Vicksburg had seen a lump of ice for weeks. Even back in February the woman who insisted on going down in history as "a young lady of New Orleans" recorded that an "egg is a rare and precious thing." Now, in June, she could at least be grateful for one advantage; she heard of "others dipping up water from the ditches and mudholes," whereas the cellar in which she lived contained two large underground cisterns of clean, cool water, "and every night in my subterranean dressing-room a tub of cold water is the nerve-calmer that sends me to sleep in spite of the roar."

Otherwise the young lady from New Orleans lived only for the comfort of reading the *Daily Citizen.* On June 13 her diary described the *Citizen* as "a foot and a half long and six inches wide"; editorially, the paper exhorted: "The undaunted Johnston is at hand." On the eighteenth the *Citizen* was "printed on wallpaper" and "therefore has grown a little in size"; again it spoke hopefully: "But a few days more and Johnston will be here."

June 20 found a cry ringing through the shattered streets of Vicksburg: "It's going to be a very bad day today!" The young lady from New Orleans feared that want of good food was breaking down H——; "I know from my own feelings of weakness," she added, "and mine is not an American constitution." Then on the twenty-first of June:

. . . I had gone upstairs today during the interregnum to enjoy a rest on my bed and read the reliable items in the *Citizen* when a shell burst right beside the window in front of me. Pieces flew in, striking all around me, tearing down masses of plaster that came tumbling over me. When H——— rushed in I was crawling out of the plaster, digging it out of my eyes and hair. When he picked up a piece large as a saucer beside my pillow, I realized my narrow escape. The window frame began to smoke, and we saw the house was on fire. H——— ran for a hatchet, and we put it out. Another [shell] came crashing near, and I snatched up my comb and brush and ran down here [to the cellar]. It has taken all afternoon to get the plaster out of my hair, for my hands were rather shaky.

A few days later a piece of bursting shell "tore open the leg of H———'s pantaloons." Shells struck the quarters of the *Daily Citizen*, scattered the type, and splintered the floor, but three issues were afterward published. The Baptist Church crumbled, the libraries of the Episcopalian and Presbyterian clergymen were "badly worsted." Benjamin D. Lay, surgeon-in-charge of the city hospital, reported sadly that on June 10 shells blew up the surgeon's room and destroyed "the entire stock of drugs, except some morphine and quinine." Fire from the Yankee mortars "blew three rooms into one"; a surgeon's leg had to be amputated immediately. Cheerlessly Lay decided that to remove the hospital now "would cause more deaths than the enemy's shells" and must be reckoned "almost certain death" for at least twenty patients. With a new outfit of drugs "and the use of a carpenter and brickmason for a couple of days," Lay decided that he could make out.

A symbol of Vicksburg's cruel and bitter plight Mrs. Loughborough found in another quarter:

One evening I noticed one of the horses tied in the ravine writhing and struggling in pain. He had been very badly wounded in the flank by a Minié ball. The poor creature's agony was dreadful: he would reach his head up as far as possible into the tree to which he was tied, and cling with his mouth, while his neck and body quivered with pain. Every motion, instead of being violent as most horses' would have been when wounded, had a stately grace of eloquent suffering that is indescribable. How I wanted to go to him and pat and soothe him! His halter was taken off and he was turned free. He went to a tree, leaned his body against it, and moaned, with half-closed eyes, shivering frequently throughout his huge body as if the pain were too great to bear.

Then he would turn his head entirely around and gaze at the group of soldiers that stood pityingly near, as if he were looking for human sympathy. The master refused to have him shot, hoping he would recover, but the noble black was doomed. Becoming restless with pain, the poor brute staggered blindly on. My eyes filled with tears, for he fell with a weary moan, the bright intelligent eyes turned still on the men who had been his comrades in many a battle.

Mrs. Loughborough saw an ax handed to a bystander "and suddenly turned away from the scene."

With destruction, hunger, exposure, death, Gregory thought the great mystery was why "many did not become insane."

2.

Yet morale within the invested city held up, perhaps with credit to no one more than to Colonel Edward Higgins, who commanded the Confederate river batteries. Thirty-one pieces of heavy artillery and thirteen pieces of light artillery strung along three miles of Vicksburg bluffs Higgins could list from memory—the eight ten-inch Columbiads, the eight "banded and unbanded thirty-two-pounder rifles," the single Dahlgren and Blakely gun (which burst at the muzzle on the twenty-second of May), the Whitworth and twenty-pound Parrott, the three smoothbore forty-two-pounders and two smooth bore thirty-two-pounders, the eight-inch siege howitzer, the ten-inch mortar. Colonel Andrew Jackson, Jr., of the 1st Tennessee Artillery commanded the upper batteries, from Fort Hill to the upper bayous; the center batteries in front of the city were under Major F. M. Ogden of the Louisiana Artillery Battalion; and the lower batteries were held by the 1st Louisiana Artillery under Lieutenant Colonel D. Beltzhoover. In the official reports, however, the greatest "labors and dangers" of the siege fell to young Andy Jackson.

After the assaults on the twenty-second of May, Pemberton fretted over his defenses in the rear of Vicksburg and ordered eleven of the light pieces withdrawn from the river front. For four days thereafter Yankee mortars pounded the city, and Pemberton called the eight-inch siege howitzer, the smoothbore thirty-two-pounder, the twenty-pound Parrott, and the Whitworth to the forts facing Grant's lines. Thus depleted, on the twenty-seventh of May, Higgins' river defenses faced a severe test. Down the Mississippi, approaching Andrew Jackson's 1st Tennessee Artillery in the upper batteries, sailed the Yankee gunboat *Cincinnati,* mounting fourteen guns.

That constant worrier Sherman had provoked the action. His fidgetiness always erupted finally. Grant could drink, shake off his hangover and cares with the same motion, but not Sherman! He had to write most, if not all, of his own dispatches, Byers said; he left his staff "little or nothing to do." Demons of unrest seemed forever nibbling at him, so that "he was last in bed at night, first in the saddle in the morning." When the guns from Jackson's upper battery prevented him from extending his right flank, Sherman decided that the Confederates had switched eleven guns from the river to the land side. Actually the guns had been lowered from their carriages to avoid naval fire. But an idea fixed in Sherman's head was tantamount to a demand that something be done about it. Somewhat prissily, Admiral Porter commented: "It being a rule with the navy never to refuse a request from the army, the *Cincinnati* was prepared for the adventure."

Western boys were proud of the *Cincinnati*, for she was Western-river built, with two-and-a-half-inch plating forward extending to about amidships. Unhappily, the after part was unprotected, a circumstance that young Andy Jackson found greatly to his liking. Jackson opened with rifled and smoothbore guns, pouring in eight- and ten-inch shot that plunged into the gunboat's magazine, tore through her bottom, ripped away the bulwarks of hay and logs, and knocked dead her pilot. Lieutenant George M. Bache, the *Cincinnati*'s square-jawed commander, refused to haul down her flag when the pole was shot away, "but nailed it to the stump." Jackson raked the gunboat with grape, compelling her to close her bow portholes; Bache swung her stern toward the battery, hoping to escape this devastation. But Bache was done. Filling rapidly with water, her casualties numbering twenty in killed and wounded, the *Cincinnati* tried to limp downstream. She sank finally, about twenty-five yards from the bank, in three fathoms of water, drowning another fifteen men. "She was a complete wreck," reported Captain James W. Barclay of the 1st Missouri Cavalry, who inspected her afterward, "the shots from our batteries having completely riddled her." Higgins felt elated; not only did the engagement result in "the complete repulse of the enemy," but many Yankees also were "killed in the portholes by our sharpshooters." Higgins had added "to the garland of Vicksburg's victories another bright chaplet," extolled an appreciative Pemberton. The repulse of the *Cincinnati* proved rather a secondhand triumph. Under cover of night, when the river fell, Sherman stripped the boat of her guns and used them to improvise a battery. To Porter, who never really believed that he lost under any conditions, this act "finally accomplished what the *Cincinnati* had not time to do."

For Higgins, disaster followed swiftly. On June 1 fire swept the magazine of the center battery, and any man who could be spared from the guns ran ammunition to safety. Then for a week the Yankees turned "an incessant fire from the mortar flats on the city and batteries." Again fretful, Pemberton withdrew two more field pieces to the rear. Federal sharpshooters, slipping across to the Louisiana shore, bothered Higgins until one of Major Ogden's light field pieces drove them off; but now the Yanks placed a ten-inch gun a mile or so above the river bend and, supported by the mortars and a brisk fire from the gunboats, smashed away at the upper batteries. Just when the river defenses were having trouble no matter where they turned, Pemberton decided that Higgins's ten-inch mortar had better be shifted to the rear.

Meanwhile Grant anchored a thirty-pound Parrott next to the ten-inch gun above the river bend and placed several mortars some five hundred yards nearer the upper batteries. Higgins could claim now that his boys along the bluffs were fairly busy, for in addition to manning the guns they served as city guards, firemen, river police, and almost nightly "reliefs were . . . under arms as infantry in the trenches." Even the unvarnished prose of Higgins's official report could not disguise the lively action along the river front:

[June 17, 18, 19] . . . The guns on the Louisiana shore fired very rapidly in the morning and evening. Our batteries replied slowly.

[June 21] . . . The enemy mounted a 100-pounder Parrott gun on the Louisiana shore, under the bank of the river, at a point about 500 yards above the mortar boats. It opened upon the city during the evening, doing a great deal of damage. [This was the day when the estimate of Yankee shells falling on Vicksburg reached 150,000.]

[June 22–27] . . . Firing from the guns on the Louisiana shore was kept up on the city and batteries with great vigor. Our guns replied slowly and with deliberation, but in consequence of the timber on the Louisiana shore affording ample means of masking batteries, it was difficult to arrive at any satisfactory results.

On the twenty-eighth the ten-inch Brooks gun in the upper battery "burst one of the bands and also at the breech." But this was the sort of calamity Higgins had learned to expect now; and in the midst of the disaster the Yankees let loose again with the one-hundred-pound Parrott.

3.

In a sentimental mood, Gregory spoke of "the heroic texture of the beleaguered population"; then, realistically, he faced the truth: "Powerless to resist the tide of events, their only refuge is indulgence of a desperate hope, whose alternative is despair and madness." Johnston would come to the city's relief—this was the "desperate hope"! Mrs. W. W. Lord told of a Sunday at the height of the bombardment when "a St. Louis man . . . named Bob Lomar" reached Vicksburg "dressed as a fisherman with his skiff full of leaves." Mrs. Lord thought him "a most daring man." He had brought, he said, dispatches from Johnston to Pemberton.

Under close questioning, however, Lomar grew evasive, then said, to forestall further inquiry: "My [life] hangs, don't for fear you make me break my word. I can only tell

you that in three or four days you will have the biggest
kind of cannonade and see the forces which are already in
the line in your rear."

Mrs. Lord believed Lomar, and a courier, "only three
days from Gen. Johnston," arriving that same Sunday
strengthened her conviction. "We are all in the highest
spirits . . . [although] no more came from him than
hope." Afterward skeptical minds asked whether Lomar
"may be in the employ of both sides and take the same
information to the enemy." Mrs. Lord refused to credit
such charges; Lomar had "looked like a reliable, daring
man." But her journal would hint at suspicion, distrust,
and despair: "Still in this dreary cave. Who would have
believed that we could have borne such a life for five
weeks? The siege has lasted forty-two days and yet no relief—every day this week we have waited for the sound of
Gen. Johnston's guns, but in vain."

20. TWO PIECES OF ADVICE

IN A letter on the seventeenth of May Joe
Johnston had tried to give Pemberton a bit of military
advice:

> . . . If Haines' Bluff is untenable, Vicksburg is of
> no value and cannot be held. If, therefore, you are
> invested in Vicksburg, you must ultimately surrender.
> Under such circumstances, instead of losing both
> troops and the place, we must, if possible, save the
> troops. If it is not too late, evacuate Vicksburg and its
> dependencies, and march to the northeast.

"Evacuate Vicksburg!"
Pemberton, shocked and obstinate, found the letter from

Johnston like a thorn in the flesh of his hand. He summoned his generals around him and asked "the free expression of their opinions" as to the "practicality" of what Johnston suggested. It was unanimously agreed, he stated with satisfaction, that it would be "impossible to withdraw the army from this position with such morale and material as to be of further service to the Confederacy." Pemberton's official report, written in August, contained numerous sentences indicative of the mood he had carried into this council of war: "I believed it to be in my power to hold Vicksburg. . . . I knew, perhaps better than any other individual, under all the circumstances, its capacity for defense. . . . With proper economy of subsistence and ordnance stores I knew that I could stand a siege."

In this spirit, on the eighteenth of May, Pemberton rejected Johnston's advice. And on the next day Grant moved. Within four days two Union assaults had been beaten back, but Grant, securely wedged between the armies of Pemberton and Johnston, had repeated the tactical brilliance by which, earlier in the campaign, he had divided Pemberton and Bragg.

Johnston must have groaned. From the moment Grant's army had crossed the Mississippi at Grand Gulf, and Pemberton no longer could fight from behind the natural obstacles of water, swamp, and forest, Grant, the man of action, at every point had outfought, outfoxed, and overshadowed Pemberton, the man of events. Although Johnston still felt poor in health from wounds he had suffered a year before at Seven Pines, he could see clearly that if Pemberton's judgments had come "five or six weeks earlier" they "might not have seemed unreasonable." Johnston was far from being a fool—"Grant told me," Sherman said, "that he was about the only general on that side whom he feared"—and Pemberton's very obstinacy in falling back into Vicksburg instead of coming out toward Jackson, where Johnston might have joined him more readily, simply revealed once more that there was little of tactical leadership and less of strategic insight in Pemberton.

Now Pemberton desperately needed to be rescued. A dispatch from Pemberton to Johnston, dated the twentieth of May, reflected the change in tone: "At present, our main necessity is musket caps. Can you send them to me by hands of couriers and citizens? An army will be necessary to relieve Vicksburg, and quickly. Will it not be sent?" Next day another letter from Pemberton spoke of Grant's stepped-up sharpshooting and artillery fire, and hinted: "The men credit, and are encouraged by, a report that you are near, with a strong force."

The courier who bore these messages informed Johnston that Pemberton required a million caps. Two hundred thousand caps had been sent, Johnston wrote back; other shipments would be continued as the material arrived. Then Old Joe came to grips with *his* quandary: "Bragg is sending a division. When it comes I will move to you. Which do you think is the best route? How and where is the enemy encamped? What is your force?"

Johnston's reply, taking four days to pass through the lines, reached Pemberton on the twenty-ninth—but the two hundred thousand musket caps had been captured en route. The loss seemed a severe blow. For days Pemberton had been employing any device to get caps—emptying the cartridge boxes of the enemy dead, even floating caps across the river in hollow logs. Wilbur Crummer told of capturing a ten-year-old boy who had endeavored to guide six men, each laden with ten thousand caps, through the swamps around Vicksburg. Cocking one eye, the lad said: "I guess they won't hurt me much, coz I'se so little." But Pemberton lost the caps, and that did hurt.

In other quarters, too, Pemberton had begun to feel the pinch; food rations had been cut in half, and Confederate ordnance officers scurried after unexploded Parrott shells from Union guns so that the shells could be recapped.

Sergeant Osborn Oldroyd testified that eating ground peas and meal "was very unhealthy, as it was almost impossible to bake the mixture thoroughly so that pea flour and meal would be fit for consumption." Still, cheerily, Pemberton wrote to Johnston on the twenty-ninth: "My men are in good spirits, awaiting your arrival."

On the same day, in a much less optimistic mood, Johnston wrote: "I am too weak to save Vicksburg. Can do no more than attempt to save you and your garrison. It will be impossible to extricate you unless you co-operate and we make mutually supporting movements." Anxiety within the city, the mounting number of dead and wounded, the ever increasing weariness that began to show, Oldroyd said, in men "much reduced in flesh," began to wear on Pemberton's nerves. If, as Jefferson Davis once declared, Vicksburg was "the nailhead that held the South's two halves together," the structure of the Confederacy wobbled. Pemberton's letter of June 3 to Johnston was filled with bad news: he could obtain no word of Johnston's position, and very little information concerning Grant's; ten messengers bearing musket caps were reported captured. With a rising note of urgency, Pemberton asked: "In what direction will you move and when? I hope north of the Jackson Road."

June 7—the twenty-first day of the siege—brought dark clouds, a dismal rain, and silence from Johnston. Morale within the city dampened with the weather; four scouts, instructed "to penetrate if possible the enemy's lines," all failed; growlingly, pressure to lift the siege increased. For Pemberton there would be even less cheer in the hedging note that Johnston dispatched that day: "Co-operation is absolutely necessary. Tell us how to effect it, and by what routes."

"I shall endeavor to hold out as long as we have anything to eat," Pemberton replied to Johnston on the tenth. "Can you not send me a verbal message by a courier crossing the river above or below Vicksburg, and swimming across again opposite Vicksburg?"

Grant's noose around the neck of Pemberton drew tighter. Reports from all sectors of the line revealed how close the Union sap-rollers were approaching Pemberton's outer fortifications. On the twelfth the Rebel supply of meat had been almost exhausted, reducing Sergeant Oldroyd in time to the necessity of making "a hearty breakfast on fried rats," although he must confess that he "found the flesh very good." On the fifteenth, Pemberton wrote Johnston that without relief he could hold out no longer than twenty days; and on the same day Johnston informed Richmond: "I consider saving Vicksburg hopeless."

The reply that Old Joe received to this dispatch was sharp and immediate. Snapped Secretary of War Seddon: "Your telegram grieves and alarms us. Vicksburg must not be lost, at least without a struggle. The interest and the honor of the Confederacy forbid it. . . . You must hazard an attack. It may be in concert with the garrison, if practicable, but otherwise without. By day or night, as you think best." In Vicksburg, on the nineteenth, Grant's shells fell from three thirty until eight in the morning. Sleepless and disconsolate, Pemberton learned that Grant's sap line had advanced to within twenty-five feet of the Confederate redan on the Graveyard Road, and other saps were coming uncomfortably close on the Jackson and Baldwin's Ferry roads. Once more Pemberton tried to plead with Johnston: "I hope you will advance with the least possible delay. My men have been thirty-four days and nights in trenches, without relief, and the enemy within conversation distance. We are living on very reduced rations, and, as you know, are entirely isolated. What aid am I to expect from you? The bearer, Captain [George D.] Wise, can be confided in."

Earlier, from Seddon, Johnston had received a second dispatch, telling him that "it were better to fail nobly daring than, through prudence even, to be inactive." Old Joe must have wondered if Seddon were writing editorials on the sly for the Richmond newspapers. With the letter from the Secretary of War in his pocket, the "desperate hope" of Vicksburg received Captain Wise.

Once more Johnston fell into an advice-giving mood.

2.

Meanwhile Grant joked with his men. All along the Union lines, good stories were told. Wilbur Crummer's favorite concerned the day when a mess of beans that was to be the dinner for the 45th Illinois had just been lifted from the fire. A piece of shell whirred overhead and crashed through the bottom of the kettle. Two soldiers, still holding the pole in their hands, "looked at each other in disgust," then one turned to the waiting, hungry soldiers. "Boys," he said, "your beans have gone to hell!" Jake Wilkin of the 130th Illinois, who recalled Grant at Vicksburg as "a stern man, at times a melancholy one," remembered an occasion when this description was not quite appropriate:

> . . . A member of the company discovered a bee tree near the camp and the boys obtained permission to cut it down. When it fell, it broke near the place where the bees had deposited their honey, but they were so hostile it was impossible to get the tempting treasure. The men took their camp kettles, and with torches marched in. But the bees as often charged and drove them back. . . . Finally a bald-headed, ill-tempered, quarrelsome, profane fellow swore that he was going to have that honey anyhow. And he ventured in with his cap pulled over his head and face, and in spite of being stung, began to dig out the honey. The bees peppered him on the hands and face

until finally he could stand it no longer and, dropping his spoon, began to strike right and left, first with his hands, but at last he jerked off his hat, jumped up and down, and swore profusely. The bees, of course . . . began to strike the top of his bald head.

"I don't think," Wilkin concluded, "Grant ever saw that soldier afterward that he did not smile."

The Mississippi countryside provided compensations that made more bearable the blistering sun, the myriad insects, the one shirt that often became "more like a necklace than a shirt." June brought an abundance of blackberries, peaches were ripening, figs were almost ready to pick. General Orme told his wife in a cheerful spirit: "We have young chickens frequently &, what is more, we have milk for our coffee & milk to drink." Orme, however, was a newcomer to Vicksburg and Grant could have apprised him that many of the soldiers "had lived so much on chickens, ducks, and turkey . . . the sight of poultry, if they could get bacon, almost took away their appetite." Even though Corporal William Camm of the 46th Illinois felt that his commanders were "a set of old grandmothers," the sparse entries in Camm's diary could not conceal a sense of wonderment: "I saw Spanish moss growing on the trees for the first time today. They were hanging heavy with it." Or: "My headquarters are made of a magnolia tree."

Visitors swarming into Vicksburg supplied another divertisement. Agents of the Sanitary and Christian Commission, according to Cadwallader, brought "immense quantities" of food, clothing, and hospital supplies, and "governors of the state vied with the humblest citizens in expressions of gratitude and contributions to the comfort and welfare of the men at the front." From Chicago came "something unheard of before"—the Lombard brothers, Julius and Frank, who had "acquired more than merely local fame in concert singing." All headquarters and hospitals were visited by the Lombards, and "the lines at camp were made vocal at night for several weeks" with "uproarious encoring and applauding." Patriotic and sentimental songs were favorites; Cadwallader considered them "excellently—exquisitely—rendered." Comic songs drew a fair share of requests, but the ballads and home songs were the true comforters to the "thousands on thousands" who were "alternately convulsed with weeping and laughter." The Lombard brothers, Cadwallader believed, brought "many a poor homesick private . . . healthy sentiments and inspirations in place of morbid, unhealthy ones."

But Grant, who possessed little ear for music—he knew only two tunes, Grant said, and one was "Yankee Doodle" and the other wasn't—felt more cheered by the progress of the night diggers behind their sap-rollers. In the air was a sense of impending climax that all felt. In such moments, when the pulsebeat at headquarters seemed to quicken, Rawlins grew more relaxed. Grant's orders were clear, brisk, pointed; he expressed himself in writing with a flow that went with his need for movement, his love for action; and there was small prospect of finding the General "where the wine bottle has just been emptied." Not only to the members of the staff at headquarters, not only to Sherman and McPherson and Logan, but also to the man in the trenches was the emergence of Grant during the Vicksburg campaign comprehensible. The sight of Grant standing quietly—"stolid he stood—erect; about five feet eight, with square features, thin closed lips, brown hair, brown beard, both cut short and neat"—made S. H. M. Byers believe he appreciated the sort of man he fought under:

> . . . There was no McClellan, begging the boys to allow him to light his cigar by theirs, or inquiring to what regiment that exceedingly fine-marching com-

pany belonged to. There was no Pope, bullying the
men for not marching faster, or officers for some trivial
detail remembered only by martinets. There was no
Bonaparte, posturing for effect; no pointing to the
Pyramids, no calling the centuries to witness. There
was no nonsense, no sentiment; only a plain businessman of the republic. . . .

Some called Grant a born soldier; to Byers he "was nothing of the kind." Rather, "he was simply a man of correct
methods and a fixed will." Under other circumstances he
might have been called "a born railway director, or a
born anything to which he had once in good earnest turned
his hand."

The feeling of the impending climax lingered. Cavalryman Tupper explained to his parents how a fort was approached: "A deep ditch is dug up to their ditch just outside the works; then [we] dig through or under this and
then under the fort; the drift is usually 3½ feet high by 2
or 2½ feet wide, and when [we] cut in [we] have an iron
rod 5 or 6 feet long with which [we] test the ground around
[us] to see that [we] are not approaching any countermines
of the enemy. Countermines are sometimes dug, and . . .
the work of the besieging party has to be abandoned." The
work of ditching, Davis reported to *Harper's Weekly*, went
on in temperatures that seemed "to give color to the story
of the maternal African who, having left one of her progeny
on the sunny side of a convenient sandhill, found it necessary to gather the melting 'Pick' in a washtub."

The diggers labored in reliefs, each for an hour at a
time. Major Andrew Hickenlooper drew the picture they
made: "two picking, two shoveling, and two handing back
the grain sacks filled with earth." Through a reddish clay
of "remarkable tenacity, easily cut and requiring but little
bracing," the main gallery was carried in forty-five feet,
with other galleries opening off at either end at a forty-

five-degree angle for a distance of fifteen feet. To protect the diggers when Yankee sharpshooters were unable to reach the Confederates by direct firing and Yankee artillerymen found it impossible "to gauge their shells so as to cause the explosion immediately behind the Confederate parapets," the Coehorn mortar was created from short sections of gum trees "bored out and hooped with iron bands." Here, Hickenlooper testified, was a most serviceable weapon when the sap reached the vicinity of the parapet. These "novel engines of warfare," accurately charged "with just sufficient powder," could lift six- or twelve-pound shells over the parapet "and drop them immediately behind."

On the twenty-second of June, Grant believed that Johnston had crossed the Big Black and moved to attack. Grant hustled down to the trenches on the Jackson road where his line faced the brigade of the Confederate Ransom. The lines here ran so close, Grant recalled in later years, that the men sometimes "exchanged the hard bread of the Union soldier for the tobacco of the Confederate." But Grant's interest right then was in how soon the hill where Ransom lodged could be mined and charged.

3.

During these days Captain George Wise, traveling as Pemberton's courier, headed for Johnston's headquarters. Wise reached there on the twenty-seventh. Old Joe gave the captain some succinct advice to carry back to Pemberton:

"Surrender!"

21. "FORT HELL"

THE Secretary of War, grateful for the daily communications from Dana evaluating the progress of the siege, wrote: "I cannot thank you as much as I feel for the service you are rendering. You have been appointed an assistant adjutant-general, with rank of major."

But even with this new authority, Dana found it difficult, in the closing days of June, to give Stanton a clear understanding of the movements of Joe Johnston. On June 22 Dana felt that "Joe Johnston's plan is at last developed"; the Confederate had begun to throw his army across the Big Black, and Sherman with thirty thousand troops had moved forth "to settle the question." Obviously Johnston must approach along the Benton or Jackson road, which, for the greater part, "winds along very narrow and precipitous ridges, heavily wooded, where a column cannot deploy." Here Sherman intended to force a fight. On the twenty-third Dana assured Stanton that additional information "confirms my former reports"; Johnston's forces were "now all the other side of Big Black," and "an intelligent spy" estimated the strength of the Confederate army at three divisions "with one battery only to each."

Dana lacked confidence in this intelligence, confessing that "the whole operation is a puzzle here." In another day the situation seemed changed: "The report that Joe Johnston has crossed Big Black, or was crossing, was erroneous. Sherman can find no trace of him." But on the twenty-fifth Dana believed again that the news of Johnston's movements was "authentic"; the Confederate operated somewhere between Canton, Bolton, and Bridgeport with "thirty-five thousand as about the limit of total troops" and with "no new reinforcements from Bragg . . . as far as we are informed."

On the twenty-fifth Grant felt ready to exert the pressure

under which Vicksburg must capitulate. That was the way with Grant, Sherman said—"he don't care a damn for what the enemy does out of his sight, but it scares me like hell!" So Grant left Johnston to Sherman while his own steady eyes and half-chewed cigar pointed straight ahead toward Pemberton within his Gibraltar of the Mississippi. Deserters coming into the Union lines had increased in numbers, supporting Grant's hunch that the right succession of blows now would enable him once more to defeat the Rebels in detail. All the Confederate deserters, said Captain Henry S. Nourse of the 55th Illinois Infantry Volunteers, "told the same tale of being worn out with sleeplessness and fatigue; of hospitals crowded with sick and wounded; of women and children slain in the city by fragments of shells." Before Johnston struck, before in a last rash effort Pemberton attempted to cut his way out of the beleaguered city, before relief in any form might reach the weary dwellers who still retreated "like woodchucks into their burrows" among the clay hills of Vicksburg, Grant sensed the moment to move.

Perhaps buoyed by Grant's confidence and good spirits, Dana sketched for Stanton the situation before Vicksburg that morning. On Sherman's front, "everything is advancing favorably"; McPherson "has a mine, with three trenches extending thirty-five feet under the great fort in his front, which is now being tapped, and will probably be exploded before my next dispatch"; Ord, tightening McClernand's loose command, had widened and connected trenches, "making it practicable to move men and artillery through them." On the extreme left, Herron continued "to press on with zeal" and the last Rebel rifle pits had been captured the previous evening; along the river front, Porter hammered the city from a battery of three rifled guns and four smoothbores.

Misty, hot, winged with insects, morning crept deeper into the valley of the Mississippi. Awake early, Grant rode down the lines, looking for Major Andrew Hickenlooper. On a bluff 250 feet above the water, Grant glimpsed the towering bulk of Fort Hill. Five flags had flown over this spot—French, Spanish, English, American, and Confederate—for this hill had guarded the great river's bend since the first occupation by the white man. Here the first settlement of Vicksburg had been planted; here the first printing-press in Mississippi had been established; here, on the twenty-seventh of May, Rebel guns had supported the river batteries in sinking the *Cincinnati*. As a military outpost for the Spanish, the hill had born the name of Fort Nogales; by nightfall Grant's boys had renamed it "Fort Hell."

Hickenlooper began the morning in an apologetic frame of mind. Digging under Fort Hill the night before, his men had been frightened by the noise of an exploding Confederate countermine, had fled, and had not come back. He would have "them rush it ahead this a.m.," Hickenlooper reported to Grant. Already on hand was twenty-two hundred pounds of powder supplied by the navy—eight hundred pounds to go under the main gallery and seven hundred pounds to go under each of the two lateral galleries. The navy also had delivered fuses to lay down in double strands from each of these three deposits—"to cover the possible contingency," Hickenlooper explained, "of one failing to burn with the desired regularity and speed."

With the waning morning, tension mounted. The Rebel garrison on Fort Hill, alert to the Yankee objective, threw hand grenades and rolled shells with lighted fuses over the parapet into the trenches in front of the fort. The Confederates sank a countermine "in hopes of tapping the gallery," and Hickenlooper's men "could distinctly hear the conversation and orders given" by the Rebel commander. Pluck, sense, speed afoot counted most for the Yankees as, in gunny sacks slung over their shoulders, they lugged forward the powder, twenty-five pounds at a time. Reaching exposed ground, a man paused, judged the interval between the explosion of shells, then dashed ahead. "So well were these movements timed," Hickenlooper said, "that, although it required nearly one hundred trips with the dangerous loads, all were landed in the mine without a single accident."

Grant's order set three o'clock as the hour for blowing up the fort. In the trenches, when noon came, then one o'clock, corps commanders brought up reserves and stood ready. Along twelve miles of investing line, Yankee musketry and artillery poised to cover the assaulting columns. Ten picked men from the pioneer corps were to go first, followed by volunteers from the 23rd Indiana and the 31st and 45th Illinois.

2.

One thirty. Grant and his staff come up to wait. Reporters stand aside in a little group. Davis of *Harper's Weekly* sketches the scene before him. Two o'clock. The sight in front of Vicksburg, Hickenlooper thinks, is "one of the most remarkable ever witnessed. As far as the eye could reach right and left could be seen the long columns of blue moving to their assigned positions behind the besieger's works." Two thirty. For thirty days—by sunlight, in rain, at night—ears have grown accustomed to artillery and musketry in the Yankee lines booming and rattling almost constantly. Now, suddenly, the sound subsides. Hickenlooper feels "a deathlike and oppressive stillness" pervading Grant's whole command. Eyes turn, "riveted" on the huge Confederate redoubt. It is three o'clock.

Grant nods.

To Wilbur Crummer, waiting to charge with the other volunteers from the 45th Illinois, the spectacle becomes awesome: "Huge masses of earth were thrown in the air, and the ground was shaken as by an earthquake. As soon as the earth was rent, a bright glare of fire issued from the

burning powder, but quickly died away." Hickenlooper
sees the fort "gradually breaking into fragments and growing less bulky in appearance until it looked like an immense fountain of finely pulverized earth, mingled with
flashes of fire and clouds of smoke, through which could
occasionally be caught a glimpse of some dark objects—
men, gun carriages, shelters." Moving closer to Grant,
Cadwallader finds "a yawning crater where the mine had
been."

3.

Confederate soldiers, hurled into the air, came down into
the Union lines. Six Rebels, buried under the falling dirt,
were found as skeletons years afterward when the ground
was converted into a cottonfield. A Negro boy named
Abraham fell among the company of the 45th Illinois—
badly frightened, but otherwise unharmed.

"How far did you travel, boy?"

"Don't know, Massa," Abraham answered. " 'Bout free
miles, I guess."

The smoke and dust cleared partly. A command: "Forward!" Under the lead of the chief engineer, the pioneers
plunged ahead. Next out of the trenches charged the 23rd
Indiana, the 31st and 45th Illinois. Where once had stood
the A-shaped fort loomed a hole, perhaps large enough to
hold eighty men. Running up to the crater, Wilbur Crummer found that the Rebs still could fight:

> . . . The enemy had come up from behind the big
> pile of earth thrown out by the explosion, and as we
> went into the crater, they met us with a terrible volley
> of musketry, but on the boys went, up and over the
> embankment with a cheer, the enemy falling back a
> few paces to an inner or second line of breastworks,
> where are placed cannon loaded with grape and

canister, and these cannon belched forth their death-dealing missiles. . . . The line wavers, staggers, then falls back into the crater. The enemy charges on us, but we repel them at the west bank, and a hand-to-hand conflict rages for hours. . . .

Dana described the fighting as "galling." Cavalryman Tupper saw a Rebel colonel [Eugene Erwin] jump up onto the parapet, wave his sword, call on his men to follow. Yankee guns poured fifty-seven bullet holes into him. "Now," Tupper commented cynically, "he ought to have his name spelled wrong in the newspaper and then he would be a hero." But down in the crater Crummer discovered heroes on every side:

> . . . Hand grenades and loaded shells are lighted and thrown over the parapet as you would play ball. . . . A dozen men [are] being killed and wounded at one explosion. [I] wonder that anyone in that hot place is left. . . .

The boys from the 45th Illinois "grab these shells and fling them back." The reporter for the *Chicago Tribune* watched "the colors of the regiment placed on the parapet of the fort . . . literally torn to pieces by the shots of the enemy." Crummer said:

> . . . A cypress log, with portholes cut on the under side, was brought into the crater. . . . A solid shot from a cannon hit the log, hurled it with terrific force against the colonel and his small command. . . . A detail of about two companies hold the crater for two hours or more, their rapid firing causing the rifles to become hot and foul, and the men weary and worn, when two other companies slip in and take their places. . . .

Hour after hour, as the bloody battle "to hold that little piece of ground" continued, Crummer could only think: "What a terrible sacrifice!" Someone had blundered, either Grant or McPherson. Hunger, fatigue, days and nights of constant shelling, had not broken the Rebel fighting spirit. In a rare understatement, Confederate General Louis Hébert reported that the enemy was "promptly met and signally repulsed." Logan, watching one of his wounded men carried away, virtually wept:

"My God! They are killing my bravest men in that hole!"

4.

By ten o'clock next morning Federal casualties at Fort Hill were estimated between sixty and one hundred. "We have made no progress in the work whatever," Dana wrote Stanton, "and have not been able either to plant a battery or open a rifle pit, or even to ascertain what is the real practical value of the fort of which we have just got possession of one corner, and cannot tell whether the adjoining works are not enfiladed against fire from it." Grant's real problem now was preventing the Rebels from concentrating on McPherson's front. Steele, who commanded during Sherman's absence up the Big Black, and Ord were both prodded to press their siege works to give McPherson some respite.

About the only person who seemed to have gained from the mining of Fort Hill was Abraham, the Negro lad who had been blown " 'bout free miles." Davis sketched the grinning Abraham for *Harper's Weekly*, and the Negro, fascinated at seeing his likeness take form on paper, scrutinized the drawing carefully, then cried: "Yah, yah! de Lord, dis chile shore—Massa, give me a quarter." Colonel Coolbaugh of McPherson's staff handed Abraham a silver half-dollar; thereafter, Davis told his readers, "the delighted African . . . made tracks for the Negro quarters near in a style showing that he was but little the worse for his aerial voyage."

But for Grant the afternoon of June 26 simply produced new worries. Dana now informed Stanton that a "spy from Canton," reaching Haines' Bluff, had brought word of thirty-five thousand troops, with Johnston "personally in command," placed under "marching orders." Another ten thousand reinforcements from Bragg were expected by the thirtieth, if not before. The entire force, the spy insisted, would move to fight Sherman next week. The Confederates were reported "zealous" for battle and were well supplied with corn that they had brought by rail from Grenada. Dana considered this information of sufficient seriousness to justify running up to Bear Creek to visit Sherman's headquarters. He was enormously impressed by what he found, and a subsequent dispatch to Stanton spoke of Sherman's "amazing activity and vigilance pervading his whole force." In a country "exceedingly favorable for defense" Sherman had "occupied the commanding points," opened rifle pits wherever advantageous, obstructed main roads and crossroads, and "ascertained every point where the Big Black can be forded between the line of Benton on the north, and the line of railroad on the south." Sherman's shrewd and rapid movements of troops delighted Dana: "By deploying them on all the ridges and open headlands, he produces the impression that his forces are ten times as numerous as they really are."

Obviously Dana's glowing report would not hinder Sherman's military future. Sherman, too, was coming fast—a general of major stature—and Dana recognized that fact. This was not the angry, redheaded man who had stomped out of a White House conference with Lincoln in 1861, shouting at his brother John: "You have got things in one hell of a fix!" This was not the diffident, untested colonel at First Bull Run, when "for the first time in my life I saw cannon balls strike men and crash through the trees . . . and realized the always sickening confusion as one approaches a fight from the rear." This was not the general of the "nervous-sanguine temperament" who had so feared his first command that he had suffered hallucinations and a mental breakdown, and would have been shunted into obscurity except that for political reasons Halleck had decided to give him a second chance. Rather, this was the Sherman who had admired the flair of Grant at Henry and Donelson, who had stood by Grant after Shiloh, and now at Vicksburg was finding a pace, a rhythm. It would take another campaign with Grant in Tennessee before the mold of Sherman would be fully set; and then would come Atlanta, the march to the sea.

But always underneath with Sherman there would remain the trace of the schoolteacher, an affection for this part of his past. So it proved at Vicksburg. Watching, waiting for Johnston, Sherman learned that close to his headquarters lived the Wilkinson family, formerly of New Orleans. Sherman had taught a Wilkinson boy at the academy in Alexandria—could this be his family? Sherman's curiosity drove him to the house. He inquired for Mrs. Wilkinson, and

> . . . an elderly lady answered that she was the person.
> I asked her if she were from Plaquemine Parish,
> Louisiana, and she said she was. I then inquired if
> she had a son who had been a cadet . . . and she
> said yes . . . and . . . he was inside of Vicksburg,
> an artillery lieutenant. I then asked about her husband, whom I had known, when she burst into tears,
> and cried out in agony: "You killed him at Bull Run,
> where he was fighting for his country!" I disclaimed
> killing anybody at Bull Run; but all the women
> present (nearly a dozen) burst into loud lamentations,
> which made it most uncomfortable for me, and I drove
> away.

Forty-eight hours found McPherson still without either batteries or rifle pits on Fort Hill. Rumors spread and persisted that Rebel troops under Price and Kirby Smith intended to seize Milliken's Bend in an effort to provision Vicksburg from that quarter.

On the twenty-eighth of June, Dana could not disguise his irritation at the fact that the siege progressed so sluggishly. A Rebel mine, sprung in front of Steele, "threw the head of his sap into confusion generally." McPherson accomplished nothing, while enemy hand grenades inflicted wounds that were "frightful." The same missiles slowed down Ord; "the brightness of the moonlight" hindered Herron. "The heat of the weather," Dana wrote Stanton in a snappish mood, "the unexpected length of the siege, the absence of any thorough organization of the engineer department, and the general belief of our officers and men that the town must presently fall into our hands without any special effort or sacrifice, all conspire to produce comparative inactivity and inefficiency on our part."

In letters to parents, to wives, to sweethearts, soldiers generally expressed the same wish that possessed Orme: "I should like very much to have them surrender before the 4th of July so that we could have a grand military celebration on that day." Grant enjoyed the derisive taunts Yankee now flung at Reb across the lines: "We are holding you as prisoners of war while you are feeding yourselves." Grant's boys boasted that they would be eating dinner in the city on the Fourth, and the *Vicksburg Daily Citizen* jeered, in reply, that in cooking a rabbit the best recipe was "First ketch your rabbit." Dana questioned deserters, learned that "extreme dissatisfaction exists among the garrison," and he also believed that "the city will be surrendered on Saturday, July 4, if, indeed, it can hold on so long as that." Word reached Vicksburg that the Rebels under Lee had invaded Pennsylvania, although as yet there was no mention of the town of Gettysburg. Grant ended the month of June with what, for him, constituted a rare act—the calling of an informal council of war among his corps commanders. Should he try another assault or wait for the exhausted garrison to collapse? The "council" voted to wait, to Grant's obvious satisfaction. There was still no verified news of Johnston's intentions; Sherman remained poised menacingly at Bear Creek.

At noon on July 1 the thermometer went above one hundred degrees. Inside Vicksburg, deserters said, soldiers were eating mule meat. Dana hinted to Stanton: "If enemy do not give up Vicksburg before sixth instant, it will be stormed on that day." McPherson marked the arrival of the new month by exploding a second mine under Fort Hill. Another six Rebels were blown into Union lines, but, added the realistic Dana, "McPherson has not yet got possession of the fort." Wilbur Crummer told the story of a soldier severely wounded, given up by the medical staff as beyond help, and placed under a tree to die. There a comrade found him, nursed him through the long, painful night, and the soldier survived. This was a story that Wilbur Crummer liked very much, as he was the wounded soldier.

5·

For John C. Pemberton—only his most intimate friends in the Confederate army felt free to call him Jack—July 1 became a day of harsh, bitter reality. In his stocking feet "Old Pem" stood five feet ten and one half inches, a slender man, austere, with proud eyes set in deep sockets, hair "more black than brown," stern, and also "hardy and tough." His grandson would describe him as "quiet rather than untalkative"—and for the boy who had excelled in Latin and Greek and who, at West Point, at least had shared with Grant proficiency in mathematics and horsemanship, there was indication of the man of introspective and mystical depth. His sister would admit: "Never was there so reticent a family as ours." Pemberton was the native Pennsylvanian who had supported the South and whose "poor worried mother" had written her daughter: "I have a great fear now that, so many of the officers knowing John's sentiments, they may take some summary steps with him and dismiss him before he resigns. Of the two cases, that would be the worst. Some think that, after all, there may be no fighting—pray Heaven it may be so."

But there had been fighting—a lot of fighting—and now Pennsylvania-born Lieutenant General Pemberton, C.S.A., waited at headquarters for a verdict. He had abandoned all hope of relief from Johnston. Should he surrender the city or attempt to cut his way out? To each of his divisional commanders, and through them to each of the brigade commanders, he had put the question with characteristic bluntness. Alone, he read their answers.

Major General Carter L. Stevenson, speaking for all but one of his brigade commanders—for Barton, Cumming, Reynolds, but not for Stephen D. Lee—must tell Pemberton: "My men . . . are necessarily much enfeebled, and . . . would be unable to make the march and undergo the fatigues . . . [of] a successful evacuation of this city." Hard-bitten Major General John H. Forney could give his commander no brighter hope: his men were so impaired in physical condition and health "by their long confinement in narrow trenches, without exercise and without relief," that they could not be expected to do more. Brigadier General Louis Hébert, whose Mississippians had repulsed Logan's forces at Fort Hill scarcely a week before, must report, in utter candor, that his men *"could not fight and march ten miles in one day."* Hébert, a man quickly impassioned, wrote:

> . . . Left to their choice to "surrender" or "cut their way out," I have no doubt that a large majority would say "cut out." But the question to my mind is

not between "surrender" and "cutting out"; it is, are my men able to "cut out." My answer is *No!* . . . Most of my brigade are Mississippians, who I am confident will leave the ranks and, throwing away their arms, make their way home the moment we leave our works. So long as they are fighting for Vicksburg they are as true soldiers as the army has, but they will certainly leave us so soon as we leave Vicksburg. If caught without arms by the enemy, they will be no worse off than other prisoners of war. If they succeed in getting home, they will not be brought back to the army for months, and many not at all, as the homes of many are within Federal lines. . . .

The chorus for surrender mounted. The colonels commanding the 37th, 40th, and 42nd Alabama, the 35th and 40th Mississippi, and the 2nd Texas signed the same statement as a group: "Our men are not such as to enable them to make the marches. . . ." With pride, however, Colonel Ashbel Smith spoke later for the 2nd Texas Volunteers: "The men bore with unrepining cheerfulness and undaunted spirit the fatigues of almost continual position under arms, of frequent working parties by night and day, the broiling of the midday sun in summer with no shelter, the chilling night dews, the cramped inaction at all times in the trenches, short rations, at times drenched with rain and bivouacking in mud, together with the discomforts inseparable from their having no change of clothing and an insufficient supply of water for cleanliness, tired, ragged, dirty, barefoot, covered with vermin, with a scanty supply of ammunition, almost hand to hand with the enemy, and beleaguered on every side, with no prospect and little hope of relief . . . it appears to me no commendation of these soldiers can be too great."

But to the end one voice dissented—the voice of Brigadier General Stephen D. Lee, pleading with Pemberton:

I do not think it is time to surrender this post and garrison yet. Nor do I think it practicable to cut our way out. . . .

I still have hopes of Johnston relieving the garrison.

One voice, however, was not enough.

22. "WE HAD CAUGHT OUR RABBIT"

AN EXCHANGE of letters between Grant and Pemberton followed. The Confederate proposed an "armistice for several hours," a meeting of three commissioners on both sides. Grant replied that a conference of commissioners was quite unnecessary; he had no terms beyond "the unconditional surrender of the city and garrison." A personal meeting between the two generals was arranged for three o'clock on the afternoon of July 3—on a hillside in front of McPherson's headquarters, where, Grant said, "near by stood a stunted oak tree." William E. Strong, of Grant's staff, was in the group that assembled promptly at the appointed hour. "The day was hot and sultry," Strong recalled. "The silence was oppressive." At three twenty Pemberton still had not appeared. Grant, clearly annoyed, said nothing.

At last Pemberton arrived in a huffy mood. Dismounting within thirty feet of Grant's party, the Confederate advanced a few paces, then stopped. His face gave no clue that he recognized Grant; he seemed determined that Grant should speak first. "The silence," Strong said, "was extremely embarrassing."

Colonel Montgomery, of Pemberton's staff, who had met Grant the previous evening, introduced the two generals.

They shook hands. Then, in what Strong described as "an insolent and overbearing manner," Pemberton spoke.

"What terms of capitulation do you propose to grant me?"

"Those terms stated in my letter of this morning," Grant answered.

Pemberton grew excited, blustered: "If this is all you have to offer, the conference may as well terminate."

"Very well," Grant said. "I am quite content to have it so." He turned quickly, called for his horse.

General John S. Bowen, who had accompanied Pemberton to the meeting, intervened. Bowen and Grant once had been neighbors in Missouri, and Grant "knew him well and favorably." It was Bowen's thought that two or more officers should "retire and talk the matter over informally and suggest such terms as they might think proper." Grant assented, for, after all, he could "not be bound by an agreement by his subordinate officers." The subsequent proceedings had an almost comic-opera character that Strong recognized:

Generals McPherson and A. J. Smith, General Bowen and Colonel Montgomery separated from the party and sat down to talk over the terms, while Grant and Pemberton went away by themselves and likewise sat down. Both were facing us [that is, Ord, Logan, Rawlins, and Lieutenant Colonel James H. Wilson, who had come to the conference with Grant]. General Pemberton showed by his manner that he was laboring under great excitement; Grant was, as usual, perfectly cool and sat smoking his cigar and pulling up tufts of grass. Generals Grant and Pemberton had been engaged in conversation about fifteen minutes when they returned to the tree of rendezvous, and were soon joined by Generals McPherson, Smith, Bowen, and Colonel Montgomery.

Part Three: CITY OF CAVES

The proposition made by the Rebel officers and Smith was promptly declined by General Grant, but he agreed to send General Pemberton his final terms by ten o'clock that night. The interview then terminated, having lasted about an hour and a half.

The proposal which, Grant said, he had "unceremoniously rejected," would have permitted the Confederate army "to march out with the honors of war, carrying their small arms and field artillery." Back at headquarters, however, Grant faced up to the realities of the situation. An insistence upon unconditional surrender would give him over thirty thousand prisoners to transport to Cairo— "very much to the inconvenience of the army on the Mississippi"—and afterward the Rebels must be transported by rail to Washington and Baltimore and then to the exchange base at Aiken's landing below Dutch Gap on the James River, "all at very great expense." The matter was further complicated by the fact that "the Confederates did not have Union prisoners to give in exchange," and, as Hébert already had suggested to Pemberton, Grant suspected that many of the Rebs "were tired of war and would get home just as soon as they could."

Under the circumstances the letter that Grant had promised Pemberton by ten o'clock that evening found the Union general more temperate in terms. "As soon as rolls can be made out," the substance of Grant's conditions stated, "and paroles be signed by officers and men, you will be allowed to march out of our lines, the officers taking with them their side arms and clothing, and the field, staff, and cavalry officers one horse each. The rank and file will be allowed all their clothing, but no other property."

Time had mollified somewhat Pemberton's aggressiveness, but, in reply, he asked Grant, in addition to allowing his officers to retain side arms and personal property, to assure him that "the rights and property of citizens" would be respected. Once again Grant picked up his pen. He did not "propose to cause any undue annoyance or loss," but he would not place himself "under any restraint by stipulation." He gave Pemberton to nine o'clock on the morning of July 4 to accept his terms or "I shall regard them as having been rejected, and shall act accordingly."

2.

A high hill running along the river to the north of Vicksburg was known as the Devil's Backbone. The Confederate signal station here, under the charge of "an alert and intelligent Creole named Mathew H. Asbury," commanded a Federal station on the isthmus, and, Gregory said, "every motion of its flags and lamps was readily seen." Asbury made the watching of the Federal flags "the business of his life," but his greatest moment came on the night of July 3 as Pemberton and Grant negotiated terms of capitulation "and an ominous and awful quiet reigned over all the scene—less welcome, no doubt, to the hearts of many than the utmost fury of the bombardment." Waiting on the Devil's Backbone, Asbury saw the Federal lamps flash and begin swinging, and "letter by letter and word by word" the Creole traced out the message being sent to Porter. Then, Gregory recounted:

> . . . Asbury mounted a horse and dashed into town, and found a grave council of generals in silent session at Pemberton's headquarters, awaiting the verdict. With intense feeling he laid before them the intercepted dispatch which fulfilled their hopes or their fears. With never a word more the council of war broke up—the stroke had fallen. . . .

Through the Federal trenches on July 4—the forty-seventh day of the siege—ran a mounting excitement. Sergeant John Hughes, Jr., Company G, Iowa Volunteers, noted in his diary at seven o'clock that morning that if Grant's terms were accepted, all Confederate forts were to display white flags by eleven o'clock. Four hours later Hughes's diary contained the jubilant entry:

"White flags are displayed!"

Despite all Mrs. Lord had suffered, when on July 3 she heard that Generals Pemberton and Bowen had conferred with Grant, she wondered: "What could it mean?" and her heart filled with "a sickening dread and anxiety." Generally, however, the rumor had been circulated that the purpose of the meeting was to protest against the constant firing on the hospital, and, reassured, Mrs. Lord had taken to her "hard bed." In the morning, at about half past eight,

> . . . before I was dressed, Mr. Lord came into the cave, pale as death, and, with *such a look of agony* on his face as I would never wish to see again, said: "Maggie, take the children home directly, the town is surrendered, and the Yankee army will enter at ten o'clock." . . . After two years of trial and disappointed hopes, the tears will come and my heart sinks within me with sorrow. I was speechless with grief. . . . As I started up the hill with . . . the children the tears began to flow and all the weary way home I wept incessantly, meeting first one group of soldiers and then another, many of them with tears streaming down their faces. . . .
>
> You can imagine our feelings when the U.S. army entered, their banners flying and their hateful tunes sounding in our ears. Every house was closed and filled with . . . mourning hearts. You may be sure that none of us raised our eyes to see the flag of the enemy, in the place where our own had so proudly and so defiantly waved so long.

Theodore R. Davis, sketch pad in hand, tried to capture

for his readers of *Harper's Weekly* the spirit of that moment: "The sturdy ironclads, trimmed from stem to stern with the many fluttering pennants and signal flags of the code, the Jack-tars in their prettiest togs—white—and the jubilant crowd on the levee, whose noisy greeting was only equaled by the p-a-c-k-like explosion of the unshotted guns that told noisily of the stated amount of thunder due the anniversary of our country's birth." Grant remembered that when his boys had boasted they would dine in Vicksburg on the fourth, the *Daily Citizen* had sneered: "First ketch your rabbit." Now, exulantly, Grant could say: "We had 'caught our rabbit.'" But, Davis confessed, one aspect of the day eluded him: "Sketching the scene, the thought came—Oh! could I portray the heat! The pencil can not; words may. 'Twas *very* hot."

Mrs. Lord said proudly that Confederate soldiers wrapped their battle flags around their bellies rather than surrender them, but, as a rule, the Confederate surrender was orderly, quiet, dignified. Colonel T. N. Waul of Waul's Texas Legion would write simply of the moment in his official report: "At ten o'clock of the day of capitulation the command marched out of the entrenchments with their colors flying and band playing. Having saluted their colors, they stacked their arms and returned—prisoners under parole—into camp." With a similar proud eloquence Colonel Edward Higgins would record that on July 3 "at five p.m. the last gun was fired by the river batteries in defense of Vicksburg."

To his wife General Orme wrote: "With great pride and pleasure I announce my arrival at this celebrated point." He was now camped, Orme said, "in the beautiful yard of a British subject—a man who has a fine house, a British flag on it, and no sympathy for the loyal North, but a great respect for the suffering South." The Rebels had surrendered, the general thought, "from sheer want of something to eat"; and wherever he went, the people and Rebel soldiers "are very bitter on General Pemberton. . . . They denounce him as a traitor and as everything else despicable and mean."

Well had she feared the coming of the Yankees, Mrs. Lord decided—"All that day they were streaming through town and in and out of my house and *so* drunk." By night the house seemed "in such ruins." But Gregory felt that the Federal army of occupation, led by Logan's division, "conducted itself in an exemplary manner." It was true that an officer, "walking up the iron stairway of the court-house, and noticing the name of the Cincinnati maker molded on it, damned the impudence of a people who thought they could whip the United States when they couldn't even make their own staircases," but this was an isolated incident. Otherwise, "the boys in blue entered by the north end of Cherry Street, and made a grand procession as they stepped by in extended line, their flags waving, their officers glittering in full uniform, and the air torn with the glad shouts that went up from victorious throats." A group of officers, returning from the courthouse, chanted the "Star Spangled Banner" and brandished a Confederate signal flag they had found. Gregory said: "I well remember the silent general in the midst of them, who *must* have been Grant."

Meanwhile in Brandon, a town on the railroad beyond Jackson, a man rose in the plaza and asked a group of fifty fellow citizens to join him in a mission. His object: to hang Pemberton as a traitor.

23. MEMORIES AT MOUNT McGREGOR

THE old General was dying. Huddled in his shawls and stocking-cap, he sat on the porch of his summer home at Mount McGregor, near Saratoga, New York. All that life had taught him in sixty-three extraordinary years he could express now in five simple words: "Man proposes and God disposes." With this quotation he had begun months ago to write his *Memoirs* in the hope that the royalties therefrom might free his family of debt. He had become a very sick man with the worsening of the cancer at the base of his tongue. There were periods when he was unable to talk; other periods when his only nourishment was liquid.

Visitors to Saratoga often journeyed to Mount Mc-Gregor, bringing their children or sweethearts, so that in later years they could boast of having seen the old General in person. They had heard that not so long ago he had suffered a severe hemorrhage and had seemed on the point of death; now they believed he might live for months. But the old General knew how wracking to his withering body were these sultry July days of 1885. In his labors to complete his *Memoirs* he battled his most relentless foe—Time. On the twenty-third day of the month he would be dead, but he would win the other struggle by a week.

Some who came to stare also whispered. "Son," a father would say to a thin-boned lad in a Buster Brown suit, "up there on the porch sits General Grant, for two terms President of the United States." Or one businessman would ask another: "How could he be so duped in that investment business even by a partner as unscrupulous as Ferdinand Ward?" Grant's family had been bankrupted—and a lot of other people with them who trusted a President, a war hero—for Ward's fantastic manipulations had resulted in a swindle that reached the staggering amount of $16,725,-466.

But the old General neither saw nor heard the whisperers. He neither saw nor heard the rumble of the ice wagon in the morning, or the flashes of summer lightning behind Mount McGregor, or the ground haze that came when evening cooled the breezes. In his eyes and in his ears these were the roll of drums, the movements of blue-clad columns with the glint of sun on their bayonets, clouds of battle smoke hanging like mist over distant valleys.

Sometimes the old General was betrayed by his own pen. He had begun one passage:

> The campaign of Vicksburg was an accidental one forced on by circumstances beyond the controll [sic] of anyone. It was commenced in 1862 on true military principles: moving from a base of supplies always covered and with every facility for rapid communication with it. The President, and Secretary of War, were induced to give a separate and independent command to an officer whom the Army did not think competent for it, to opperate [sic] against the same point. To forestall this, with the knowledge and approval of my superior, General Halleck, I sent a most competent officer, with nearly half my movable forces, by the river, in conjunction with my land operations. . . .

Suddenly the old General knew this was wrong. He crossed out the whole passage, and, not attaching first importance to a bitterness two decades behind him, began anew: "The campaign of Vicksburg was suggested by circumstances. The election of 1862 had gone against the prosecution of the war. . . ." Now he felt at ease. This passage he would publish.

So, in those dwindling days of July 1885 the old General clung to his memories. With a preciseness of expression that characterized so many of his war dispatches, he told his physician in a memorandum: "A verb is anything that signifies to be; to do; to suffer. I signify all three."

2.

The "most competent officer" received by telegram from Grant news of the negotiations for the surrender of Vicksburg. By Grant's direction, Sherman said, general orders were given "to my troops to be ready at a moment's notice to cross the Big Black and go for Joe Johnston."

Out from Vicksburg on the fourth marched Ord's XIII Corps, heading for the railroad bridge over the Big Black; the XV sped to cross the river by Messinger's Ferry; the IX, under Parkes, aimed at Birdsong's Ferry. Bolton was the point set for meeting. Sherman led his own troops across the river on the fifth and sixth, joined Ord's corps at Bolton, and learned that the IX had been delayed at Birdsong's.

Johnston, receiving notice of Pemberton's capitulation on the eighth, hurried in full retreat for Jackson. In weather "fearfully hot" and with "water scarce," Sherman found that Old Joe "in retreating had caused cattle, hogs, and sheep to be driven into the ponds, and there shot down, so that we had to haul their dead and stinking carcasses out to use the water." On the tenth Johnston's army reached Jackson and "turned at bay behind the entrenchments." Sherman closed the lines around the town, holding the center with his own troops, with Ord on his right and Parkes on his left. Jackson was shelled on all sides next day; Lauman's brigade, however, "got too close and was very roughly handled and driven back in disorder." Ord blamed Lauman for the loss, and, with Sherman's consent, relieved him of command. The sun blistered everything it touched; Sherman, continuing to press the siege, used "our artillery pretty freely"; but on the morning of the seventeenth Johnston and his army had slipped out of Jackson. Steele's division chased fourteen miles to Brandon only to find that Old Joe "had carried his army safely off." Sherman gave up: "Pursuit in that hot weather would have been fatal to my command." Grant told him to send Parkes to Haines' Bluff, Ord back to Vicksburg, and to camp his own corps near the Big Black "with the prospect of a period of rest for the remainder of the summer."

Part Three: CITY OF CAVES

3.

In the White House, on the thirteenth of July, the President of the United States wrote Grant a letter:

My dear General
    I do not remember that you and I ever met personally. I write this now as a grateful acknowledgement for the almost inestimable service you have done the country. I wish to say a word further. When you first reached the vicinity of Vicksburg, I thought you should do, what you finally did—march the troops across the neck, run the batteries with the transports, and thus go below; and I never had any faith, except a general hope that you knew better than I, that the Yazoo Pass expedition, and the like, could succeed. When you got below, and took Port-Gibson, Grand Gulf, and vicinity, I thought you should go down the river and join Gen. Banks; and when you turned Northward East of the Big Black, I feared it was a mistake. I now wish to make the personal acknowledgement that you were right, and I was wrong.
                                        Yours very truly
                                        A. Lincoln

This letter, so rich in the generosity of spirit that distinguished Lincoln, did more than praise Grant. Across the miles between Washington and Vicksburg it was as though Lincoln stretched out his hand, touched Grant's shoulder, and declared his greatness. Perhaps at times the General drank too much. But in every crisis he kept his head. He won.

It seemed to many, as it seemed to Sherman, that with the great defensive victory at Gettysburg and the great offensive victory at Vicksburg, coming only a day apart, the war should have ended; but, Sherman blustered, "the Rebel leaders were mad, and seemed determined that their people should drink of the very lowest dregs of the cup of war, which they themselves had prepared." So there remained Spottsylvania, the Wilderness, Richmond—other names to engrave on the sword that young Freddy Grant loved to wear fastened at his waist by a broad yellow belt.

4.

Finally, for the old General in his shawls and stocking-cap on the porch at Mount McGregor remained another memory. An April morning, 1865. Appomattox Court House.

The conference had ended. Grant came down the steps of the porch, moved toward Lee, and lifted his hat in a salute. The officers on Grant's staff raised their hats also. And then Lee, too, lifted his hat, respectfully. . . .

And Grant, in victory, thought first of Galena. Of Galena and Julia. In the mornings he would soon be lacing her shoes.

Bibliography

I. MANUSCRIPTS

BROWNING, ORVILLE H.: Diary, MS, Illinois State Historical Library, Springfield, Ill.

CADWALLADER, SYLVANUS: *Four Years with Grant*, MS, Illinois State Historical Library.

COMSTOCK, CYRUS B.: Papers, MS, Library of Congress, Washington.

DICKEY, CYRUS E.: Papers, MS, Illinois State Historical Library.

GRANT, ULYSSES S.: *Personal Memoirs*, MS, Library of Congress.

——: *Headquarters Records*, MS, Library of Congress, 62 vols.

HUGHES, JOHN, JR.: Diary, MS, Library of Congress.

LORD, MRS. W. W.: *Journal kept during the Siege of Vicksburg, May–July, 1863*, MS, Library of Congress.

McCLERNAND, JOHN A.: Papers, Illinois State Historical Library.

McPHERSON, JAMES B.: Papers, MS, Illinois State Historical Library.

ROACH, MRS. M. P. H. to C. A. DANA, Jan. 11, 1865, MS, Southern Historical Collection, Chapel Hill, N.C.

SCHWARTZ, ADOLPH(?): *Biography of General John A. McClernand*, MS, Illinois State Historical Library.

SHUMWAY, Z. P.: Papers, MS, Illinois State Historical Library.

SMITH, W. W.: *Diary of a Visit to General Grant's Headquarters, 1863*, MS, Library of Congress.

TUPPER, FRANCIS W.: Papers, MS, Illinois State Historical Library.

YATES, RICHARD: Papers, Illinois State Historical Library.

II. NEWSPAPERS AND MAGAZINES

Century Magazine
Charleston Mercury
Chicago History
Chicago Tribune
Cincinnati Commercial
Frank Leslie's Illustrated Newspaper
Harper's New Monthly Magazine
Harper's Weekly
Journal of the Illinois State Historical Society
Mississippi Valley Historical Review
New York Times

BIBLIOGRAPHY

New York Tribune
Philadelphia Weekly Times
Vicksburg Daily Citizen

III. PUBLISHED SOURCES

ADAMS, GEORGE WORTHINGTON: *Doctors in Blue*. New York: 1952.

ANGLE, PAUL M.: *Here I Have Lived: The Story of Lincoln's Springfield*. New Brunswick, N.J.: 1950.

Annals of the War, written by Leading Participants North and South, Originally Published in the Philadelphia Weekly Times. Philadelphia: 1879.

BADEAU, ADAM: *Military History of U. S. Grant*. New York: 1868–81. 3 vols.

BALLARD, COLIN R.: *The Military Genius of Abraham Lincoln*. New York: 1952.

BASLER, ROY P., ed.: *The Collected Works of Abraham Lincoln*. New Brunswick, N.J.: 1953. 8 vols.

Battles and Leaders of the Civil War. New York: 1884–8. 4 vols.

BROOKS, VAN WYCK: *The Flowering of New England*. New York: 1936.

BUTLER, BENJAMIN F.: *Autobiography. Butler's Book*. Boston: 1892.

BYERS, S. H. M.: "Some Recollections of Grant." See *Annals of the War*.

CAMM, WILLIAM: "Diary, 1861–1865," *Journal of the Illinois State Historical Society* (Vol. XVIII).

COPPÉE, HENRY: *Grant and His Campaigns*. New York: 1866.

CRAMER, JESSE GRANT, ed.: *Letters of Ulysses S. Grant to his father and his youngest sister, 1857–78*. New York: 1912.

CRUMMER, WILBUR F.: *With Grant at Fort Donelson, Shiloh and Vicksburg*. Oak Park, Ill.: 1915.

DANA, CHARLES A.: *Recollections of the Civil War*. New York: 1898.

DAVIS, THEODORE R. See *Harper's Weekly*.

DAWSON, GEORGE FRANCIS: *Life and Services of General John A. Logan as Soldier and Statesman*. Chicago and New York: 1887.

FISKE, JOHN: *The Mississippi Valley in the Civil War*. Boston and New York: 1900.

FORBES, STEPHEN A.: "Grierson's Cavalry Raid." See *Transactions of the Illinois State Historical Society for the Year 1907*.

GLADDEN, WASHINGTON: *Recollections*. Boston: 1909.

GOSNELL, H. ALLEN: *Guns on the Western Waters*. Baton Rouge, La.: 1949.

GRANT, ULYSSES S.: *Personal Memoirs*. New York: 1953.

GREEN, ANNA MACLAY: *Civil War Public Opinion of General Grant*. Reprinted from the *Journal of the Illinois State Historical Society* (Vol. XXII). Springfield, Ill.: 1929. Pamphlet.

GREENE, FRANCIS VINTON: *Campaigns of the Civil War*. New York: 1884.

GREGORY, EDWARD S.: "Vicksburg During the Siege." See *Annals of the War*.

HAY, THOMAS ROBSON: "Confederate Leadership at Vicksburg," *Mississippi Valley Historical Review* (Vol. XI).

HENDRICK, BURTON J.: *Lincoln's War Cabinet*. Boston: 1946.

HICKENLOOPER, ANDREW: "The Vicksburg Mine." See *Battles and Leaders of the Civil War*.

HOWE, M. A. DE WOLFE, ed.: *Home Letters of William T. Sherman*. New York: 1909.

JOHNSTON, JOSEPH E.: *Narrative of Military Operations*. New York: 1874.

LEWIS, LLOYD: *Sherman, Fighting Prophet*. New York: 1932.

——: *Letters from Lloyd Lewis*. Boston: 1950.

——: *Captain Sam Grant*. Boston: 1950.

LIVERMORE, MARY A.: *My Story of the War*. Hartford, Conn.: 1889.

LONGLEY, CHARLES L.: "Champion's Hill." See *War Sketches and Incidents*.

LOUGHBOROUGH, MRS. JAMES M.: *My Cave Life in Vicksburg*. New York: 1864.

McCOOK, DANIEL: "Second Division at Shiloh," *Harper's New Monthly Magazine* (Vol. XXVIII).

MERCUR, JAMES: *Attack of Fortified Places*. New York: 1894.

MEREDITH, ROY: *Mr. Lincoln's Camera Man: Mathew B. Brady*. New York: 1946.

Military Essays and Recollections, Illinois Commandery, Loyal Legion of the United States, Vol. II. Chicago: 1894.

NICOLAY, HELEN G.: *Lincoln's Secretary*. New York: 1949.

NOURSE, HENRY S.: "From Young's Point to Atlanta." See *The Story of the Fifty-fifth Regiment Illinois Volunteer Infantry in the Civil War*.

Official Records. See *War of the Rebellion*.

OLDROYD, OSBORN H.: *A Soldier's Story of the Siege of Vicksburg*. Springfield, Ill.: 1905.

OLMSTEAD, FREDERICK LAW: *The Cotton Kingdom*. New York: 1953.

ORME, WILLIAM WARD: *Civil War Letters of Brigadier General William Ward Orme—1862–1866*, reprinted from the *Journal of the Illinois State Historical Society* (Vol. XXIII). Springfield, Ill.: 1930. Pamphlet.

PEMBERTON, JOHN C.: *Pemberton, Defender of Vicksburg*. Chapel Hill, N.C.: 1942.

PITNAM, BENN, ed.: *The Assassination of President Lincoln and the Trial of the Conspirators*. Facsimile edition. New York: 1954.

PORTER, DAVID, D.: *Incidents and Anecdotes of the Civil War*. New York: 1885.

BIBLIOGRAPHY

——: *Naval History of the Civil War*. Hartford, Conn.: 1886.

PORTER, HORACE: *Campaigning with Grant*. New York: 1897.

POST, LYDIA MINTURN, ed.: *Soldiers' Letters from Camp, Battle-field and Prison*. New York: 1865.

SANDBURG, CARL: *Abraham Lincoln, The War Years*. New York: 1939. 4 vols.

SCHOFIELD, JOHN M.: *Forty-six Years in the Army*. New York: 1897.

SHANKS, W. F. G.: "Recollections of Sherman" and "Recollections of Grant," *Harper's New Monthly Magazine* (Vol. XXX).

SHERMAN, WILLIAM T.: *Memoirs of General William T. Sherman*. New York: 1875. 2 vols.

STARR, LOUIS M.: *Bohemian Brigade*. New York: 1954.

The Story of the Fifty-fifth Regiment Illinois Volunteer Infantry in the Civil War. Clinton, Mass.: 1887.

STRONG, WILLIAM E.: "The Campaign Against Vicksburg." See *Military Essays and Recollections*.

THOMAS, BENJAMIN P.: *Abraham Lincoln*. New York: 1952.

Transactions of the Illinois State Historical Society for the Year 1907. Publication Number Twelve of the Illinois State Historical Library. Springfield, Ill.: 1908.

TROLLOPE, ANTHONY: *North America*. New York: 1951.

War of the Rebellion: . . . Official Records of the Union and Confederate Armies. Washington, D.C.: 1880–1901. 128 vols.

War Sketches and Incidents, as related by companions of the Iowa Commandery, Military Order of the Loyal Legion. Des Moines, Ia.: 1893.

WELLES, GIDEON: *Diary*. Boston: 1911. 2 vols.

WHITNEY, HENRY C.: *Life on the Circuit with Lincoln*. Boston: 1892.

WILEY, BELL IRVIN: *The Life of Johnny Reb*. Indianapolis: 1943.

WILKIN, JACOB W.: "Personal Recollections of General U. S. Grant." See *Transactions of the Illinois State Historical Society for the Year 1907*.

WILLIAMS, T. HARRY: *Lincoln and His Generals*. New York: 1952.

WILSON, JAMES HARRISON: *Life of John A. Rawlins*. New York: 1916.

——: *Under the Old Flag*. New York: 1912. 2 vols.

"A Woman's Diary of the Siege of Vicksburg," *Century Magazine* (Vol. XXX old series; Vol. VIII new series).

Notes on the Sources

WHEREVER specific reference is made to *The Collected Works of Abraham Lincoln* (New Brunswick, 1953, 8 vols.), the citation is shortened to *Collected Works*, followed by the volume in Roman figures and the page or pages in Arabic figures. The *Official Records of the War of the Rebellion* (Washington, D.C., 1880–1901, 128 vols.) are listed as *O.R.*, with similar designations of volume and page.

INTRODUCTION

LINCOLN to Schurz, Nov. 24, '62, *Collected Works*, V, 509–11, original in the Schurz Papers, Library of Congress; Annual Message to Congress, Dec. 1, '62, *Ibid.*, 518–37. The editorial "Have We a General Among Us?" appears in *Harper's Weekly* (Volume VII), Jan. 17, '63, p. 34; the editorial "The Opening of the Mississippi," *Ibid.*, Jan. 24, '63, p. 50; the account of the marriage of Tom Thumb to Lavinia Warren, *Ibid.*, Feb. 21, '63, p. 114.

1. PORTRAIT OF A GENERAL

WHEREAS many sources were used to create the portrait with which this chapter opens, especially helpful was Horace Porter's *Campaigning with Grant* (New York, 1897), pp. 7, 13–15. Jacob W. Wilkin's "Personal Reminiscences of General U. S. Grant" appears in *Transactions of the Illinois State Historical Society for 1907*, pp. 131–40. See also Lincoln to Hamlin, Sept. 28, '62, *Collected Works*, V, 444; Lincoln to Schurz, Nov. 24, '62, *Ibid.*, 509.

The reporter for the *Chicago Times* was Sylvanus Cadwallader, and his manuscript *Four Years with Grant* is in the Library of the Illinois State Historical Society, Springfield, Illinois. This remarkable manuscript was rediscovered for modern scholarship by the late Lloyd Lewis; and an annotated edition of this work is being prepared for publication by Benjamin P. Thomas, who generously supplied the author with a typescript copy. Cadwallader's preface, written at Fall River Mills, California, is dated June 1896—thirty-four years after the Vicksburg campaign—but there are indications of labor on the manuscript during the succeeding six years. Cadwallader stated that his objective was to contribute "something to the great volume of unwritten history"; his recollections, written "very near to the close of a busy life," must claim mistakes insofar as they were prepared "hundreds of miles from any public library" with only Grant's *Memoirs*, the biographies by Coppée and Richardson, and the files of the *New York Herald* to verify dates. Portions of the manuscript were read and verified as essentially accurate by General James H. Wilson in February 1905.

In reporting on the Cadwallader manuscript for a prospective buyer, the reader for Arthur H. Clark Company wrote: "Mr. Cadwallader may be a little prejudiced in Grant's favor, although he discusses Grant's weakness in regard to intemperance and its serious results, but at the same time it seems to me he has explained satisfactorily a number of points on which others have criticized Grant." Cadwallader all but idolizes Grant on occasion, yet the circumstances that brought Cadwallader into Grant's Department as an emissary for Storey & Worden, publishers of the *Chicago Times*, were not favorable and are discussed in a later chapter. Cadwallader, however, wished to escape from the ill-health that he attributed to his former desk job as city editor of the *Milwaukee Daily News*, and he traveled into Mississippi determined to keep an open mind toward Grant. From 1862 to 1865 Cadwallader served as correspondent first for the *Chicago Times* and then the *New York Herald;* from 1864 to 1866 he was correspondent-in-chief for the Army of the Potomac and of the *Herald's* Washington Bureau. The incident of the trip to Cairo will be found in Chapter I of the Cadwallader manuscript.

The *Personal Memoirs of U. S. Grant*, originally published in two volumes in 1885, has been reissued in a one-volume edition with notes and an introduction by E. B. Long (New York, 1953), from which the quotations in the present work are drawn. The manuscript of the *Memoirs* is in the Library of Congress, and contains a number of interesting passages deleted from both published editions.

For a detailed study of Grant's first years in the West, from Ironton to Shiloh, Volume III of *Lincoln Finds a General*, by Kenneth P. Williams (New York, 1952), is a thoughtful work. T. Harry Williams's *Lincoln and His Generals* (New York, 1952) is a penetrating analysis of the emergence of Lincoln as a commander-in-chief, yet an earlier work, *The Military Genius of Abraham Lincoln*, by the British authority Colin Ballard (New York, American edition, 1952), remains of great value. Ballard brought first emphasis to Lincoln's growth as a military leader, and Williams has added modern research, wit, and sophistication.

Specific references:

On Ironton command, Grant to Kelton, Aug. 9, '61, *O.R.*, III, 432; for Grant and *Hardee's Tactics*, *Memoirs*, pp. 128–9; Battle of Wilson Creek, *O.R.*, III, 61–2; on Jesse Grant's anger at his son's repeated shifting of command, *Letters to Grant*, edited by Jesse Grant Cramer (New York, 1912), pp. 53–5; for Grant at Paducah, *The Mississippi Valley in the Civil War*, by John Fiske (Boston and New York, 1900), p. 45; on Frémont, *Memoirs of General William T. Sherman* (New York, 1875, 2 vols.), I, 196–7.

On the Battle of Belmont, *Memoirs*, pp. 139–43, and Fiske, pp. 47–51; on battles at Donelson and Henry, *Memoirs*, pp. 144–61, and Fiske, pp. 52–69; Grant's comment on Pillow is quoted in Carl Sandburg's *Abraham Lincoln, The War Years* (New York, 1939, 4 vols.), I, 466; the four issues of *Harper's Weekly* featuring the fall of Donelson appeared in March 1861 (Volume VI).

For Grant's account of Shiloh, *Memoirs*, pp. 169–92; for reminiscences of the battle, Daniel McCook, "Second Division at Shiloh," *Harper's New Monthly Magazine* (Volume XXVIII); for conditions and attitudes after the battle, *Soldiers' Letters from Camp, Battle-field and Prison*, edited by Lydia Minturn Post (New York, 1865), p. 170; for the meeting between Grant and Sherman, Sherman's *Memoirs*, I, 254–6.

2. THE DISGRUNTLED BRIDEGROOM

GRANT's account of the meeting in Springfield is in his *Memoirs*, pp. 124–5. A curious volume filled with hero worship for "the Gallant Egyptian" is *Life and Services of General John A. Logan as Soldier and Statesman*, by George Francis Dawson (Chicago and New York, 1887), and material has been drawn from pp. 4–6, 10–12. Much helpful background information on the home-town relationships between Lincoln and McClernand exists in Paul M. Angle's readable *Here I Have Lived: The Story of Lincoln's Springfield* (New Brunswick, reissued 1950), pp. 217, 226, 232. Insofar as Sherman figured prominently in the Grant-McClernand controversy, an important reference is Lloyd Lewis's *Sherman, Fighting Prophet* (Boston, 1950), pp. 255–8. Lincoln's comment (to Washburne) on McClernand is quoted in Sandburg's *Abraham Lincoln, The War Years*, II, 52.

Lincoln's remarks on his experiences in the Black Hawk War were included in a speech in Congress, July 27, '48, *Collected Works*, I, 509–10; for Lincoln's advice after Belmont, see Lincoln to McClernand, Nov. 10, '61, *Ibid.*, V, 20–1. The original of Lincoln's letter to McClernand is in the Robert Todd Lincoln Collection, Library of Congress. Grant's reactions to McClernand at Donelson and Shiloh are drawn from the *Memoirs*, pp. 153, 178.

Lincoln's comment in 1861 on the importance of Vicksburg is in David D. Porter's *Incidents and Anecdotes of the Civil War* (New York, 1885), pp. 95–6; the account of the capture of New Orleans and Far-

NOTES ON THE SOURCES

ragut's river expedition are drawn from Porter's *Naval History of the Civil War* (Hartford, 1886), pp. 246–64; see previous citation on Cadwallader. Stanton's "confidential" order to McClernand and Lincoln to McClernand, Oct. 20, '62, are in *Collected Works*, V, 468–9; the original letter is in the Illinois State Historical Library.

For the battles from Iuka to the end of the Vicksburg campaign, the reader is referred not only to the published volumes of the *O.R.*, but also to the sixty-two volumes of *Headquarters Records*, General Grant Papers, Library of Congress. See also, for affair at Iuka, *Memoirs*, pp. 210–14; for movement into Holly Springs, *Ibid.*, pp. 219–20.

3. "TIRED OF FURNISHING BRAINS"

FOR episodes involving Gabe Bouck, bedevilment of 124th Illinois, and looting at Oxford, see Cadwallader manuscript. For treatment of freedmen, see *Memoirs*, p. 221; for comment on McClernand, *Ibid.*, p. 222.

Byers's story about Sherman appears in *Annals of the War*, pp. 342–56. The report on Sherman's insanity appeared in the *Cincinnati Commercial*, Dec. 11, '61. See also Porter's *Campaigning with Grant*, pp. 290–1; W. F. G. Shanks, "Recollections of Sherman," *Harper's New Monthly Magazine* (Volume XXX); *Memoirs*, pp. 222–4.

4. A BLEAK YULETIDE

GRANT'S order, expelling Jews, is in his *Headquarters Records*, Library of Congress; for Cadwallader's explanation of the ban, see Cadwallader manuscript; for comment by Jesse Grant, see Washburne Papers, Library of Congress, and *Letters from Lloyd Lewis* (Boston, 1951), p. 24; for Rosecrans's religious discussions, see Williams's *Lincoln and His Generals*, p. 186; for remark by General Dumont, see Lewis's *Sherman, Fighting Prophet*, p. 168–9; for Jesse Grant's attitude on religion, see Lewis's *Captain Sam Grant*, p. 49; for Grant and religion, see Porter's *Campaigning with Grant*, p. 494; for revocation of order, see Halleck to Grant, Jan. 20, '63, *O.R.*, XXIV, Pt. 1, 9.

The best source of material on Pemberton is *Pemberton, Defender of Vicksburg*, by John C. Pemberton (Chapel Hill, 1942). In a foreword Douglas Southall Freeman scored "those of Grant's biographers who failed to see that they did not add glory to the winner at Vicksburg if they depreciated Grant's adversary"; but Mr. Pemberton's method has been rather to build up the loser at Vicksburg by knocking down Pemberton's adversary. Even Freeman must concede that Pemberton did not compare with Hannibal or Marlborough; nor did he compare with Grant. However, Mr. Pemberton had access to the unpublished papers of his grandfather and has used them richly. Generals Taylor and Early are quoted in *Pemberton, Defender of Vicksburg*, p. 22; the letter from Patty to John is in turn quoted in a letter from Mrs. Pemberton to her daughter-in-law, *Ibid.*, pp. 23–4; the editorial opinions regarding Pemberton appear *Ibid.*, p. 43.

5. BILLY'S BEDEVILMENTS

FOR Sherman's operations against Vicksburg, see Sherman's *Memoirs*, I, 285–95, Porter's *Naval History*, pp. 283–8, and *O.R.*, XVII, Pt. 1. The Cadwallader manuscript is the source for discussion of the Knox affair.

Sherman did not fare as badly with some members of the press as he had feared; on January 17 (Volume VII, p. 34) the editors of *Harper's Weekly* saw Sherman as one who was "making his record at Vicksburg . . . a capable officer and a far-seeing man"; and after McClernand had replaced Sherman the editors still took an optimistic view on January 24 (*Ibid.*, 50): "Like our forefathers the English, who always began their wars by getting soundly thrashed by their enemies, and only commenced to achieve success when it was thought they were exhausted, we are warming to the work with each mishap. . . ."

Porter in his *Naval History*, p. 284, wrote that immediately on his arrival at Cairo he informed Grant of Lincoln's intended command for McClernand. Within "a few days," by Porter's account, Grant hustled up to Cairo to propose and work out the details of Sherman's expedition. The whole interview, reported Porter, "lasted just half an hour"— proof, in a way, that Porter lived history faster than he could tell about it.

For Sherman's operations in Arkansas, see Sherman's *Memoirs*, I, 296–303, Porter's *Naval History*, pp. 289–94, and *O.R.*, XVII, Pt. 1.

6. DECISION AT YOUNG'S POINT

SEE Grant to Halleck, Jan. 20, '63, *O.R.*, XXIV, Pt. 1, 8–9; Halleck to Grant, Jan. 21, '63, *Ibid.*, 9; Grant to Kelton, Feb. 1, '63, *Ibid.*, 11–14. McClernand's letter to Lincoln, Jan. 7, '63, is in the Robert Todd Lincoln Collection, Library of Congress, and quoted in *Collected Works*, VI, 70. See also Lincoln to Banks, undated, original in the New York Historical Society, and Lincoln to Stanton, Jan. 23, '63, original in the Abraham Lincoln Association, *Ibid.*, 73–4, 76–7. Grant's part of the Knox affair is drawn from Cadwallader. The comparison of Grant to Napoleon is Byers's.

7. FIGHTING THE RIVER

McCLERNAND's letter to Lincoln, undated, is in the Robert Todd Lincoln Collection, Library of Congress, and quoted in *Collected Works*, VI, 49; Lincoln to McClernand, Jan. 8, '63, original in the Robert Todd Lincoln Collection, *Ibid.*, 48–9. The general to whom Lincoln reputedly confessed he had "wrestled" with God over Vicksburg was Daniel E. Sickles; the letter is dated July 5, '63, and is quoted in Henry C. Whitney's *Life on the Circuit with Lincoln* (Boston, 1892), p. 274, but does not appear in the *Collected Works*. Mary Livermore's description of Grant appears in *My Story of the War* (Hartford, 1889), pp. 309–10. Cadwallader is the source for the story of the smallpox scare.

For progress on canal, see *O.R.*, XXIV, Pt. 1, 17 *et seq.* For the passage of the batteries by the *Queen of the West*, *Ibid.*, 336–9, and Porter's *Naval History*, pp. 296–7.

Lincoln to Dix, Jan. 29, '63, original in Brown University Library, *Collected Works*, VI, 83; for Olmstead's visit to Grant's headquarters, see "Letter to the Editor," *Harper's Weekly*, June 6, '63 (Volume VIII), p. 355; for Trollope's opinions on Western men, see *North America* (New York, 1951), pp. 400–1; for Olmstead's part in strengthening the Medical Corps, see *Doctors in Blue*, by George Worthington Adams (New York, 1952), pp. 16–17.

8. THE HARES AND THE TORTOISE

A. M. BODMAN's account of the adventures of the *Queen of the West* appeared under date of Feb. 15, '63, in the *Chicago Tribune;* it is more convenient to the general reader in H. Allen Gosnell's *Guns on the Western Waters* (Baton Rouge, 1949), where it is extensively quoted, pp. 179–89. See also, for capture of *Queen of the West*, *O.R.* XXIV, Pt. 1, 341–9, and for capture of the *Indianola*, *Ibid.*, 361–7.

Civil War Public Opinion of General Grant by Anna Maclay Green, reprinted from the *Journal of the Illinois State Historical Society*, Volume XXIV (Springfield, 1929, pamphlet), is a helpful reference. See also Gideon Welles *Diary* (Boston, 1911, 2 vols.), I, 387, and Orville H. Browning *Diary*, Illinois State Historical Society Collections. For the reaction to Grant's order banning Jews, see *New York Times* editorial, Jan. 18, '63; for Grant as a commander, *Cincinnati Commercial*, Jan 23, '63. Grant's *Memoirs* were drawn on for his reaction to Northern "croakers," p. 231; for the expedition to Lake Providence, *Ibid.*, pp. 233–4; for the Yazoo Pass Expedition, *Ibid.*, pp. 234–6. Wilson's opinions of Grant appear in his two-volume work *Under the Old Flag* (New York, 1912), I, 138–9; his correspondence with Rawlins during the expedition is in *O.R.*, XXIV, Pt. 1, 371–91. Davis's sketch at Lake Providence is in *Harper's Weekly* (Volume VIII, p. 187).

9. BATTLE IN THE BAYOUS

PORTER'S *Incidents and Anecdotes of the Civil War* is a principal source for reconstructing the expedition to Steele's Bayou and again is generously reprinted in Gosnell's *Guns on the Western Waters*, pp. 147–76; for Sherman's role in this expedition, see *O.R.*, XXIV, Pt. 1, 431–7, and Sherman's *Memoirs*, I, 306–11.

10. THE BIG GAMBLE

WHEREAS the short portrait of Stanton with which this chapter opens has come from many sources, an always admirable and reliable book is Burton J. Hendrick's *Lincoln's War Cabinet* (Boston, 1946); and for a portrait of the Brook Farm that Dana knew, Van Wyck Brooks's *The Flowering of New England* (New York, 1936) is unsurpassed. The opportunity to read in manuscript Louis Starr's *Bohemian Brigade* (New York, 1954) gave me a feeling for Dana that I am certain could not be derived from any other source. Dana's own *Recollections of the Civil War* (New York, 1898), hereinafter cited as *Recollections*, is a lively document, and the student of the period recognizes how heavily the later work draws from Dana's letters to Stanton in *O.R.*, XXIV, Pt. 1, 63–117.

Nicolay's letter to his wife, Therena, is quoted in Helen G. Nicolay's *Lincoln's Secretary* (New York, 1949), p. 168; General Butler's claim that he could have had Grant's command appears in *Butler's Book* (Boston, 1892), p. 550. For Dana's early support of Stanton, see *Recollections*, pp. 4–5; for his break with Greeley, *Ibid.*, pp. 1–2; for his early experiences in Washington, *Ibid.*, pp. 11, 16–17; for his speculation in cotton and subsequent assignment to Grant's department, *Ibid.*, pp. 18–28. Cadwallader relates the story of Duff's stormy reaction to Dana's coming; Dana's first reactions to Mississippi are in his *Recollections*, pp. 28–9. At the close of the Vicksburg campaign, under the dates of July 12, '63, and July 13, '63, Dana wrote two long letters to Stanton giving his judgment of the generals and staff officers he had observed in action, among the most incisive of all the documents for which he was responsible; these letters are reprinted in full in the *Recollections*, pp. 63–77, and are the source of many judgments the author attributes to Dana here and in subsequent chapters.

The sources from which the author has developed the reactions to Grant's new plan of attack are Grant's *Memoirs*, pp. 237–9; Sherman's

Memoirs, I, 316–18; Dana's *Recollections*, pp. 30–2; Wilson's *Under the Old Flag*, I, 158–62.

For the running of the batteries, see Dana's *Recollections*, pp. 37–8; Wilson's *Under the Old Flag*, I, 162–4; Sherman's *Memoirs*, I, 317–18; Grant's *Memoirs*, pp. 240–1; *O.R.*, XXIV, Pt. 1, 67. For Logan and the dusky dancers, see Cadwallader; for portrait of Grant and Julia at running of batteries, see Wilkin in *Transactions of the Illinois State Historical Society for 1907*, p. 134.

11. TENSING FOR THE SPRING

FOR Grant's attitude toward McClernand, see Dana's *Recollections*, pp. 32–3, and *O.R.*, XXIV, Pt. 1, 75 *et.seq.*; for McClernand's delay, *Ibid.*, 80; for an account of the Grierson raid, see Stephen A. Forbes: "Grierson's Cavalry Raid," *Transactions of the Illinois State Historical Society for 1907*, pp. 99–130; *O.R.*, XXIV, Pt. 2, 519–53.

Porter gives a lively account of the fight at Grand Gulf in his *Naval History*, pp. 313–15; for this engagement and events leading to the crossing at Bruinsburg see also Dana's *Recollections*, pp. 42–4, and Grant's *Memoirs*, pp. 248–54. The reports on the Battle of Thompson's Hill appear in *O.R.*, XXIV, Pt. 1, 581–682. For Freddy's arrival in Grand Gulf, see *Memoirs*, p. 255; for Dana's letter on life in camp, see *Recollections*, pp. 49–50; for the exchange of letters between Dana and Stanton, see *O.R.*, XXIV, Pt. 1, 83–4.

12. GUNS, WHISKY, AND TACTICS

SEE *O.R.*, XXIV, Pt. 1, 711–12, 714–15, 743–6, 722–5, for the reports of Davis, Force, Beaumont, and Crocker on the engagement at Raymond. See *Memoirs*, p. 262, for Grant's account of his meeting with Sherman. Cadwallader is the source for Oglesby's barrel of whisky and the tent scene between Duff and Grant. See Joseph E. Johnston's *Narrative of Military Operations* (New York, 1874), pp. 172–6, for his transfer to Mississippi. Thompson's letter to Pemberton describing the reaction to the council of war is quoted in *Pemberton, Defender of Vicksburg*, pp. 146–8.

Jacob Thompson later would go to Canada as a Confederate agent, and would be suspected strongly of having engineered in large part the plot to assassinate Lincoln. At the subsequent trial of Booth's fellow conspirators, Grant would be called as a Government witness to give this testimony regarding Thompson:

I met Jacob Thompson, formerly Secretary of the Interior under President Buchanan's administration, when the army was lying opposite Milliken's Bend and Young's Point. A little boat was discovered coming up near the opposite shore, apparently surreptitiously, and trying to avoid detection. A little tug was sent out from the navy to pick it up. When they got to it, they found a little white flag sticking out of the stern of the rowboat, and Jacob Thompson in it. . . . He pretended to be under a flag of truce, and he had therefore to be allowed to go back again. . . . He professed to be in the military service of the rebels, and said that he had been offered a commission—anything that he wanted; but . . . he preferred having something more like a civil appointment, and he had therefore taken the place of Inspector General. . . .

The Government's case against Thompson collapsed completely (Cf. Benn Pitman: *The Assassination of President Lincoln and the Trial of the Conspirators*, facsimile edition; New York: 1954; p. 37).

Sherman's report on the destruction of Jackson will be found in *O.R.*, XXIV, Pt. 1, 754; the story of the intercepted message is in Grant's *Memoirs*, p. 268; the tale that Grant occupied the bed used the night before by Johnston may be apocryphal. For the confusion in orders between Pemberton and Johnston, see *O.R.*, XXIV, Pt. 1, 270 *et seq.* Cadwallader tells how Hovey beat Logan to the field of battle.

13. CHAMPION'S HILL

VISITORS to Mississippi today, searching for Champion's Hill, will find it largely cut away to provide a level surface for a new highway.

For all of the reports on the Battle of Champion's Hill see *O.R.*, XXIV, Pt. 2, 6–128; for Grant's comments, see *Memoirs*, pp. 269–73. The reminiscences of Charles Longley appear in *War Sketches and Incidents* (Des Moines, Ia.: 1893), pp. 208–14; those of S. H. M. Byers in *Annals of the War*, pp. 342–56; those of Dana in *Recollections*, pp. 53–5; those of Crummer in *With Grant at Donelson, Shiloh and Vicksburg*, pp. 104–6. For Sherman's adventure in Bolton, his meeting at Black River Bridge with Grant, see Sherman's *Memoirs*, I, 323–5; for Grant's meeting with Halleck's messenger, see Grant's *Memoirs*, p. 274; for the reports on the battle, see *O.R.*, XXIV, Pt. 2, 128–42.

14. McCLERNAND CLAIMS A VICTORY

THE ninety-seven reports on the siege of Vicksburg (May 16–July 4, 1863) will be found in *O.R.*, XXIV, Pt. 2, 146–424. See also Grant's *Memoirs*, pp. 276–7; Crummer, pp. 110–15; Sherman's *Memoirs*, I, 326–8; Cadwallader. The messages that passed between

Grant and McClernand are in the McClernand Papers, Illinois State Historical Library. For a detailed reference to the unpublished biography see notes for Chapter Seventeen.

15. LIFE IN THE DITCHES

CADWALLADER tells the story of the difficulty that arose between Rawlins and Grant's manservant. For Dana's comments to Stanton concerning McClernand, see *O.R.*, XXIV, Pt. 1, 87–8. The *New York Times* for May 26, 1863, tried to evaluate Grant as a general; the *New York Tribune* for June 29, 1863, is also quoted. For Sherman's remarks, see Howe's editing of the *Home Letters* (New York: 1909), p. 265; see also Welles's *Diary*, p. 320. Major Andrew Hickenlooper's "The Vicksburg Mine" appears in *Battles and Leaders of the Civil War* (New York: 1884–8, 4 vols.), III, Pt. 2, 539–42. Crummer, *With Grant at Donelson, Shiloh and Vicksburg*, p. 118, describes sap-rolling; the letters of Private Francis W. Tupper are in the manuscript collection of the Illinois State Historical Library; the exploits of "Coonskin" Foster are retold in *Battles and Leaders*, III, Pt. 2, 541, footnote.

The papers of Cyrus Comstock in the Library of Congress consist of seven volumes of letters and reports and a notebook and diary dated 1863–7. The letters of Lieutenant Cyrus E. Dickey, written to his sister, Mrs. M. Ann Wallace of Ottawa, Illinois, are in the Illinois State Historical Library. The quotations attributed to Edward S. Gregory in this and succeeding chapters are drawn from "Vicksburg During the Siege" in *Annals of the War*, pp. 111–33. Mrs. James M. Loughborough's *My Cave Life in Vicksburg* (New York: 1864) was a little book that understandably became a best-seller, appearing a few months after the end of the siege.

A fine account of life within the city of caves emerges from the fourteen typescript pages of Mrs. W. W. Lord's diary for June and July 1863, now in the Library of Congress. The woman who would identify herself only as "a young lady of New Orleans" permitted her diary to be published in the *Century Magazine* for September 1885. In an appended editorial note George W. Cable commented:

> Just a quarter of a century ago a young lady of New Orleans found herself an alien and an enemy to the sentiments of the community about her. Surrounded by friends and social companions, she was nevertheless painfully alone. In her enforced silence she began a diary intended solely for her own eye. A betrothed lover came suddenly from a neighboring state, claimed her hand in haste, and bore her away, a happy bride. Happy, yet anxious. The war

was now fairly upon the land, and her husband, like herself, cherished sympathies whose discovery would have brought jeopardy of life, ruin, and exile. In the South, those days, all life was romantic. Theirs was full of adventure. At length they were shut up in Vicksburg. I hope some day to publish the whole diary; but the following portion is specially appropriate to the great panorama of battle in which a nation of readers is just now so interested. I shall not delay the reader to tell how I came by the manuscript, but only to say that I have not molested its original text. The name of the writer is withheld at her own request.

16. ON FANNING A GENERAL TO SLEEP

For Dana's estimate of the progress of the siege, see *O.R.*, XXIV, Pt. 1, 90–2.

Cadwallader supplies the source of the extraordinary adventure that befell Grant on his trip to Satartia. In *Under the Old Flag*, I, 210, Wilson refers somewhat obliquely to the incident: "Before the end of the first week in June, he [Grant] started by steamer to visit an outlying detachment on the Yazoo, but before reaching his destination he 'fell ill,' which, but for the timely action of Dana and the firmness and devotion of Rawlins, might have proved a great misfortune to Grant and his army." Whisky had been flowing freely around headquarters from the start of the siege, and on the day the truce was declared so both sides could bury their dead Private Richard Puffer of the 8th Illinois Infantry wrote to his sister: "Logan ordered out a keg of whisky & from what I can learn they had a big drunk" (Cf. *Chicago History*, Summer 1949, II, 120–1).

There are witnesses who declare that Grant was a total abstainer, and they vary from William Cullen Bryant, who based his evidence on "friends who profess to be acquainted with him," to men of the military significance of General John M. Schofield. In *Forty-six Years in the Army* (New York, 1897), p. 111, Schofield wrote: "At length I ventured to remark that he [Grant] had not tasted his wine. He replied: 'I dare not touch it. Sometimes I can drink freely without any unpleasant effect; at others I cannot take a single glass of light wine.' A strong man, indeed, who could thus know and govern himself." The blunt truth was that Grant became a much stronger man, and much more likely to "know and govern himself," when Julia was around. Otherwise moments of indiscretion continued; and in July 1864 the harried Rawlins would write his new bride: "The God of Heaven only knows how long I am to serve my country as the guardian of the habits of him whom it has honored" (Cf. Wilson, *Life of John A. Rawlins*, p. 249).

17. "A JACKASS IN THE ORIGINAL PACKAGE"

IN SUPPORT of Cadwallader's account of the aftermath of Grant's drunk, Wilson states in *Under the Old Flag*, I, 210–11:

> It was upon this occasion that Rawlins, in the late and silent hours of the night, wrote his remarkable letter of June 6, 1863, appealing to Grant's sense of duty and propriety. And it was the next morning that this fearless and faithful staff officer took measures for the exclusion of wine and liquor from the headquarters encampment by personally searching every suspected tent and ruthlessly breaking every bottle he found over a near-by stump. . . . Although Grant said something about keeping a case of champagne, which a friend had sent him to celebrate the capture of Vicksburg with, he allowed Rawlins to have his way without further objection.

The letter McClernand wrote Grant is in the McClernand Papers, Illinois State Historical Library; the letter from Halstead to Chase is quoted in Benjamin P. Thomas's *Abraham Lincoln* (New York: 1952), pp. 372–3; for Lincoln's defense of Grant, see Lincoln to Arnold, May 26, '63, *Collected Works*, VI, 230–1, original in possession of the Chicago Historical Society. Dana's letters to Stanton, June 5–11, appear in *O.R.*, XXIV, Pt. 1, 93–7. Rawlins's letter censoring Grant for being where the "wine bottle has just been emptied" is quoted in Lewis's *Sherman, Fighting Prophet*, p. 283. For Grant's angry comments on Confederate shells, see *Memoirs*, p. 281.

McClernand's letters to Warmoth and to Yates will be found, respectively, in the McClernand Papers and the Yates Papers, both in the Illinois State Historical Library. Wilkin, as cited in *Illinois Transactions for 1907*, is the source of the Aus Griffin story. The *Civil War Letters of Brigadier General William Ward Orme, 1862–1866* appeared originally in the *Journal of the Illinois Historical Society* (Vol. XXIII) and were later reprinted separately. For the letters of Sherman and McPherson commenting upon McClernand's "Congratulatory Order," see *O.R.*, XXIV, Pt. 1, 162–4; also for subsequent correspondence and supporting evidence, *Ibid.*, 164–83.

The manuscript copy of the *Biography of John A. McClernand*, in the Illinois State Historical Library, is possibly the work of Adolph Schwartz, who advanced from major in the 2nd Illinois Light Artillery to McClernand's chief-of-staff. Evidently written in the fall of 1863, with McClernand's blessing and assistance, it is hardly an unbiased document. It is just as well for McClernand's place in history that it remains unpublished. Lincoln's letter to McClernand, Aug. 12, '63, is in *Col-*

lected Works, VI, 383; the original is in the Illinois State Historical Library.

18. A SADISTIC WIDOW

THE Manuscript sources of Tupper, Cadwallader, and Dickey have been previously identified.

The editorial "The Western Boys" will be found in *Harper's Weekly* (Vol. VII) for June 13, 1863, p. 370. The account, with illustrations, of the hardships that befell Gordon, and a reprint of the correspondence in the *New York Times* concerning the Widow Gillespie, appear in *Harper's Weekly* (Vol. VII) for July 4, 1863, pp. 429–30. The quotation from Frederick Law Olmstead's *The Cotton Kingdom* (New York, 1953) appears in a footnote, p. 476. Captain Nourse tells the story of the picture lost at Shiloh and returned at Vicksburg in *The Story of the Fifty-fifth Regiment Illinois Volunteer Infantry in the Civil War* (Clinton, Mass., 1887), pp. 242–3.

19. "RATS AND OTHER SMALL DEER"

SEE previous citations for Gregory, "the young lady from New Orleans," Mrs. Loughborough, and Mrs. Lord. Crummer, *With Grant at Donelson, Shiloh and Vicksburg*, pp. 149–50, quotes the note thrown across the picket line. The *Vicksburg Daily Citizen* for July 2, 1863, berated the extortioners. For Lay's report on the destruction of the hospital, see *O.R.*, XXIV, Pt. 2, 423; for Higgins's reports on the operations of the river batteries, *Ibid.*, 336–9.

20. TWO PIECES OF ADVICE

FOR Johnston's appraisal of his negotiations with Pemberton from May 17 through the period of the siege, see the Johnston *Narrative*, pp. 185–204; Captain Wise's account of his meeting with Johnston is quoted in *Pemberton, Defender of Vicksburg*, pp. 211–14; for Pemberton's own report, see *O.R.*, XXIV, Pt. 1, 249–331.

Sergeant Oldroyd's comments on life inside the beleaguered city appear in *A Soldier's Story of the Siege of Vicksburg* (Springfield, Ill.; 1905). The "Diary of William Camm, 1861–1865" will be found in the *Journal of the Illinois State Historical Society* (Vol. XVIII), pp. 793–969. All other sources will be readily identified from former citations.

21. "FORT HELL"

DANA's communications with Stanton covering the period to the explosion at Fort Hill will be found in the *O.R.*, XXIV, Pt. 1, 105–9. Crummer details the explosion and attack in *With Grant at Donelson, Shiloh and Vicksburg*, pp. 136–42. For Dana's later reports to Stanton, see *O.R.*, XXIV, Pt. 1, 109–11. Sherman's uncomfortable meeting with the Wilkinsons is in his *Memoirs*, I, 329–30. For the reports of Generals Stevenson, Forney, Hébert, and Ashbel Smith advising surrender, see *O.R.*, XXIV, Pt. 2, 345–6, 368, 374, 393; for Lee's dissenting opinion, *Ibid.*, 348.

22. "WE HAD CAUGHT OUR RABBIT"

GRANT's own account of the surrender negotiations is in *Memoirs*, pp. 290–4; for Strong's reminiscences of the surrender scene, see his chapter "The Campaign Against Vicksburg" in *Military Essays and Recollections, Illinois Commandery, Loyal Legion of the United States*, Vol. II (Chicago, 1894). The sources for Gregory, Mrs. Lord, and Orme have been given; the diary of John Hughes, Jr., is in the Library of Congress.

23. MEMORIES AT MOUNT McGREGOR

THE quotation of the unpublished paragraph in Grant's *Memoirs* is taken from the manuscript copy in the Library of Congress. Sherman's *Memoirs*, I, 331, supplies an account of his pursuit of Johnston. Lincoln's letter to Grant, July 13, '63, appears in *Collected Works*, VI, 326; the original is in the Historical Society of Pennsylvania archives.

Index

Abraham (Negro blown up at Fort Hill), 281, 283
Adams, Charles Francis, 19
Alabama regiments (37th, 40th, 42nd), 289
Alexandria, La., 95, 98, 100, 285
Alexis, Grand Duke, 253
Allegheny Mountains, 15, 36, 251
Alton Penitentiary, 69
Appomattox Court House, Va., 15, 56, 301
Arkansas, District of East, 111
Arkansas Post, 139, 142; expedition to, 70–4. *See also* Hindman, Fort
Arkansas River, 71
Army Medical Corps, 92
Arnold, Isaac N., 241
Asbury, Mathew H., 293
Atlanta, Ga., 285
A. W. Baker, 91
"A Young Lady of New Orleans," describes life in Vicksburg during siege, 229–30; when shells explode, 260–1

Bache, George N., 264
Baker's Creek, 174, 175, 177, 187, 192
Bald Head, 151, 152
Baldwin's Ferry, Miss., 200, 243
Ballard, Colin, 242
Ball's Bluff, Battle of, 37
Baltimore, Md., 292
Banks, Nathaniel P., viii, 5, 34, 64, 77–9, 89, 118, 159, 160, 197, 243, 300
Barclay, James W., 264
Barnum's Museum, ix
Barton, Seth M., 288
Baton Rouge, La., 64, 254
Baxter Bayou, 93, 107
Bayou Pierre, 154–5
Bear Creek, 40, 284, 287
Beaumont, T. W., 164
Beauregard, Pierre G. T., 20, 61, 168, 174
Belmont, Battle of, 13–14, 15, 29, 41, 242

Beltzhoover, D., 263
Benton, 142, 152
Benton, William P., 210
Berwick Bay, 91
Bethel, Battle of, 36
Big Black River, 64, 139, 140, 159, 162, 167, 170, 171, 173, 195, 196, 198, 220, 221, 228, 232, 243, 254, 276, 277, 283, 284, 299, 300
Bill (Grant's manservant), 219
Birdsong's Ferry, Miss., 299
Black Bayou, 116, 124, 125, 128
Black Hawk War, 29
Black River, 95
Black River Bridge, x, 204, 245; battle at, 197–8
Blair, Frank P., Jr., 67, 176, 186, 196, 198, 205, 232, 233, 242, 248
Blair, Montgomery, 131
Blenheim, Battle of, 78
Blue Wing, 70, 71
Bodman, A. H., 69; describes attack on Gordon's Landing, 95–9; meeting with *Indianola*, 101; chase after *Webb*, 101–2; escape of *Era No. 5*, 102–3
Bolivar, Tenn., 36, 40, 42
Bolton Station, Miss., 173, 174, 176, 196–7, 277, 299
Boomer, George B., 189, 213
Boston, Robinson & Co., 88
Bouck, Gabriel, 41–2
Bowen, John S., 155, 191–2, 291, 294
Bowling Green, Ky., 12
Brady, Mathew, 28
Bragg, Braxton, 35, 37, 59, 68, 148–9, 168, 221, 268, 277, 284
Brandon, Miss., 296
Brent, Joseph L., 100
Bridgeport, Miss., 196, 198, 277
Brook Farm, 133, 135, 137, 138, 162
Brown, George: commands *Indianola*, 100; joins *Era No. 5* against *Webb*, 101–2; fights Confederate fleet, 103–5
Browne, Junius Henri, 69
Browning, Orville H., 106
Brownsville, Tenn., 36

i

INDEX

INDEX